Taggart, Jean E.

Pet names

$22.50

DATE			

Preface

The purpose of this book is to bring together suitable Foreign and English names for naming that important member of the American family -- the Pet.

The languages used in the book are: French, German, English, Italian, Spanish, Dutch, Chinese, Japanese, Korean, Lapp, Norse, Icelandic, Teutonic, Old French, Old German, American Indian, Scandinavian, Russian, Slavic, Polish, Persian, Arabic, Egyptian, Welsh, Irish, Scotch.

The breeds of the dogs selected are those recognized by the American Kennel Club. They have been grouped according to the country of their origin. This is an arbitrary grouping since authorities do not agree on exact origins. The names are given in the language of the country of origin. The arrangement is so that in any language list, the English equivalent is almost in alphabetical order, underlined, so that knowing the English name to be translated, makes it easier to use that list. It will enable the reader to search from English to Foreign Language and vice versa. Many other combinations may be made with the aid of "How to Coin Names," page vii.

Sources are: Books on Mythology, Folklore, Nature, Astronomy, Word Origins, History, Biographies, Encyclopedias, Christian Names, American Kennel Club names reduced to the 'call' name of the dog; Champions; Pets in Literature, in Children's books, in Zoos, owned by famous people, living or dead, on T.V. in the Movies, in the News.

The author is most grateful to the following publishers and persons who kindly let me use material in their books, or who helped me in translation.

R. Ellis, Keeper of the Brooklyn Zoo, for his list of names given to the animals in the Brooklyn Zoo, New York, by the keepers of the Zoo.

Henry P. Davis, editor, The Modern Dog Encyclopedia, for permission to use some dog names found in the encyclopedia.

Gaines Dog Research Center, New York City, for permission to use some of the dog names in their pamphlet, "A Name to Fit Your Dog."

Harbor Cities Kennel Club, Hollywood, California, for use of Kennel names reduced to the call name of dogs found in their yearly programs.

Mr. William Bridges, Curator of Publications, N.Y. Zoological Society, The Zoological Park, New York, for permission to use names given to Zoo animals by keepers, as presented in his article in the New York Times Magazine, March, 1959.

The Philosophical Library, Inc., N. Y., for permission to use 22 words from "Dictionary of Word Origin" by Joseph T. Shipley, c1945, 2nd edition.

H. Ettinger, Zoological Board of Control, St. Louis Zoological Park, St. Louis, Mo., for a compilation of given names applied to animals in the Zoo.

Simon & Schuster, Inc., New York, for permission to quote various names and meanings from "What Shall We Name the Baby?," edited by Winthrop Ames. Copyright 1934 by Simon and Schuster, Inc. By permission of the publishers.

Staten Island Zoo, N. Y., for their list of Zoo Pet names.

The Librarians of the Long Beach, California Public Library and the Los Angeles Public Library.

Mr. Saleh S. Freij, who supplied and defined many Arabic names.

Long Beach, California   Jean E. Taggart
January 1962

Table of Contents

How To Use This Book

Abbreviations

Also: Other names that may be used instead of the entry name, since they have the same meaning.

Ch.   Champion, having won recognition in shows.

Dim.   Diminutive form of the name.

F. or f.   Female.

K.   Kennel, that is the Kennel name given by its owner reduced to the 'call' name for the dog.

M. or m.   Male.

Pop.   Popular, the English name as we know it.

Var.   Variant of a name.

How to Coin Names

It is hoped that these lists will stimulate the pet owner to coin his own pet name. There are numerous ways to do this, using the lists.

1.   Take two or more characteristics of your pet, join them together. Is your dog bright-eyed? Is he full of fun? Then when you look for words having these meanings you find:

     ASTA - meaning starry-eyed.
     BLISS - meaning joyous, happy.

     This becomes ASTABLISS, your own private name for your own special pet.

2.   Use two appropriate names, or words, that sound alike, have the same inner letters, or the same beginning letter.

     KING PIN
     SILVER SPARK

3.   The definitions of the names will help you coin
      new names. The Arabic word LAMA 'AN means,
      "flash, or the swift glance of a ladies eye." In
      this definition are the words, FLASH and SWIFT
      that might be used for a pet that moves fast. Go
      beyond this. What flashes? LIGHTNING, NORTH-
      ERN LIGHTS, FLASHLIGHT.

4.   From the special capability of the pet, you can
      find a name. A Newfoundland dog fishes, a
      Spaniel swims, so a name connected with fishing,
      the sea, the ocean, quiet streams, waves would
      be suitable.

            IRVETTE   means   'little sea friend.'
            AEGIR   means   'god of the sea.'
            TOBIAS   means   'he of the fish.'

5.   If a pet is small, find all the little words, as,
      cricket, bumblebee, fly, hummingbird, Tom
      Thumb, elf, Rumpelstiltskin, crumb, corkscrew,
      button, mite, gremlin. Does he have curly hair?
      Why not, deckle, lacy, fluted, ruffles, crinkles?
      For a tempestuous dog there are suitable words
      taken from the idea of wind: Chinook, blizzard,
      whiff, puff, blast, flury, Sirroco, whistle, roar,
      wail, blast, bluster, breeze. From these words
      you get the feeling of smallness, curliness, or
      movement.

6.   Characters in a book have been used for litters of
      puppies, or a family of animals. Those in "Little
      Black Sambo," by Helen Bannerman were used for
      a litter of black puppies. BLACK SAMBO, BLACK
      MUMBO, BLACK JUMBO.

7.   Kennel names have been prefixed with a word like
      MIGHT, as MIGHTY MAN, MIGHTY MIDGET, for
      two dogs of the same litter. SILVER SONG,
      SILVER SPARK, SILVER FLEECE are toy poodles.
      RIVETS is the son of IRON MAN, both Beagles.
      NEEDLESS TO SAY and NO FOOLIN' are the sons
      of TOM FOOLERY. MUSIC MAESTRO is the
      parent of DISC JOCKEY and STOP THE MUSIC,
      all Collies. TRULY FAIR is the mother of the

Champion YOURS TRULY.

8.   Words belonging to each other are fun to use:
COWBOY, LARIAT, a lasso rope, BROOMTAIL, a
wild she-horse, BRONCO, a lively, wild horse,
ROUNDUP, cattle gathered, BRAND, the mark of
the ranch.

9.   Other subjects may be found in Mythology, the
names of gods and goddesses; Astronomy, the con-
stellations, planet names; Meterology, shooting
balls, fire balls, meteorites, cold front, warm
front, bolide; Oceanography, -sea water, blue sea,
green sea, yellow sea; in the Ballet,-the terms
used, the ballet names; in signals,-beacons, light-
houses, flares, rockets, red light, "All's well..,"
SOS; Animals that light up in the dark, -as fire
beetle, firefly, glowworm; Flowers; Playing cards,
Famous battles, Holidays, Spices. There are
many others. Ask your public librarian, your
school librarian for books on these subjects.

10.   Kennel prefixes you may use:

PRINCESS	PRINCE	DUTCHESS	DUKE
CURLY	LITTLE	SILVER	MERRIE
GAY	HAPPY	CHIEF	FLEET
GRACIOUS	GENTLE	HIGH	BOLD
OUR	MY	JUST	BASHFUL
TARRILONG	DAPPER	TOP	WEE
BEAU	FITZ..(son of)	GREVE..(count)	SHO..(little)
MAC, MC..(son of)	YUKI..(snow)	SCHARF.(sharp)	QUEEN
PADDY...(every Irishman)	IBN..(son of)	UM..(mother of)	KING

BIRDS

BIRDS

Aviary, Cage and Backyard Birds

BALTIMORE ORIOLE

    ARCHITECT — It builds the best nest.

    MRS. SEAMSTRESS — It sews drooping edges of leaves with fine grass.

    WILL YOU. . .
    WILL YOU. . . — Oriole's song. Or, WILL.

BENGALEE

    SPLASH — It looks as though someone had taken a paint brush and daubed his feathers.

    MUD PIE — The feathers look as though mud had been splashed all over him.

BLACKBIRD

    ARCHY — In honor of "archaeopteryx," the first known bird and taken from the first letters of the name.

    ZIT KA TANKA — The American Indian name for 'blackbird.'

    STOP LIGHT — Redwing blackbird has red feathers on shoulders.

BLUEBIRD

    COCHE — The American Indian name for the 'blue sky.'

    SPECKLES — The young have speckles on their breasts.

    WINSOME — A bluebird was called this in the "Burgess Bird Book for Children," by Thornton Burgess.

BLUEJAY

    BABY — It can scream, scold, act like a

BLUEJAY (continued)

bad child.

CLOWN	It's full of fun.
FEATHER CREST	On the top of the head is a feather crest.
JOLLY	He is a humorous fellow.
KITTA	The Greek word for 'blue jay.'
MIMIC	This bird imitates the songs of other birds.
MISCHIEF	The bluejay is mischievous.
PLANTER	He hides acorns like a squirrel.
RACKET	He is noisy.
RICKRACK	His bib looks as though it had been trimmed in blue rickrack.
SCOFFER	He scolds and scoffs.
SCREAMER	Jays scream, shriek.
SHRIEKER	Bluejay shrieks.
SLANDERER, the	The Jay is abusive.
SOOTY	The color of the Jay.
TEASER	Jay is mischievous, teasing, scoffing all the time.
TOP KNOT	He has a crest.

BOWER BIRD

BLUE BOY	He is dressed in blue and picks up blue articles.
BALLET DANCER	He rises on his toes, walks on his toes as he sings like a wheel spinning.
INTERIOR DECORATOR	This bird lines the nest with fancy bits.

BOBOLINK

BUTTER BALL	This bird gets quite fat before he flies South for the winter.
YELLOW BRIDE	Her coloring.

BOBOLINK (continued)

YELLOW GROOM	His coloring.

BUDGERIGAR

DEW DROP	It is a small bird.
DIGGER	The Australian word for 'buddy.'
PANCHO	Name given by a pet lover.
MR. MICKEY	Name given by a pet lover.
MR. POO	Name given by a pet lover.
PETER PAN	Name given to a cobalt blue budgie. Peter Pan was a fairy, and the budgie is small and sprightly.
SHORTY	He is so small.
SIR KIETO	Name given by a pet lover.
SOCRATES	It acts as though it were very wise.
TINY TIM	A small bird. He sings the "Star Spangled Banner."
TOPPER	Tops them all.
TUFFY	It can be tough.
WINKIE BLUE	Name given by a pet lover for a blue budgie.
WOODY	Name given by a pet lover.

BULFINCH

PAINTED DESERT	It looks like the Painted Desert.
SUNSET	The Desert Trumpeter has pink colored feathers like the sunset.

CANARY

BILLE	The canary in "Everyday Miracle," by Gustav Eckstein.
CAPTAIN JINKS	A canary who could whistle his own name in "Dody and Cap-tin Jinks," by Helen Ferris.
CLOUDY	A canary in "Everyday Miracle."
CONCERTO	A canary that sings all the time.

CANARY (continued)

CRUSTY	A canary in "Everyday Miracle."
GUINEA	Appears in "Everyday Miracle."
HILDA	A canary in "Everyday Miracle."
HINGE	A canary in "Everyday Miracle."
JENNY LIND	A singing canary.
ONE TWIN	A canary in "Everyday Miracle."
PART-IN-THE-MIDDLE	A canary in "Everyday Miracle," so called because his feathers parted naturally, right down the center of his back.
PEPPY	A canary in "Everyday Miracle."
PINKIE'S MAN	A canary in "Everyday Miracle."
PIPPINELLA	The green canary in Dr. Doolittle's stories by Hugh Lofting. It appeared as prima donna of a canary opera.
PRINCESS, the	Appeared in "Everyday Miracle."
PUCK	Billies mate in "Everyday Miracle."

CARDINAL

BLACK BEARD	It looks as though it had a beard.
CHEER	The way it sings, "cheer, cheer, cheer."
CHIP	This is it's call, short and thin.
FLAME	Red crested, or red headed.
PARTY CLOTHES	It wears a bright red dress.

CATBIRD

RED FEATHER	For the cluster of red feathers.
REDDY	Same reason.

CHICKADEE

ACROBAT	It clings to a tree twig in a reverse position, and goes round and round as it looks for insects.

CHICKADEE (continued)

BLACK CAP	On top of the head is a black spot, like a cap.
BOW TIE	A black streak in front of its neck makes it seem to be wearing a bow tie.
CHEERY	It is a happy bird.
CROWN	The black spot on top of its head is like a crown.
DEE DEE	Or, just DEE. This is part of its call.
HIGH COLLAR	It wears a high collar in front.
ROUND N' ROUND	He pecks each twig for insect eggs and goes round and round it.
KITCH	The Chippewa Indians called him 'Kitch Kitch Ga Ne Shi.'

CHIMNEY SWIFT

SPEED DEMON	This bird flies faster than most birds.

COCKATOO

COCKY	From his name and from the crest of the greater sulphur crested cockatoo. Name given to a cockatoo in the Bronx Zoo.
INDIAN SUMMER	Wears the fall color of orange in his crest.
MILDRED	In the Staten Island Zoo.

COWBIRD

NEST SNATCHER	This bird lays the eggs in the nests of smaller birds.
PARASITE	It depends on others to care for her young, if they will.
SHIFTLESS	It uses any nest it can find.
TICK SNATCHER	It sits on animal's backs; picks off ticks.

CRANE

BLAIR	The whooping crane call is like the blare of an automobile.
O JE JAK	An American Indian name for the sand hill crane.
RUSTY	Name of the whooping crane in "The Whooping Crane," by Robert M. McClung.
WHOOPER	This is taken from the word, 'whooping.'
BALLET DANCER	The Sandhill crane makes high kicks and leaps at mating time.

CROW

BLACK MARAUDER	Crow is a thief, a marauder, yet he is also the farmer's friend.
BLACK LEG	Crow robs the nest of the smaller birds.
CAW	The crow's call.
CHICKAMY CRANY CROW	In "Little Mr. Thimblefinger and his Queer Country," by Joel C. Harris.
FEARLESS	A crow is fearless; he laughs at scarecrows, too.
HIDE & SEEK	Crow plays tricks on his enemies.
HO SA	The American Indian name for "little crow."
JOHNNY CROW	Name of a crow in "Johnny Crow's New Garden," by Leslie Brooke.
MIME	Crows are mimics.
MISCHIEF	A crow is mischievous.
SCAVENGER	Crow picks up anything.
THIEF	Crows have thieving propensity, similar to kleptomania in humans. They like bright shiny

CROW (continued)

	objects to hide away.
VENTRILOQUIST	Some crows can throw their voices so that their enemy will hunt for them in the wrong direction.
WHISTLER	A crow is able to whistle.

DOVE

CHENOA	"White dove" in American Indian language.
COO	The mourning dove coo's softly.
LA PALOMA	The mourning dove in Spanish.
MOURNER	The mourning dove sounds sad and mournful as though he had lost his last friend.
ROO	A turtle dove says, "Roo coo, roo coo."

DUCK

AH AH WEH	The American Indian name for 'duck.'
ALICE	The white duck in the Freddy Stories by Walter Brooks.
DAB DAB	The duck in the Dr. Doolittle stories by Hugh Lofting.
EMMA	A duck in the Freddy Stories.
JEMIMA PUDDLE DUCK	The duck in the story of the same name by Beatrix Potter.
MRS. SIEVE	A duck lets the water run out from the tongue when scoops up water, mud and insects.
LUDO	The duck in "Wonderful Adventures of Ludo," by Jack Roberts. This green duck went around the world.
PEPPI	In "Peppi, the duck," by Rhea Wells.
PING	The Chinese duck in the "Story

DUCK (continued)

	about Ping," by Marjorie Flack.
POLLY PUNK	"Ponk" for short, in "Story of Mrs. Tubbs," by Hugh Lofting.
REBECCAH	Rebeccah Puddle Duck is the sister-in-law of Jemima and her story is told in the "Tale of Jemima Puddle Duck," by Beatrix Potter.
SHEE KEEB	American Indian name for 'duck.'
SHY	The Black Duck is shy.
UNCLE WESLEY	A duck in the Freddy stories by Walter Brooks.

EAGLE

CHE HE TA	American Indian for 'eagle.'
KEE HU	American Indian for 'eagle,' or 'falcon.'
KEN DA WA	American Indian for 'eagle.'
WE PIA GAH	American Indian for 'golden eagle.'

FALCON

BELLE	Bells are used to reveal the whereabouts of the trained hawk.
ELSU	A flying falcon.
FALCO	Latin for 'falcon.'
FINIST	Name given to a falcon in "The Feather of Finist, the Falcon," in the Russian Wonder Tales.
SPEEDY	The prairie falcon in "Pets Wild and Western," by Elmo N. Stevenson.

FINCH

FRECKLES	The crimson finch has markings like freckles.
ROUGE	The Zebra finch has rouge (red) splashes.

FINCH (continued)

SLOPPY JOE — The Black Ringed finch looks as though it wore two bibs edged in black.

SAILOR — House finch swoops, sails through the air.

FLICKER

ANT EATER — The flicker does eat ants.

BLACK BIB — It has a black spot on its breast like a bib.

BLACK MUSTACHE — It looks as though he had a mustache.

BUZZ — By his buzzing noise, he scares people.

FLICKUP — Taken from his name.

KEE YEE — His notes sound like this.

WHITE SPOT — When he flies the white spot on his back shows.

WICK WICK — The call of the bird.

YOU SEE! — Some think he says this when he calls.

GOLDFINCH

BELLE — The goldfinch has a bell song.

BLACK CAP — The black spot on his head.

CHEERIO — Goldfinches are happy birds.

CHIC — His call goes like this, "Per-chic-Or-Ree."

THISTLEBIRD — It lines its nest with thistle down.

WILD CANARY — It is wild, and it sings with a bell-like song, like the canary.

YELLOW JACKET — It wears a yellow coat.

GRACKLE

BLACK BILL — The grackle is all black, he has a black bill.

NOISY ONE — It is especially noisy.

GRACKLE (continued)

YELLOW EYE   It has yellow eyes.

GROSBEAK

CHEEPER   It cheeps.

PINKY   The male has a pink breast.

RED BIB   The male rose-breasted gros-
                          beak has a red breast.

RED PATCH   As above.

SLEIGH BELLS   His notes resemble the jingling
                          of sleigh bells. (Evening Gros-
                          beak.)

SUNFLOWER   It is the color of sunflowers,
                          yellow, and it likes sunflower
                          seeds.

SUNBURN   His feathers are so rosy they
                          look as though he were sun-
                          burned.

GULL

CORKY   The gull is as buoyant as corks.

STREET CLEANER   The gull assists in eating the
                          waste along the waterfront.

TAG   The gulls play tag with each oth-
                          er when bathing.

TOPGALLANT   The gull's name in "Topgallant,"
                          by Marjorie Medary.

TOUGHIE   Herring Gull-he is just that.

HAWK

KILLY KILLY   The war cry of a day hawk.

ONE EYE   A Swainson's hawk.

RUFOUS REDTAIL   A hawk in "Rufous Redtail," by
                          Helen Garrett.

SCREAMER   The day time hawk screams.

WHEELER   The day time hawk wheels in the
                          sky.

HUMMINGBIRD

ANNA	From the Anna's Hummingbird, the California species.
COQUETTE	It's a pretty little thing.
DAZZLER	It's bright plumage is dazzling in the sun.
DEWEY	It takes its bath in the morning dew.
FIRE	His plumage looks as though it were on fire. He is a firey fighter too.
FLOWER	When the bird darts at a blossom the wings look like a few bright petals of the flower.
FLUTTER	The wings flash and flutter.
GLITTER	Small scales reflect the light in prismic hues.
HELICOPTER	He can fly straight up and down, backwards and forwards.
HONEY	He is lovely to look at and takes honey from the flowers.
HUMMER	The buzzing or humming of the bird.
JEWEL	He looks like a cluster of bright jewels.
MINI	From "Minima" meaning "smallest."
NEEDLE	The beak looks like one as he darts at his enemy.
OI NA	American Indian word for 'jewel.'
RAINBOW	The many colors of his feathers.
SCRAPPER	He puts up a good fight.
SWORD BEARER	His bill is 5 inches long.
WEB THIEF	This bird tries to take the spider's web with its bill to make the nest, and often succeeds.
WHIRLYBIRD	The name for a helicopter.

HUMMINGBIRD (continued)

WHISTLING WINGS The male Broad-tailed Hummingbird makes a sound like 'a rap-
idly revolving circular saw when
rubbed by a splinter,' or, 'a
shrill screeching noise' with his
wings in flight.

JACKAL

TABAQUI "The dish-licker," in the Jungle
Book by Rudyard Kipling.

KITE

CHIL In the Jungle Book, by Rudyard
Kipling.

MACAW

"GENERAL" Name given to a blue and gold
macaw.

HAMMER CRACKER His powerful beak crushes nuts
that would take a hammer.

MACK Name given to a scarlet macaw
and comes from the first part of
the bird's name.

POLLY Pronounced 'Pawley,' and is a
blue and gold macaw in "Everyday Miracle," by Gustav Eckstein.

POP A Hyacinthine macaw in the
Bronx Zoo.

MAGPIE

BLINKY A black billed magpie in "Pets
Wild and Western," by Elmo N.
Stevenson.

MANAKIN

GRANDMA The black-headed manakin looks
as though it had on a cap and
shawl.

RUFFLES Its feathers are ruffled.

MAMMY It looks like a southern mammy.

MEADOW LARK

    COLORATURA   It has a gay, flute-like song.

MOCKINGBIRD

    GRAY COAT   It wears a gray outfit.

    IMITATOR   This bird imitates the songs of other birds.

    KING OF SONG   He can sing so many songs.

    MELODY   He sings many songs.

    MIMIC   He imitates the other bird songs.

    MOONLIGHT SONATA   He sings during the night.

    QUAKER   The suit is gray.

    WHISTLER   He whistles.

    OPERATIC STAR   He can sing so many songs.

MYNAH

    JERRY   A talking bird that lived 20 years.

    JOHNNY   Was used as a test for the book "Pet Myna," by All-Pets.

    INKEY   He is coal black.

    INK SPOT   The same idea.

    LITTLE BIT   A champion talker that knew more than 40 phrases.

    RAFFLES   A famous Mynah belonging to Zetta and Carveth Wells that could whistle the "Star Spangled Banner." He came from the Malayan Jungle.

    TIONG   Javan Hill Mynah in the St. Louis Zoo.

    TOMMY   Javan Hill Mynah in the St. Louis Zoo.

NUTHATCH

    CIRCLE BIRD   He goes round and round the tree as he goes up it in his search for food.

    MR. UPSIDE DOWN   He works up and down the trunk of the tree upside down.

NUTHATCH (continued)

YANK
Or, HANK, which sounds like the call of the white breasted nuthatch.

OWL

ATTIC
The elf owl hides in the top of a tall cactus in the daylight. He climbs to the very top.

BARNEY
He lives in old barns.

BILLY OWL
The name local residents call the burrowing owl.

CROO
The love note of the California Coast Screech Owl.

DAMPER
He flies on silent wings.

DICTATOR
The horned owl is aggressive.

FUZZY
Owlets are fuzzy and white. The name of the owl in "Little Prairie Dog," by Jene Barr.

GLADSTONE
Name of a tame owl.

GHOST FACE
The snowy owl has a face like a ghost.

GLORIA
A Screech owlet.

HOME LOVER
The barn owl likes to live in peace.

HOO WHO YOU?
From its call.

HOW DO YOU DO?
The burrowing owl is always bowing.

KEE, KAICK
The call of the burrowing owl.

KNOCK KNEES
The barn owl looks as though he had knock knees.

LADY
When the owl moves across the floor, she picks up her feathers, like a lady holds up her gown.

MA KOTCH
American Indian for 'owl.'

ME ATH WA'
American Indian for 'owl.'

MONKEY
The barn owl's face appears like a monkey.

OWL (continued)

NIGHT FLIGHT	Owls fly at night.
NOCTURNE	Owls fly at night.
OGRE	Owl looks like an ogre.
OLD MR. BROWN	The owl in the stories of Beatrix Potter.
OLD MAN	The face of the barn owl is like that of an old man.
POOK POO	The calls of the burrowing owl.
RUFFLES	The face of the barn owl is bordered in brown ruffles.
SCREE EE EE	The way the barn owl hisses as he goes through the night.
SENTRY	Owl, as he sits quietly watching for prey.
SHADOWS ON THE MOON	The owl flying, with no sound, across the moon.
SHIVERS	Owl makes you shiver with his sad, quavering call.
SNOW WHITE	The snowy throat of the barn owl.
THREE CORNERS	The barn owl's face is three cornered.
TIGER	The great horned owl is the tiger of the air, for he is savage.
TOO TOO	The owl's name in the Dr. Doolittle's stories by Hugh Lofting.
TOOTHLESS	Owl looks like a toothless old woman.
TUFFY	There are tufts on top of owl's head.
WA CIN TON	American Indian for 'wise owl.'
WHOO EET	The call of the California saw whet owl.
WORRY WART	The great gray owl looks worried.

OWL (continued)

| WAIST COAT | An owl that is a pet throws back his breast feathers just as a man throws open his coat. |

PARRAKEET

BUTTERCUP	Its feathers are yellow.
CINNAMON	The wings are cinnamon color.
EGBERT	A yellow parrakeet that performed in the colored feature picture "Bill and Coo."
FEISTY	Full of energy.
GRAYWINGS	The wings are grey and the body blue.
MAIZE	Pronounced MAISIE for a yellow parrakeet.
MR. PEEPERS	The way it calls, it peeps.
MICKEY	An Australian Shell Parrakeet.
PETE	A character in "Pete, the Parrakeet," by Irma S. Black.
POLLY	A female Australian shell parrakeet.
RUBY	A red-eyed, white feathered bird.
SKYE	A bird as blue as the sky.

PARROT

ACROBAT	He rolls and tumbles in the pool when bathing.
CIRCUS	His circus colored plumage.
CORNELIUS EXLECTUS	A Sacred Temple parrot.
CAPTAIN HOOK	Parrot uses his upper mandible as a hook to raise himself up. He is a Captain because he is found on ships as a pet.
GAUDY	He has feathers of many gaudy colors.

PARROT (continued)

> GREEN WAVES   The blue fronted Amazon has feathers that resemble green waves.
>
> LOUELLA   The parrot in the Carolyn Haywood stories.
>
> MR. PINCER   He cracks nuts with his bill.
>
> MRS. HINGE   The bill is connected to the skull by a hinge.
>
> POLLYANDREW   In "Mr. T. W. Anthony Woo," by Marie Hall Ets.
>
> SNOWSHOES   This parrot walks as though he wore snowshoes.
>
> TOTO   In "T's Triumph," by Claire Huchet Bishop.

PENGUIN

> ADELA   From "Adelie," the scientific name.
>
> ANDY   Name of a penguin in the Bronx Zoo.
>
> ANNIE   Name of a penguin in the Bronx Zoo.
>
> BEAU BRUMMEL   He is always dressed like a dandy.
>
> CLOWN   Penguin is a funny, humorous animal.
>
> EMPEROR   Comes from the species name, 'Emperor Penguin.'
>
> JOHNNY PENGUIN   Appears in "Johnny Penguin," by Dorothy Bryan.
>
> KING   From the species named 'King Penguin.'
>
> PADDLEWINGS   In "The Penguin of Galapagos" by Wilfred S. Bronson.
>
> MARY   A penguin in the Bronx Zoo.
>
> WILLIAM   Penguin in the Bronx Zoo, sometimes called Willy.

PENGUIN (continued)

"HAVE TUX"   He wears a black and white suit that looks like a tuxedo. He will travel with the rest because he likes to look at the scenery.

TOBAGGAN   He takes rides down slopes into the sea.

PIGEON

HERMAN   Rocketed to stardom in M.G.M.'s 'The Gazebo,' and received the Patsy award given to a top performing movie animal star.

LU CHIH   The American Indian name for 'pigeon.'

LUTE JA   An American Indian name for 'pigeon.'

COLUMBA   Taken from the scientific name, 'Columba Livia.'

MEALY   A racing pigeon.

MR. AND MRS.   Pigeons in "Everyday Miracle,"
   NORTH   by Gustav Eckstein.

THE NEIGHBORS Pigeon in "Everyday Miracle."

RED   Pigeon in "Everyday Miracle."

RUCH KA SCHA KA   American Indian name for 'white pigeon.' Could be reduced to RUCH, or KA, etc.

WHITEY   Appeared in "Everyday Miracle."

PEACOCK

JEWEL CASE   It has beautiful colored feathers in the tail, and 'eyes' that look like jewels.

MOR   A character in the "Jungle Book," by Rudyard Kipling.

PLOVER

BOBBY   It bobs its head as it walks.

MR. DENTIST   This bird picks food from the teeth of the crocodile.

PLOVER (continued)

RINGER	It has two rings about its neck.

QUAIL

CUH	The sounds of the quail seem like, 'cuh cuh cuh.'
WHEEE...EE	The call of the California Quail.
WHITE TIE	The quail, or bob-white has a white throat, edged in black.

RAVEN

KA KA GOS	American Indian name for 'raven.'

REDSTART

DART	It darts about.
HOPPER	He is never still.
HIPPETY	First part of Hippety Hop.

ROAD RUNNER

CHAPARRAL	Another name given to this bird.
COCK OF THE DESERT	Another name for this bird.
LIZARD BIRD	Another name for it.
MEDICINE BIRD	Another name for it.
MISTER X	The bird makes an X when he walks.
MYSTERY	The X left in the sand after he walks by seems a mystery to those who don't know what made it.
PAISANO	Pronounced 'pi-sano,' meaning "fellow countryman," a name given to it by the Mexicans.
PERRP	The sound the road runner makes is like a purr.
RUNNING CUCKOO	Another name for this bird.
SHARP BILL	It has a sharp, pointed bill.
SLY ONE	He has canny devices with which to kill his prey.

ROAD RUNNER (continued)

TRICKSTER	For the same reason.
WAHPT	American Indian name meaning, 'great runner.'
WAR BIRD	Another name for this bird.

ROBIN

BROWN EYES	The ground robin, or towhee, for its eyes.
CHEER UP	The cheery call of the robin.
COCK ROBIN	A character in Tale of Mrs. Tiggy-Winkle, by Beatrix Potter.
HOP-STOP-LISTEN	He hops, stops, listens for the stirring of an earthworm.
MR. J.J. POMEROY	Called JJ, in the Freddy stories by Walter Brooks.
TRAVELLER	He travels a lot.
WAKE ROBIN	In the story, "Wake Robin," by John Burroughs.

SANDPIPER

SANDERLING	In the story, "Run Sandpiper Run," by Lloyd Lózes Goff.
SEESAW	As he walks, he keeps bowing, his head goes down, as his tail goes up.
TEETER	For the above reason.
TWIT TWIT	The call of the sandpiper.

SCARLET TANGER

DU TA	American Indian name for 'scarlet red.'
FLAME	The color of the feathers.
FIREBIRD	For his bright feathers.
RED LIGHT	For his bright feathers.

SEED CRACKER

BLOTTO	The black bellied has ink splotches on it.
WARRIOR	The black spots look like war

SEED CRACKER (continued)

> clouds against a red sky.

SPARROW

EVE	The Vesper sparrow is heard early in the evening.
DRY CLEANER	The sparrow rolls, flutters in the dust to clean his feathers.
SHY ONE	The white throated sparrow is shy.
SPRING	The song sparrow's song is one of the first signs of spring.
SWEET VOICE	The Vesper sparrow is called this in the "Burgess Bird Book for Children."
WHITE CHEEKS	The sparrow has white cheeks.
WHITE PATCH	In "White Patch," the sparrow is called this. A book by Olive L. Earle.

STARLING

BULLY	A fighter.
FIESTY	A fighter.
JACOB	Coat has many colors, just like Jacob's in the Bible.
STRUTTER, or OLD STRUTTER	From the way he walks.

SWALLOW

CINNAMON	The breast feathers are cinnamon color.
GRAY APRON	The Purple Martin has breast feathers of gray.
HURRY UP	The Tree Swallow sounds like this when he is hurrying his mate to finish the nest.
PURPLE COAT	The Purple Martin has purple feathers.
SAILOR	He is always sailing through the air.

SWALLOW (continued)

STEEL	Feathers have a steel blue in them.

SWAN

WHISTLER	The call of the Whistling swan.

TAILOR BIRD

DARZEE	In the Jungle Book by Rudyard Kipling.
STITCHER	Because it stitches a cradle of leaves.
SINGER	Because it not only sings a song, but it stitches as a Singer sewing machine.

THRUSH

"CHUCK"	The call of the Hermit Thrush.
DARK EYES	The Hermit Thrush has dark eyes.
DOTTY	The polka dots on its feathers.
FLUTE	His song sounds as though he were playing a flute.
LEE	From the song of the wood thrush which is 'e-o-lee.'
POLKA	From the dots on his feathers.
SHORTY	The wood thrush is short and has a short bill.
SHY ONE	The Hermit thrush.

TITMOUSE

JAUNTY	He looks jaunty.
QUAKER GRAY	Feathers are a soft gray.
TUFFY	He has a fine showy crest.
ZEEEE	He has only one note which he sings high.

TOUCAN

GROWLER	In the St. Louis Zoo.

TURKEY

OSCAR   The character in "Turkey Tale,"
                                   by Frances A. Bacon.

PAL LA OOH   American Indian name for 'tur-
                                   key.'

VIREO

HAPPY   The male sings happily as it
                                   works covering the outside of
                                   the nest with lichens.

SWINGER   He makes a swinging basket
                                   nest.

TEASER   The red-eyed vireo is a teaser.

WARBLER   The Warbling virero sings six
                                   or eight notes. The male sings
                                   while he sits on the nest.

WAXWING

BONNET BIRD   In Maine he is called this for
                                   his crest.

FRIEND   Helps the other birds, feeds
                                   baby birds whose parents are
                                   lost or dead.

SILKY   Its plumage is silky. His tail
                                   is silky.

SPECTACLES   The black lines on his head
                                   make it look as though he had
                                   glasses.

WAXY   From the name given it in "Pets,
                                   wild and western" by Elmo Ste-
                                   venson.

WILD CHERRY   The Cedar waxwing likes to eat
                                   cherries.

WISE ONE   He appears to be wise.

WEAVER

RUDOLPH   He has a red bill, nose, like the
                                   red nosed reindeer.

WHISTLER'S   She has a white cap.
MOTHER

WHIPPOORWILL

BIG MOUTH	It stretches it from ear to ear.
HOLCHKO	Hopi Indian name for 'poor will,' the sleeping one.
LONESOME	It sounds lonely.
NIGHT WATCHER	It comes out at night.
WHITE NECKLACE	It wears white feathers around its neck.

WOODPECKER

AMIGO	He is a friendly bird. AMIGA for feminine.
CHISLER, the	Noisy when he taps.
DINNER JACKET	The downy woodpecker has a white front, black and white wings.
DRILLER	Sounds as though he was drilling.
FERAO	The scarlet woodpecker in the Jungle Book, by Rudyard Kipling.
HAMMER & TONGS	Husband and wife. Woodpecker goes at his work with hammer and tongs.
KNOCK KNOCK	A noisy bird.
MR. CARPENTER	You can hear him work.
PERKY PECKER	He is just that.
POLE SITTER	The red headed woodpecker often is seen sitting on telephone poles, fence posts, and at the tops of dead trees.
RED HEAD	He has a red head.
TAT TAT	From the noisy Rat-tat-tat that he makes.
TREE SURGEON	He keeps the tree well by eating insects on it.

WREN

DUMMY	The Marsh wren builds a dozen dummy nests to fool his enemies, so he is no dummy.

WREN (continued)

HAPPY	The House wren sings happily as she builds her nest.
HOUSEWIFE	The House wren seems like a typical housewife, busy, happy.
LIMMERSHIN	The winter wren in the Jungle Book, by Rudyard Kipling.
TEA KETTLE	The Carolina wren, whose voice is so loud, can be heard everywhere. So can the tea kettle which sings too.

YELLOW THROAT

BLACK MASK	The male Northern Yellow Throat has a black face.
WHITCHETY	The way the male sings.

YELLOW WARBLER

SEE WEET	From the call of the bird, "See see see weet."
SILVER	He has a silver colored nest.
SWEET SWEET	After the song or call of the bird.
THREE DECKER	Warbler builds floors over the eggs that the cowbird puts into her nest, and sometimes has three rows of eggs.
YELLOW JACKET	His yellow coat.

CATS

CATS

ABYSSINIAN   PERSIAN
ANGORA   RUSSIAN BLUE
BURMESE   SIAMESE
MANX   TABBY
TORTOISE SHELL

Names

ABSALOM — Name given to a male Siamese, meaning 'Father is peace.'

ABYGAIL — Name given to a female Abyssinian, meaning, "My father is joy."

ADONIS — Name given to a male Grand Champion meaning, "a favorite." In Greek Mythology Adonis was a favorite of Aphrodite, the goddess of love and beauty.

AGFA — Name given to a Siamese cat. "Ag" was used as a short name.

AGRIPPINA — Belonged to Agnes Repplier, the author, who wrote about her in "Agrippina." In Roman history Agrippina was the mother of the Roman emperor Nero.

AJAX — Name given to a male Siamese, meaning 'strong.' Ajax was a mighty warrior of the Greeks.

AL HAKIM — Name given to a male Himalyan seal point.

ALABASTER — Given to a golden eyed, white male long haired cat. It means, 'white, translucent.'

ALEZAN — Name given to a champion female Siamese.

ALLY PALLY   Name given to a Siamese cat.

AMBER   The golden male cat in "Danger, Crazy Cats," by Murray Robinson.

AMDOS YANKEE   A seal point, masculine Siamese.

AMURU   Name given to an Abyssinian.

ANDROMACHE   Name given to a female Persian cat. She was the wife of Hector in Greek legend. She is one of the finest characters in Homer.

ANGELA   Name given to a female long haired cat, meaning "angelic."

ANGUS SILKY   Sire of Gamma, which belonged to Pamela Mason. Angus means 'of great virtue.'

ANNA   Means 'grace.' A Siamese belonging to Pamela Mason.

ANSON   Name given to a Burmese and an Abyssinian. It means, 'born of God.'

APOLLINARIS   A cat that belonged to Mark Twain. Probably pertaining to 'apollonian' which is 'serene, poised, majestic,' a cult of Apollo.

APRILIS   Name given to a female Persian and probably coined from the word April.

ARCHIBALD BUCHANAN   Name given to a tom cat belonging to Pamela Mason. Archibald means, 'very valiant' and Buchanan was the 15th president of the U. S.

ARIEL   A female cat belonging to Andrew Lang, which hid spools, keys, pens, pencils, scissors under the rugs. In Shakespeare's Tempest, Ariel is a spirit of the air who is required to use his magic to help Prospero.

ATOSSA	Or Toss, belonged to Matthew Arnold, who wrote a poem about this Persian cat, called "Poor Matthias."
AUGUSTA	Means 'imperial.' Mary E. Wilkins, the author, owned this cat.
AUTUMN PRINT	A blue point Siamese cat.
AZTEC	Name given to a male silver tabby.
BABOU	In "The Long Cat," by Colette, story of a short haired black cat, which was nicknamed the 'long cat.'
BACK TALK	Name given to a kitten.
BALLERINA	Name given to a blue eyed white Persian.
BAMBEYLING	Name given to a champion blue point male Siamese.
BANDIT II	Name given to a silver Persian male cat.
BANGUR BAN	Ban means 'white.' "The White Cat and the Student," from a Gaelic poem, translated by Robin Flower.
BASIL	Meaning 'kingly' was given to a Siamese.
BANJO	Name given to a Chinchilla owned by Ella Wheeler Wilcox, author.
BEAU PEEP	Name given to a smoke Persian, meaning 'beautiful' Peep.
BEAUTY	Given to a blue, short haired cat.
BELLE	Means beautiful, given to a double champion Persian cat.
BELLA ADORADO	A four times champion Blue Cream. Means, 'adoring and beautiful.'

BES MUDI	"Bes" means cat. It belonged to Errol Flynn, and was a Siamese.
BETTY JO	A female kitten in "Smudge," by Clare T. Newberry.
BIBÉ	In "Love adventures of a French cat," by P. J. Stahl.
BILLY BOY	Name given to a white, long hair.
BINGY	Name given to a gray Persian.
BIT O' HONEY	Name given to a male cream.
BLUE TANGO	Name given to a blue pointed Siamese.
BLONDIE	Name given to a Siamese.
BONNIE CLAIRE	Female, grand champion Persian name, meaning 'illustrious, little good one.'
BONNIE JEAN	Name given to a female double champion blue point Siamese cat, meaning, 'gracious little one.'
BLACKY	A cat that belonged to Matthew Arnold.
BLATHERSKITE	A cat that belonged to Mark Twain, meaning 'to talk nonsense.'
BLU ACRE FANCEE	Name given a double Grand champion female blue Persian.
BLUE MICKY	A blue point male Siamese that was a Champion.
BLUE TANGO	Name given a male seal point Siamese.
BLUEGRASS	Becky Boone, daughter of Daniel Boone, owned this cat in "Becky and Her Brave Cat," by Miriam E. Mason.
BON JOE	Means, 'good, witty,' a name given to a male black smoke cat.
BONETTA	Name given to a female, white, long hair, meaning, 'good.'

BONETTE	A female Manx cat.
BOOTS	A female cat in "Danger, Crazy Cats," by Murray Robinson.
BOUHAKI	The first cat known to have a name was given this one. It belonged to King Hana in the 11th dynasty, Egypt. It was a Theban cat who sat with gold earrings in its ears at the foot of its master, King Hana. In "Agrippina," by Agnes Repplier.
BOY	A champion blue eyed Manx cat that was white.
BROWN VELVET	A Burmese.
BRUN BOY	A Siamese, probably chocolate pointed.
BRUN MALVANA	A female chocolate point Siamese.
BOY BRUTUS	A silver Tabby, short haired, male.
BUBU BARA	Bubu means 'baby.' Name given an Abysinnian cat.
BULLFROG	Name given a chocolate pointed Siamese.
BUMRA	A Triple Champion, Burmese cat.
BUSTER	A male Persian, father of Smudge, in "Smudge," by Clare T. Newberry. He was a big red cat.
BUTTON NOSE	A female, blue, long hair.
CADUCEUS	The staff carried by Hermes, or Mercury, as messenger of the gods. Emblem of the medical profession. Name given a male, seal point Siamese.
CAESAR	Roman general, conqueror of Gaul. Name given a seal point, Siamese male.

CALLENDER	A tom cat.
CALVIN	A male Maltese given to Charles Dudley Warner by Harriet Beecher Stowe. It turned on a hot-air register to a room where it went when it wished to be alone; but he never turned it off.
CANDACE	A female Black Manx cat, meaning, 'glowing.'
CANDYTUFT	A Siamese cat.
CARBONEL	In "Carbonel, the King of the Cats," by Barbara Sleigh. He was under the witch's spell.
CHANOINE	Belonged to the author, Victor Hugo, meaning, 'canon.'
CHARRITA	The pike-faced red Persian female.
CHARMIAN	A Siamese cat.
CHARMER	A white Persian.
CHAUNCEY	In "Danger, Crazy Cats," by Murray Robinson. Means, chancellor.'
CHERI	Name given to an Abyssinian.
CHESHIRE CAT	Cat drawn by John Tenniel for "Alice in Wonderland," by Lewis Carroll, a constantly grinning cat.
CHIEF NODA PURACHUTR	A Siamese cat, probably a coined name.
CHINCHILLA	Name is derived from "sinchi," meaning, 'strong.'
CHINNIE	Name given a silver, short haired Tabby.
CHIQUITA	A blue smoke Persian cat, meaning 'little chewer.'
CHIRMON LON	Name given a Siamese seal point champion.

CHITALA	Name given a Siamese seal point.
CHO SEN	Name given a Siamese cat.
CHU CHU	A blue Persian.
CHULA	A female Siamese cat.
CINDERELLA	Name given a Chinchilla Persian.
CLENSI	Name given a Siamese.
CLOTH CAP	Name given Pamela Mason's tabby.
CLOW OF CARNE	Name given a Tortoiseshell, white cat.
COFFEE	A Siamese cat.
CONCHA	A kitten. An early father, Padre Francisco Uria, was given these four kittens by a devoted Indian - Concha, Frasquito, Lola, Pepto, and Frasquito, his favorite, leaped on the bell rope, at the time the Father died, swung the rope back and forth, tolling for the Franciscan.
COLUMBINE	Name given a cat that belonged to Thomas Carlyle, which was black. It means 'dove.'
COPPER BLAZE	Name given to a red, long hair.
CORTES	Name given to a male cream Persian. Cortés was the Spanish conqueror of Mexico.
COURAGE	Name given a female long hair.
CUDDLES	Name given a Persian cat.
DABRU	A Grand and Triple Champion Abyssinian cat, named Best Cat six times.
DAH LING	Name given a Champion Siamese. The word 'darling' drawn out.
DANDIE	Name given to a Champion Siamese.

DAPHNE	Name given to a Champion Siamese, 'sign of triumph.'
DARE DEVIL	Name given a white, long hair.
DASCO	Name given to a Siamese kitten belonging to Pamela Mason's family, and a champion.
DAVID	A black Siamese, meaning, 'beloved.'
DEBBIE	Name given a blue cream, from Deborah, meaning 'bee; industry.'
DELIA	A seal point Siamese, female, meaning 'chaste.'
DENISE	A blue smoke Persian, meaning 'serving the god of revelry.'
DESIREE	Name given a female Siamese, meaning 'beloved.'
DIANE	Name given to an Abyssinian cat, meaning, 'goddess of the moon.'
DICK	The pet name of the cat belonging to Mrs. Frances Hodgson Burnett, the author of 'Little Lord Fauntleroy.' She exhibited him at the first cat show held in New York City.
DILLY BOY	Name given a masculine frost pointed Siamese cat.
DIMPLE	Name given a Siamese cat.
DOLL	Name given a female white long hair.
DREAM OF MO LING	Name given a Siamese cat.
DRUSILLA	Name given a Champion Siamese cat, meaning 'eyes of dew.'
ECLASSITY	Name for a female Calico Manx Cat.

ELIJAH

A small tiger striped kitten so called because it was found in church at the time the minister was preaching about Elijah. Found in "Elijah, the Fishbite."

ENJOLRAS

Cat belonging to Theophile Gautier, French poet, novelist, critic, probably meaning, 'a coaxer, wheedler.'

EPONINE

A black cat belonging to Theophile Gautier.

FABIAN

A Siamese male, blue point and Champion. It means, 'to avoid battle.'

FAIRMAID

A blue pointed Siamese queen.

FANTASIE II

A male Persian cat.

FEATHER

A female white, long hair.

FEATHERS

Name of a cat that belonged to Carl Van Vechten, author, which was a Persian.

FILIGREE

Name for a Double Champion Silver Tabby. It means, 'lacy, jeweller's work, or anything very delicate.'

FINNEGAN II

Called Finne, for short name. In "Finnegan II, his 9 lives," by Carolyn Sherwin Bailey.

FIREFLY

Name given a male blue pointed Siamese.

FISH HEAD

In the story "Fish Head," by Jean Fritz, a rapscallion cat living on the waterfront.

FLAVIA

Sir Richard Steele's cat to which he alluded in the "Tatler." It means, 'flaxon-haired.'

FLEA BITE

A cat.

FLUFF

In "Joan Wanted a Kitty," by Jane Brown Gemmill.

FLUFFY	Name given a Persian cat.
FLYBALL	A gray striped kitten in "Space Cat" by Ruthven Todd.
FLYING CLOUD	Name given to a Persian.
FOLLY	Name given to a Siamese cat.
FOSS	Edward Lear's cat, about which he wrote in "the Owl and the Pussy Cat."
FRANCINE POUCETTE	Double Champion, golden-eyed white Persian cat. Francine means, 'little free one.' Pouce means 'thumb.' Poucette would be, 'little thumb.'
FRASQUITO	The kitten belonging to the Padre Francisco Uria. See under the entry 'Concha.'
FROST-E	A frost point Siamese.
FROSTY	In "Swamp Cat," by Jim Kjelgaard.
GAMMA	Meaning, 'the third letter of the alphabet.' It was Pamela Mason's first Siamese cat.
GAMMA MOON	The full name of the cat above.
GAYLA	A female white, long hair.
GIANT	A Champion male white, short hair.
GIPSY	Booth Tarkington's pepper and salt kitten.
GOLDEN DUTCHESS	A long hair.
GOLDEN NUGGET	A cream, long hair, male.
GOOD FORTUNE	In "The Cat Who Went to Heaven," by Elizabeth Coatsworth.
GRAVITY	In "Great Gravity," by Johanna Johnston.
GRIDDLEBONE	The cat in "Macavity: the Mystery Cat," a poem, by T. S. Eliot.

GRIMALKIN	The cat that belonged to Benjamin West, the artist in his biography by Marguerite Henry. It means, 'an ill tempered old woman,' or 'an old female cat.'
GRYMALKIN	Was the Devil's cat.
GRISNEZ	A Siamese cat, blue pointed.
GUMSHOES	A cat walks lightly.
GYP	A cat that belonged to Andrew Lang, the fairy tale writer.
H.R.H.	His, or Her Royal Highness. A Champion Siamese cat.
HANSA	A Champion Siamese cat, meaning, 'gracious.'
HARRIET	In "The Ninth Life," by Mazo de la Roche.
HARRLI	A tabby in "Hurrli, Bold, Proud and Amiable, Master of Elk House," by Paul Eipper.
HEATHCLIFF	A part blue Persian cat.
HEBNI	A black, short hair, grand champion.
HECTOR	A male Siamese cat, meaning, 'support.'
HEIL	A Particolor Manx cat, meaning, 'hail.'
HEINI	A Siamese cat, meaning, 'home lord.'
HIDDIGEIGEI	A Tom cat in "Songs of the Tom Cat, Hiddigeiger, a poem," by Joseph Victor Von Scheffel.
HINSE	Sir Walter Scott's cat who listened to the Arthurian legends which Scott read aloud.
HO	A Siamese cat, meaning, 'the good.'

HODGE

Dr. Samuel Johnson's cat, in "Hodge, the cat," a poem, by Susan Coolidge. Johnson wrote that Hodge doted on oysters.

HONORLORE

A blue eyed, white female, long hair.

ILO

A male Champion Siamese cat.

ITCHABODY

A cat in "The Little Leftover-Witch," by Florence Laughlin.

JAGUARUNDI

Belongs to the cat family, lives in South and Central America, and is a favorite pet of boys and girls there.

JAMES

Name of a Siamese cat, meaning, 'supplanter.'

JAY TEE

A Grand Champion, seal point, female Siamese.

JENNA

A Grand Champion Tabby.

JENNIE

The cat in "The Abandoned," by Paul Gallico.

JENTLEMAN

A Grand Champion Tabby, Silver, male.

JOSETTA

A red Tabby, long hair, meaning, 'little Jose.'

KADIS

A Tame cat that lived several thousand years before Christ, the cat in Nubia.

KANNIKA

A blue pointed, female Siamese, meaning, 'Jasmine-like blossom.'

KEDI

Means 'cat.'

KEW KING

Outstanding cat of early days when the National Cat Club ran the shows at the Crystal Palace.

KEWALO	A grand champion blue pointed male Siamese.
KHAFA SIMI BEY	Shortened to 'Shimmy.' A Siamese.
KIKI, the Demure	An Angora tabby in "Sentimental-ities, " by Colette.
KING PETER	A red Tabby, long hair, male.
KNURREMUREE	The King of Cats in Folklore.
KRISADON	A Double Champion seal point, male, Siamese.
KRISPIN	A Seal point, Siamese.
KIERROO	A Triple Champion Black Manx cat.
KUT	An Egyptian name for the male cat.
KUTTA	The Egyptian name for the female cat.
LITABOIS	A Seal point, Siamese, ancestor of the chocolate points today.
LOCKET	On the throats of many cats may be seen a small or light colored spot.
LADY FANTASIA	Shaded silver, long hair.
LADY LEEDS	For the R.R. Station at Leeds, where it was found.
LADY LYNN	A blue, female, long hair.
LANVIN	A blue point, Siamese.
LANTARA GENE	A blue point, female, Siamese.
LAUREL	A blue point Siamese.
LAVSNDEN LIBERTY	A blue Persian grand champion.
LINALE	A blue point female Siamese.
LITTLE DUTCHESS	A Persian cat.
LOCHINVAR	A male, any cat.
LORD BYRON	A black, male, long hair.

LORD OF THE MANOR	Any male cat.
LOXEY	A Triple Champion Tortie Manx.
MACAVITY	In "Macavity: the Mystery Cat," a poem by T. S. Eliot, also called the Hidden Paw, a ginger cat, tall and thin with sunken eyes the Napoleon of Crime.
MCDERMOT	Capt. Kidd's cat in Robert Lawson's book, "Captain Kidd's Cat." He wore a ruby ring in his ear, drank milk laced with rum.
MANX	The Manx cat is a tailess cat, named after the Isle of Man. The theory is that first Manx cats were brought by the Spaniards from the East, swam ashore from wrecked warships of the Spanish Armada.
MARIA	A blue Persian.
MARTY	The son of Flyball in "Space Cat," by Ruthven Todd. He and his sister Tailspin were born on the moon.
MATAPON	A cat that belonged to Emile Achard.
MAU	The Egyptians name for 'cat.' May have been inspired by a kitten's 'meow.' It is the onomatopoeic name in Oriental lands.
MAMY	A Turkish cat, meaning, "meow," probably.
MEFISTO	The cat that hated music in "Pet of the Met," by Lydia Freeman.
MEHITABEL	The alley cat in "The Song of Mehitabel," by Don Marquis.
MEOLA	In "Mr. T. W. Anthony Woo," by Marie Hall Ets.
MERLIN	The black cat in "13th is Magic,"

	by Joan Howard.
MERIT T'UNG	A Seal pointed Siamese.
MICETTO	Chateaubriand's ecclesiastical cat.
MIA	A Siamese cat imported from Bangkok in 1884.
MI LO JOIEE	A male Tabby.
MIMI	A Seal point, female, Siamese.
MINETTE	A white cat in "Love Adventures of a French Cat," by P.J. Stahl.
MING	A male Siamese cat, meaning, 'famous.'
MINNA MINNA MOWBRAY	In "The Gentle Cat," by Michael Joseph.
MISS AL LA BI	A blue pointed Siamese.
MITTENS	So called because it had 6 toes on each front paw, in "Mittens," by C. T. Newberry.
MITZIE	A Tabby in "Danger-Crazy Cats," by Murray Robinson
MRS. BERTHA MOCATTA	Cat in "Little White King," by Marguerite Steen.
MOOFA	Last of the Martian fishing cats who became Flyball's wife, in "Space Cat," by Ruthevy Todd.
MOONDANCE	A long hair, male, Grand Champion, white.
MOONSHEE	A seal point, male, Siamese.
MOONTALK	A Champion white, male.
MOONTIDE	A Grand Champion seal point Siamese.
MORGAN LE FAY	A Champion Siamese.
MORNING MIST	A smoke Persian.
MOUCHE	Belonged to Victor Hugo, meaning 'beauty patch.'
MUESSA	The favorite cat of Mohammed.

MUFF	The Persian cat in "Smudge," by C. T. Newberry. She is the mother of Smudge.
MUNGOJERRIE	The cat in "Macavity: the Mystery Cat," poem, by T. S. Eliot.
MUSH	A ginger cat belonging to Pamela Mason.
MUZZIE	A white Persian.
MYSOUFF	Belonged to Alexandre Dumas, French novelist.
NANKI POOH	A Siamese cat.
NARCISSUS	An orange eyed white, female, Domestic.
NAUGHTY SAIDEE	A Champion Siamese.
NEE YANG	A Siamese cat.
NELLIE	A maltese cat in "Nellie & Tom," by Marvin.
NELSON	A black cat, the favorite of Winston Churchill.
NERO	A male, Domestic short hair.
NEW	A Siamese cat belonging to Vivien Leigh.
NIBBLER	A Ginger Persian cat.
OGRE	A male Siamese cat.
OLIVER	In "Marshmallow," by C. T. Newberry.
OTHELLO	Cat belonging to Robert Southey, the poet.
OLAF	A Triple Champion red Tabby Manx cat.
PAGAN OF THE DARK	A champion seal point, male, Siamese.

PANDORA	A Double Champion, female, parti-color Manx.
PASHT	"Goddess of Light." Also, 'goddess of moon and love,' in Egypt, and identified with the cat.
PEPPER	A blue cream Persian cat.
PETE	A Siamese belonging to Frances and Richard Lockridge, mystery story writers.
PHO	A Siamese cat imported in 1884.
PICKLEPUSS	A red and white cat that hunts snakes, belonging to Margaret Cooper Gay. It is also called Monsieur du Piquel, and His Pickleship.
PIRATE	A white, long hair, male.
PITTAA PAT	A Siamese.
PITSCHI	A kitten that always wanted to be something else, in "Pitschi," by Hans E. Fischer.
PLATINE	A blue point short hair.
PLUTO	A black cat that had an eye put out by his master in Poe's story, "The Black Cat."
POO TOO	A Siamese cat.
PRET	A cat that belonged to Rev. J. G. Wood.
PRINCESS	A Siamese cat.
PRISCILLA	A Chinchilla, female.
PRINCE OF SIAM	Imported in 1897, a chocolated pointed Siamese.
PRITHIE PUSS	A Siamese cat.
PROMISE	A silver Tabby Persian, female.
PUDDY	The cat that got caught on a porch roof when she had her kittens. To get four kittens down she leaped from roof to nearest tree limb, a kitten held within her paw and

	teeth. This she did safely, four times.
PUDLENKA	In "The Immortal Cat," by Karel Capek.
PUFF	A ginger cat of Pamela Mason's.
PURR SON	A seal point, male, Siamese.
PUSS	Some Orientals believe that Puss derives from Pasht (Bast or Bastet), the ancient cat goddess of Egypt.
QUEEN ANN	A long hair.
QUICKSILVER	A silver tabby, female.
RA	A blue Persian, in "The Mysterious Ra," by Margaret Benson.
RABBIT	A brown Tabby, domestic, short hair.
RAG DOLL	A Persian cat, for it looks like one.
RAINBOW	In "The Rainbow Cat," by Rose Fyleman. A fairy cat with a violet nose, indigo eyes, pale blue ears, green front legs, red tail.
RAMAAHIPATI IV	A Siamese cat belonging to Greer Garson.
RAMREE RANI	A Burmese cat, female.
RAS BYANA	An Abyssinian cat.
RAS HAILU SAGAD	An Abyssinian cat. Ras means, 'head,' Hailu, means, 'sweet,' and Sagad means, 'to kneel.'
RED O'MAN	A red manx cat, male.
RENDEZVOUS	A Tortoise Shell long hair.
RHAPSODY	A black Persian cat.

RHODA	A blue pointed Siamese born in 1894, meaning, 'rose.'
RHUBARB	A movie star cat.
RIBBY	In "The Pie and the Patty Pan," by Beatrix Potter.
RIKKI	A Siamese cat.
ROBERT, Esq.	A short hair.
ROCCO	A Chocolate pointed, male, Siamese.
ROMNEY	A Seal pointed, male, Siamese.
ROYAL DOMINO	An Abyssinian cat.
RUMPEL	Cat belonging to Robert Southey.
RUSTY	A red Persian cat.
SABLE	A Siamese cat that had sable colored ears.
SADIE	A Siamese cat when young is called 'fly face.' Sometimes is called 'Flower face.'
SPRING SONG	An Abyssinian cat.
SAMPAN	A seal point, Siamese, female.
SEASHELL	A Siamese cat.
SELIMA	In "On the Death of a Favorite Cat, Drowned In a tub of Gold Fishes ..." by Thomas Gray. Meaning, 'like the moon.'
SERAPINA	The Cat in "Story of Serapina," by A. W. White. It means, "afire with love of God."
SERENADE	A blue point Siamese cat.
SARIA SHALA	An Abyssinian, female.
SEA CHANGE	An Abyssinian, female.
SHAH MINIATURE	A Siamese cat.
SHAH PASHA	A Siamese, in French, Chat-pas-chat, meaning cat-not-cat, or not

quite like cats.

SHADED SILVER	A Persian, female.
SHANNON	A Cream, female.
SHARON	A Siamese cat.
SHEBA	In "April's kittens," by Clare New-berry. The Bibical name for an ancient country in Southern Arabia.
SOAP SUDS	An orange eyed, white, female, Tripple Grand Champion, Domestic.
SIL O ETT	A Manx, red tabby, male.
SILVER MIST	A Siamese.
SILVER DENNIS	A silver Tabby, male.
SILVER DON	A Persian, shaded silver, male.
SILVER EMBLEM	A Chinchilla.
SILVER PATTERN	A short hair, Grand Champion. It won Hydon-Goodwin Challenge Award, for best short hair and domestic short hair. Silver Tabby, female, Domestic.
SILVER QUEST	A silver long hair, male.
SILVER SIGNATURE	A Chinchilla, silver, long hair. Double Champion.
SIMMY	A Royal Siamese cat, real name being Khafa Simi Bey, in "Little Kitten, Big World," by Victor and Jeanne Baldwin.
SINGUMIN	A seal point, female, Siamese.
SWIRL TIDE	A Silver Tabby, female, Champion.
SKIPPER	In "Fishing Cat," by Grayce Silver-ton Myers.
SKITTER	In "Skitter Cat and Little Boy," by Eleanor Youmans.
SKYWAY FLOWER	White, long hair, female.
SMOKY	Maltese, male, in "Danger-Crazy Cats," by Murray Robinson.

SMUDGIE	In "The Abandoned," by Paul Gallico, because of the black spot on the nose.
SMUDGE	A Persian in "Smudge," by C.T. Newberry.
SNEAKERS	For the black and white paws, likes to prowl around, in "Seven Stories about a cat named Sneakers," by Margaret Wise Brown.
SNITZ	An Alley cat.
SNOW DEAR	A long hair, white, female.
THE SNOW KING	A male in "Little White King," by Marguerite Steen.
SOLOMON	A Siamese, male, black, in Antique Cat," by Bianco Bradbury.
SKIP	A four month old black and white kitten, topped 34 competitors at the Calgary Cat club's mouser contest by whipping through a five stage maze to a cage containing live mice in 37 1/2 seconds. The performance knocked two seconds off last year's record.
SOUR MASH	Belonged to Mark Twain.
SPIDER	A male cat, silky black, with white star on chest, white feet.
SPITHEAD	Ship's cat, of which Sir Isaac Newton wrote in his Journal.
STINKY	A Persian cat, probably so named for disposition.
STRAPS	Because he ate the straps on shoes, shoulder straps, in "Straps, the Cat," by Claudia Lewis, a grey striped cat.
SUGAR 'N SPICE	A Red tabby.
SULETTE	A seal point, Siamese, female.
SUNMIST	A Cream, male.
SUNNY	A long hair, male, cream box cat.

SUSAN	A Siamese imported in 1885.
SWEETHEART	A Blue, female.
SMOKE PHANTOM	A Smoke Long Hair.
STAR SAPHIRE	A Champion blue eyed white Domestic short hair.
SWEET LORRAINE	Champion Brown Tabby Manx, female.
TA KLAEW	A Siamese cat, meaning, 'militant.'
TABITHA	A Siamese cat in "One Kitten Too Many," by Bianco Bradbury. Called Tabby, for short.
TABITHA TWICHET	A Tabby that belongs to Pamela Mason.
TAILSPIN	Sister of Marty, daughter of Flyball and Moofa. She was born on the moon in "Space Cat," by Ruthven Todd.
TAWNEY	In "Joey Patches" by M.S. Johnson.
TATOO	A silver Tabby, domestic, female.
TAYOH	A Siamese cat, male, meaning, 'lost.'
TEDDY BEAR	A blue point Siamese cat.
THISTLEDOWN	A Siamese cat.
TIAM O'SHIAN	A Siamese imported in 1885.
TICH TAYLOR	A Semi-Persian, gray and white.
TIEN	A Siamese, male.
TEXX-ESS ROSE	A seal point Siamese, female.
TOM QUARTZ	In "Dick Baker's Cat," by Mark Twain.
TOP BRASS	An Abyssinian cat.
TOPBOY	Belongs to Pamela Mason.

TOPPER	An orange eyed white male Domestic.
TOTO	A chocolate point, male, Siamese.
TUDOR	A seal point, Siamese.
TUTTI FRUTTI	A box cat, blue cream.
TREE	A Siamese which is often addressed as Trezie, and Treacle.
TYBERT	A cat in "Reynard the Fox."
UPS 'N DOWNS	A seal point Siamese, female.
VALENTINE CAT	A black cat with a white heart on its forehead in "The Valentine Cat," by Clyde Robert Bulla.
VAGABOND KING	Grand Champion white Domestic, short hair, male.
VIOLET LADY	A Grand Champion blue point Siamese, female.
VENUS DE MILO	A long hair, Cream, female.
WAMPUS	A long hair.
WAZERO ZAUDITU	An Abyssinian.
WEE SUNSHINE	A Double Champion long hair, male.
WHI TING	A seal point, Siamese.
WHITE WISTERIA	A Domestic, short hair, white.
WHITE MOORAGH	A blue eyed, white, male.
WHIFFENPOOF	A blue short hair, female.
WHITEY	White with tabby marking splashed over coat at random. Another Whitey earns $125.00 a week appearing in motion pictures.
WHISPERS	The tiger kitten in "One Kitten Too Many."

WHISPERING SAND	A Tabby, male.
WHITE ANGEL	A White female cat.
WHITE CHALK	A Champion, white haired, female.
WIDGET	In "Widget," by Clare Turley Newberry.
WILLY	Who always knew Monday in "Everyday Miracle," by Gustav Eckstein.
WONG MAU	First known Burmese cat.
WUN LON SONG	A blue point, Siamese, male.
YA RAIN	A blue point Siamese.
YAN KEE KLIPPER	A Siamese cat.
YANKEE	A seal point, male Siamese and Champion.
YUSEF	Also called "Topboy."
ZARCALA	A seal point, female, Siamese.
ZIZI	A silver grey Angora that belonged to Theophile Gautier. Ziz, in Arabic, means 'cicada.'
ZOMBIE	A Siamese cat. Also, The Zombie, which belonged to Robert Southey, and was named after the chief of the Palmares negroes.
ZORASTER	Belonged to Mark Twain. He was a Persian religious teacher.
ZUT	Belonged to Guy Wetmore Carryl.

DOGS

AFGHANISTAN-ARABIAN-AFRICAN
EGYPTIAN-PERSIAN DOGS

Afghan Hound
Basenji
Saluki
Persian Greyhound (Saluki)
Rhodesian Ridgeback

Names

Male

A 'TI BÂLAK	"Look out!"
AB	"father."
ÂB	"August."
ABDALLAH	"servant of God."
ABDUL FAROUK	"a king of Egypt." K. name given to a Ch. Saluki.
ABYAD	"white."
ÂDHÂR	"March."
AGHA	"chief."
AISH	"living."
AHMAR	"red."
'AJÎB	"strange."
AKH	"brother."
AKID	"sure."
AL KAHIR	"victorious." Also, the city Cairo.
ALADDIN	"the possessor of the magic lamp and ring, with which he commanded two jinns who gratify all his wishes."

ALHAZEN	"11th century magician. K. name given to an Afghan Hound.
ALI	"the lion of God." Commonly used as a proper name.
ALI BABA	"the poor woodchopper in "The Arabian Nights Entertainment." He used the magic words 'open sesame' to open the door that led to the fabulous wealth of the Forty Thieves." K. name given to a Ch. Afghan Hound.
ÂLIM	"learned."
ALTAIR	"any kind of bird."
ʿÂMIL	"worker."
AMÎR	"prince; leader."
ʿÂMM	"uncle."
ANF	"nose."
ARSH	"venerable; throne."
ʿAṢABI	"nervous."
AṢFAR	"yellow."
ASIL	"noble."
ASMAR	"brownish."
ASWAD	"black."
AWWAL	"first."
AYYÂR	"May."
AYLÛL	"September."
ʿAYN	"eye."
AZAD	"free; independent."
ʿAZÎM	"great."
AZIZ	"a proper name; son of a shiek."
AZRAQ	"blue."
BAHR	"sea."
BALID	"stupid."

BALK	"war council." Also: BALZ: BALTZEL.
BANTALÛN	"trousers."
BARQ	"lightning."
BÂS	"to kiss."
BATÎ	"slow."
BASIṬ	"simple."
BEDOUIN	"Arab nomad."
BÛLÎS	"policeman."
CAID	"Arab chief."
CASPARO	"master of the treasure."
ḌÂ	"lost."
ḌÂÎF	"lean; weak."
ḌÂLÎL	"guide."
DARIUS	"one who conserves, restrains; upholds the good; ruler." Name of a Persian King. Pop.: <u>Darian</u>
DÂYMAN	"Always."
DHAHAB	"gold."
DHAKI	"intelligent."
DHOLE	"wild dog." K. name given to a Ch. Saluki.
DIABLO	"devil." K. name given to a Ch. Afghan Hound
EL HOR	"the noble one." Moslems considered the Saluki a sacred dog.
ESIVED	"black."
FADALLAH	"servant boy."
FEISUL	K. name for a Saluki. Also: FEISAL: FAISAL A King of Syria in 1920; and a King of

	Iraq in 1921.
FIDDA	"silver."
FIRDUSI	"paradise." Abdul Kasim 'Mansur, greatest of all Persian poets was called 'firdusi' because of the beauty of his poetry.
GAZAL	"gazelle; deer."
GAZELLE HOUND	"another name for the Saluki, which hunts for the gazelle.
GHAYR	"different."
GRANDEUR	Name given to a Ch. Afghan Hound, meaning, "statliness, dignity, majesty, splendour, exalted rank."
HABEEL	"vanity; crazy." Also: HABIL Pop.: Abel
HABIB	"lover."
HADD	"sharp."
HADI	"quiet."
HALAN	"at once."
HARIR	"silk."
HASAN	"servant; goodly; beautiful." Faik Hassan is an artist of Modern Iraq.
HAWA	"the wind."
HAWL IL BAYT	"around the house."
HAZ	"luck."
HAZIN	"sad."
HAZIRAN	"June."
HEIBA	"gift."
HIBR	"ink."
HULU	"sweet."

HURR   "free."

IBN   "son of..."
IL AHAD   "Sunday."
IL ARB 'A   "Wednesday."
IL KHAMIS   "Thursday."
IS SABT   "Saturday."
ISLAM   "submission." The religion in
                        the Middle East.

JARAS   "bell."
JASPER   "master of the treasure." A jew-
                        el name from the red or green
                        jasper on the breast plates of the
                        Jewish high priests.
                        Also: GASPAR
                        Pop.: Jasper
JAWZI   "nut."
JOLLITY   "fun." Name given to a Basenji.
KA-ED   "General in the army."
KABIR   "big."
KA'KI   "cake."
KABUL   K. name for a Ch. Afghan Hound,
                        meaning, "from the capitol of
                        Afghanistan."

KALB   "dog." K. name given to a Ch.
                        Saluki.
KALIPH   "Caliph."
KASSIM   "Name of a hero."
KBIR   "large."
KHADIM   "servant."
KHUSUSI   "special."
KURUSH   "a King."

LATIF   "gentle."

LAYL   "night."

MA AJMAL   "how beautiful!"

MA ḤADA   "nobody; no one."

MAESTRO   "master." K. name for a Bas-
                              enji.

MAJNÛN   "foolish."

MALÎḤ   "good."

MALIK   "king." K. name given to a
                              Saluki.

MA ʿNA   "sense."

MAQAM   "dignity."

MARJAN   "previous gem." K. name given
                              to a Ch. Saluki.

MASÂFI   "distance."

MASHGHÛL   "busy."

MEKTOUB   "it is written."

MERPABA   K. name given to Saluki.

MERHABA   "hello."

MRATTAB   "tidy."

MRÂYI   "mirror."

MUHIMM   "important."

MUSTAF   "eager; or a person who goes to
                              a resort."

NÂFI   "useful."

NÂ ʿIM   "soft; smooth."

NAWʾ   "quality."

NEJEE   "we come."

NÎSÂN   "April."

NÛR   "light."

NURI   "gypsy."

OMAR	"the better." Omar Khayyam, Persian poet, wrote The Rubaiyat.
ORIBI	"a small, tan colored antelope." K. name given to a Ch. Basenji.
PATRICIAN	K. name given to an Afghan Hound, means, "of noble birth; an aristocrat."
PLAYBOY	K. name given to a Ch. Afghan Hound, meaning, "carefree."
QÂDI	"a judge."
QALB	"heart."
QAMAR	"the moon."
QAWI	"strong."
QÎMI	"value; valuable; of value.
RÂBI'	"Spring."
RAGHÎF	"loaf."
RÂÎS	"chief."
RAMÂDI	"grey."
RAMULLAH	K. name given to a Saluki in the Kennels of Ali Khan. In Hebrew, RAM means 'exalted, made high, lifted up.' ULLA, in Hebrew, means, 'servitude bondage, servile.' The meaning might be 'exalted servant.'
RASMI	"official."
RED ZEPHYR	K. name given to a Ch. Basenji.
RIKK	"small Egyptian tambourine."
ROH	"ghost; soul."
RÛH DUGHRI	"go straight."
SÂ 'AH	"clock."

SABAH	"to swim."
SABI	"boy."
SABI DHAKI	"bright boy."
SÂFAR	"to journey."
SÂFI	"pure."
SAGHÎR	"little."
SÂHIB	"friend."
SAHÎH	"true."
SAH 'RA	"desert."
SA 'ÎD	"happy."
SALÂM	"peace."
SALIM	"in good health."
SALUKI	"the name came from Salquia, an ancient town in Yemen, Southern Arabia, where armour was made. The Saluki often wears beads, amulets to ward off evil."
SAQR	"falcon."
SARDAR	"prince." K. name given to a Ch. Afghan Hound.
SARÎ	"swift."
SAYF	"summer."
SEID	"master."
SHAMS	"the sun."
SHEIK	"chief."
SHIKARI	"a hunter, aid, or guide." K. name given to an Afghan Hound.
SHITA	"winter."
SUKKAR	"sugar."
SHAH IN SHAH	"King of Kings." Ancient title of Persian Kings.
TA 'ÂL	"come!"
TABASSAM	"to smile; to be happy."
TABÎ'I	"natural."

TAEJON	K. name given to an Afghan Hound.
TAJ	"crest, crown."
TALJ	"snow, ice."
TÂNI	"second."
ṬAWÎL	"long."
TAZI	A K. name given to a Saluki.
TEEJILLAH	K. name given to an Afghan Hound.
TENZAH	"the pleasant." K. name given to a Saluki.
TOP BRASS	K. name given to a Ch. Afghan hound, meaning, "highest ranking officer."
ZAWJ	"husband."
ZIR	"button."
ZRÂR	"buttons."

Female

ABRA	"smart."
AGA	"lady."
AISHA	"favorite wife of Mohammed." meaning, 'living.'
AJRÂS	"bells."
ÂKHIR	"end of the road."
A'LAMUT	"eagle's nest." A fortress in the mountains near the Caspian sea where Hassanben Sabbah, the mystic, founded a secret order that became the terror of all the Mohammedan World.
ALIA	"heroic maiden."
ALMERIA	"princess." AL-AMEERA (lit. form)

ALZENA	"a woman."
AMBER	"the amber; jewel." K. name given to an Afghan Hound.
AL KAHIRA	"victorious." 'city of Cairo.'
ANWÂA	"qualities."
ARBÂA	"four."
'ARÛS	"bride."
'ASAFÎR	"birds."
ASHÂB	"friends."
AYESHA	"favorite." Name for Moslem girls. Also: AISHA
ASAD	"lion."
AZRAQ	"blue."
AMAL	"hope."
ASILAT	"noble born."
BADOURA	Princess in the Arabian Nights story, "Camaralzaman and the Princess."
BALÎDI	"stupid."
BARK	"lightning."
BARAKA	"blessing."
BATÎA	"slow."
BAYDA	"white."
BESELAAMA	"peace be with you."
BEYDÃ	"white."
BINT	"girl."
BURNOUS	"woolen cloak."
CAPER	K. name given to a Ch. Basenji, meaning, "to leap playfully, frisk."
CHELA	"follower."

CHICKIE

K. name given to a Basenji. 'a term of endearment.'

CLORINDA

"the renowned." The Persian poet Tasso used the name for a beautiful lady in "Jerusalem Delivered.'

COMET

K. name given to a Ch. Basenji. It implies swiftness.

DAHABI

"golden."

DĀLĪLEH

"guide."

DAMASPIA

"horse tamer."

DAQĪQA

"minute."

DARIA

"queen; wealthy." The f. of Darius, a fifth century king of Persia.

DEL

"tail."

DIN

"faith."

DOLLY

K. name given to an Afghan Hound, meaning, "Sweetheart of a gift."
Pop.: Dorothea

ESTHER

"a star." A Bible Queen, the Queen of King Ahasuerus of Persia. She saved the lives of the Jewish people in Persia. It also means, "happiness; good fortune; the planet Venus."

FATIMA

"the only daughter of Mohammed." She was the last wife of Bluebeard. Her name is a synonym for curiosity.

FI KULL MAHALL

"everywhere."

FIL BAYT

"at home."

FIKRA

"idea."

FLAGEOLETT

K. name given to a Ch. Basenji, meaning, "small flute."

FLASH OF LIGHT	connotes speed. The Arabians used names indicating speed for their Salukis. Name given to a Pharoah's favorite Saluki.
FLÛS	"money."
FURṢA	"chance; or vacation."
GANDOURA	"silk, or woolen white robe."
GAZELLE	"swift; graceful; deer."
HABIBEH	"graceful; lover."
HADÎN	"quiet."
HADIYA	"gift; present."
HADJ	"pilgrim."
ḤÂMIḌA	"sour."
HAMRA	"red."
ḤASHARA	"insect."
ḤASSA	K. name given to a Saluki.
HATASU	Shortened form for Hatishepsut, Queen of Egypt in the 15th and 16th c. B. C.
ḤAZÎRÂN	"June, the month."
HEGAB	"talisman."
HIJAB	"amulet."
HOPE DIAMOND	K. name given to an Afghan Hound, meaning, "great brilliancy."
ḤULUI	"sweet."
ḤURRA	"free."
ÎDI	"my, my hand."
IL JUM ʿA	"Friday."
IL KHARÎF	"fall, the season."
ILI	"mine."
IS ṢUBḤ	"morning."

ISIS	"Egyptian goddess, who in "The Golden Ass," by Apuleius, restores Lucius, who had turned into an ass, by giving him rose petals to eat.
JAMÎLI	"beautiful."
JARAS	"bell."
JUI	K. name given to an Afghan Hound.
JASMINE	"the flower." Also: YASMINE
KAATRAK	"goodbye."
KABÎRI	"big."
KALSÂT	"stockings."
KÂNÛN IT TÂNI	"January."
KASBAN	"winner."
KEF	"enjoyment; pleasure."
KHÂDMI	"maid servant."
KHAMSIN	"southerly wind; fifty miles an hour."
KHAYYÂT	"sisters."
KHIEBA	K. name given to an Afghan Hound, meaning, "a disappointment."
KHÎRI	"generous."
KHITTIKU	K. name given to an Afghan Hound.
LAMA'AN	"a flash, or the swift glance of a ladies eye." K. name given to a golden Saluki.
LADY	Name given to the Basenji in "Goodbye My Lady," by James Street.
LÂHAZ	"observe."

LÂJI	"refugee."
LATIF	"gentle."
LAWN GHÂMÎQ	"deep color."
LEILAH	"dark beauty; night." Also: LEILA
LILAC	"bluish, or indigo."
MA AJMAL	"how beautiful!"
MAJNÛNI	"foolish."
MALIKATUN	"queen."
MANDEB	"tears."
MARA	"woman."
MARRA TÂNI	"sometime, or next time."
MARYAN	"a frangrance name." Pop. Mary
MASHGHÛLI	"busy."
MASHHÛRÎN	"famous."
MAY	"water."
MIFTÂH	"key."
MONKEY FACE	affectionate name for all Afghan dogs.
MRATTABÎ	"tidy."
MUHARRAM	"scared, or forbidden."
MUHIMMI	"important."
MUKHTÂR	"chosen."
NAERUN	"river."
NAHÂR JAMIL	"bright day."
NÂ 'IMI	"soft."
NÂFIA'	"useful."
NAIRUN	"fire."
NAO'	"a quality."

NAOMI	"felicity; my sweetness." Friend and mother-in-law of Ruth in the Bible.
NÂR	"fire."
NIJM	"morning star."
NEFERTITI	"beauty's arrival." Most beautiful queen of Egypt, wife Pharoah Amenhotep IV.
OPHAAL	K. name given to a Ch. Afghan Hound.
QASIDA	"elegy."
RABI'	"the spring."
RÂDÎ	"satisfied."
RANA	K. name given to an Afghan Hound.
RÂS	"head."
RIJIL	"leg."
RISHA	"feather."
RUDIKI	Name given to a Ch. Afghan Hound in a Kennel.
RUMADI	"gray."
SÂ 'A	"hour."
SADIRA	"star; a constellation."
SAFRA	"yellow."
SAFRON	"yellow."
SAFFRON	"the crocus."
SAGHÎRI	"little; young."
SA'ÎDI	"happy."
SAKI	"stars."
SARI'	"speedy."
SAWDA	"black."

SHAYEB	"grey hair."
SAYY'IDI	"lady."
SCHEHERAZADE	"eldest daughter of the grand vizir of the Kingdom of Persia. She was clever; courageous; beautiful; intellectual; wise."
SELIMAH	"peace." Also: SULEIMA
SHA SHA	"king." K. name given to an Afghan Hound.
SHBÂT	"February."
SHEÉLAH	"a flame."
SHOOTING STAR	"swift."
SHUGHL	"work."
SILVER SIJAB	"good luck amulet."
SODA	"black."
SÛF	"wool."
SUNDOWN	K. name given to a Ch. Basenji.
TA'THÎR	"influence."
TARI	"soft."
TAWNI	K. name given to an Afghan Hound.
TAYER	"flying; on the wing."
UKHT	"sister."
ULEMA	"the learned."
UMM	"mother."
'UTLI	"holiday."
ÛYÛN	"eyes."
VAIZATHA	"white; white robed."
VASHTI	"fair; lovely." The Persian Queen of Ahasueras of the Medes and

	Persians.
VEGA	"the falling." Vega is the brightest star in the constellation of Lyra.
VEH	"pure."
WÂHADI	"one."
WIJJ	"face."
WINOMANA	K. name given to a Ch. Afghan Hound.
ZADA	"prosperous, increase."
ZAI EL HARIR	"silky."
ZAWJI	"wife."
ZEENAB	"name of a girl; a father's ornament."
ZOBEEDEE	"favorite wife of Harounal-Raschid in the Arabian Nights. It means, "the favored."
ZOE	K. name given to an Afghan Hound.
ZÛHÛR	"flowers."
ZULEIKA	"the fair." A favorite name of the ancient Persian poets. The heroine of Lord Byron's poem, "The Bride of Abydos."
ZAHRA	"flower."
ZEBINA	"the purchaser."

AMERICAN & BRITISH DOGS

Airedale Terrier
American Foxhound
American Water Spaniel
Beagle
Bedlington Terrier
Bloodhound
Border Terrier
Boston Terrier
Bulldog
Bull Mastiff
Bull Terrier
Chesapeake Bay Retriever
Clumber Spaniel
Coonhound
Curly Coated Retriever
Cocker Spaniel
Dalmatian
English Cocker Spaniel
English Foxhound
English Setter

English Springer Spaniel
English Toy Spaniel
Field Spaniel
Flat Coated Retriever
Fox Terrier
Gorden Setter
Greyhound
Harrier
Lakeland Terrier
Manchester Terrier
Mastiff
Norwich Terrier
Old English Sheep Dog
Otter Hound
Pointer
Silky Terrier
Staffordshire Terrier
Sussex Spaniel
Toy Manchester Terrier
Whippet
Yorkshire Terrier

Names

Male

ACE
"first at play, or to accomplish."
K. name given to a Boston Terrier.

ACE OF HEARTS
K. name given to a Boston Terrier.
Means, "first in your heart."

ACROBAT
K. name for a Dalmatian. Means,
"clown."

ADDO
"of noble cheer."

ADELPHO
"beloved brother."

ADONIS	"handsome." A beautiful youth beloved by Venus. K. name given to a Boston Terrier, a Springer Spaniel.
ADOLPH	"noble wolf." K. name given to a Boxer.
AGILARD	"formidable bright."
AGAIN	K. name given to a Boston Terrier.
AJAX	K. name given to a Boxer, meaning, "strong; courageous."
ALBAN	"white."
ALDEN	"an old friend."
ALADDIN	K. name for a Boxer.
ALEX	"helper."
ALPIN	"an elf." (Scotch)
ALVIE	"noble friend." K. name for an English Springer Spaniel.
AMBER RUST	K. name for a Cocker Spaniel.
ANDY	"strong." K. name for a Field Spaniel, a Ch. Beagle.
APPLEJACK	K. name for an English Springer Spaniel. "a cider."
ARIEL	"spirit of the air." K. name for a Pointer.
ASA	"healer."
AXEL	"divine reward."
BAILEY	"a keeper."
BAGATELLE	"trifle." K. name for a Cocker Spaniel.
BANQUO	"white."
BARON	"noble warrior." K. name for a Chesapeake Bay Retriever.
BELISARIUS	"white prince."

BEAUTIFUL JOE	mongrel in the novel "Beautiful Joe" by Marshall Saunders. K. name for and English Springer Spaniel.
BENJAMIN	"my right hand." K. name for a Bloodhound.
BERN	"strong as a bear."
BEVAN	"young archer."
BIT O'HONEY	K. name for a Boston Terrier.
BLACK ROYAL	K. name for a Flat Coated Retriever.
BLOT	K. name for a Dalmatian.
BLUE CAP	K. name for a Beagle.
BLUE VELVET	K. name for a Yorkshire Terrier.
BOLD VENTURE	K. name for a Dalmatian.
BUSYBODY	K. name for Boston Terrier, a Boxer.
BOMSIGHT	K. name for an Airedale Terrier.
BOOTS	K. name for a Cocker Spaniel, a Boxer.
BOY	K. name for a Wirehaired Terrier.
BRICK	K. name for a Springer Spaniel.
BRIGADIER	K. name for a Bloodhound.
BUCKSHOT	K. name for a Golden Retriever.
BURKE	"of the castle."
CANTATA	an English Springer Spaniel.
CASSIDY	"the ingenious."
DALE	"from the dale."
DAN	K. name for a Border Terrier, meaning, "judge."
DANDY	K. name for a Pointer, meaning, "man."
DAPPER DAN	K. name for a Ch. Beagle.

DANTE	"the lasting."
DEMI-TASSE	K. name for a Cocker Spaniel, meaning a small cup of black coffee, or the cup itself.
DEMPSEY	"the proud."
DIEHARD DANDY	K. name for a Ch. Border Terrier, meaning, "man with great strength."
DIAMOND	Name given to Sir Isaac Newton's dog, a spaniel, that caused him to have a nervous breakdown. A jewel name with a feeling of preciousness. Also, "innocence."
DISCOVERY	K. name for a Boston Terrier.
DON JUAN	K. name for a Boston Terrier. "Lord's grace."
DONALD	"proud chief."
DOUBLE FEATURE	K. name for a Cocker Spaniel of two colors.
DRUM MAJOR	K. name for a Cocker Spaniel.
DUKE	K. name for a Stafforshire Terrier, meaning, "to draw, or lead."
DUSTER	K. name for a Retriever.
DYNAMITE	K. name for a Cocker Spaniel.
ECHO	K. name given a Bluetick Hound.
ETH	"fire."
EXACT COPY	K. name for a Cocker Spaniel.
EXTERMINATOR	K. name for a wirehaired Fox Terrier.
FAGAN	"a small voice."
FANCY BOOTS	K. name for a Cocker Spaniel.
FAXON	"the thick haired."
FANE	"joyful."

FERDINAND	K. name for a Ch. English Bull-dog, meaning "adventuring life."
FILMER	"the most famed."
FIRECRACKER	K. name for a Manchester Terrier.
FLEANCE	"the rosy."
FLASH	K. name for a Boston Terrier, a Cocker Spaniel.
FORTUNE	"chance."
FORZA	Name given to a St. Bernard type of Mongrel, meaning, "to go on."
FOWLER	"catcher of birds."
FRECKLES	K. name for a Cocker Spaniel.
FRANKLIN	"a free man."
GALLAGHER	"eager helper."
GAMBLER	K. name for an English Fox Hound.
GANGBUSTER	K. name for a Boston Terrier.
GHOST	K. name for an English Setter.
GINGERBREAD	K. name for a Cocker Spaniel.
GOLDEN AMIGO	K. name for a Cocker Spaniel, meaning, "Golden Friend."
GYPSY	Name given to a Dalmatian.
HALBERT	"bright stone."
HALLOWEE'N	born on Halloween. K. name for a Cocker Spaniel.
HAMLET	K. name for a Pointer. Means, "a small home."
HAREM SCAREM	K. name for a Cocker Spaniel.
HASTING	"the swift."
HELMET	K. name for an American Foxhound.
HERBERT	"bright warrior."
HIGH STEPPER	K. name for a Boston Terrier.
HILARY	"cheerful; merry."
HOLT	"of the woods."

HONEYMOON	Name of a Ch. Black and White Coonhound.
HOWE	"eminent."
IDEAL WEATHER	K. name for an Old English Sheepdog.
INJUN SUMMER	K. name for a Cocker Spaniel.
ISA	"iron-like."
JACK TAR	K. name for an English Bulldog, meaning, "a sailor."
JACOB	K. name for a curly-coated Retriever, meaning, "the supplanter," or, "one who takes the place of." Pop.: James
JESTER	K. name for a Ch. Beagle.
JIGGS	Name given to a Bulldog.
JIP	Name of a Miniature Terrier, black and tan, a Sunnybanks dog, and that of Dora Copperfield's in the book, "David Copperfield," by Charles Dickens.
JOB	"the afflicted."
JOKER	Name for a Ch. English Cocker Spaniel.
JUMPING JACK	K. name for an English Springer Spaniel.
JUSTIN	"the great."
KING	"male monarch."
KING TUT	K. name for a Ch. Chesapeake Bay Retriever.
KNAVE, THE	K. name for an English Ch. Bull Terrier.
KRISS	K. name for a Bloodhound.

LADDIE BOY	Name given to an Airedale Terrier belonging to Warren Harding.
LANALOTE	K. name for a Dalmatian.
LIA	"dependence."
LILINE	Name of an English Toy Spaniel belonging to King Charles IX.
LITTLE CHAP	K. name for a Norwich Terrier.
LITTLE WIZZARD	Name of a Beagle that went after the morning paper, took in the morning mail, ran errands.
LLOYD	"the grey."
LUCKY LAD	K. name for a Whippet.
LUCKY STRIKE	K. name for an English Springer Spaniel.
MACK	K. name for a Plott Hound.
MADDY	"force." K. name for a Gordon Setter.
MALLARD	K. name for a Chesapeake Bay Retriever.
MATHE	a hound that was the favorite of Richard II of England, meaning "gift of the Lord."
MEDDLER	K. name for a Chesapeake Retriever.
MESSENGER	K. name for an Old English Sheepdog.
MEYER	"a steward."
MINUTE MAN	K. name for a Cocker Spaniel.
MISCHIEF	K. name for a Dalmatian, a Beagle, a Bulldog.
MR. DICKENS	Name for a Beagle Hound.
MONK	K. name for a Bloodhound.
MOUJIK	"a Russian peasant." A K. name for a Dalmatian.

MUFFIN	K. name for an English Springer Spaniel.
NIGHTSHADE	K. name for an English Springer Spaniel.
NITRO EXPRESS	K. name for a Retriever.
NO-SITCH	part bull-dog, shepherd, spaniel, St. Bernard, hound, in Phil Stong's book - "No-sitch, the hound."
NORTH WIND	K. name for a Cocker Spaniel.
NUGGET	K. name for a Cocker Spaniel.
OLD RED	K. name for a Bloodhound.
PACEMAKER	K. name for a Boston Terrier.
PATCH	K. name for an English Setter.
PETER	"a stone."
PERT	K. name for a Fox Terrier. "son of furrows."
PETER PAN	Wire-haired terrier belonging to Calvin Coolidge.
PITCH	K. name for a Smooth-haired Fox Terrier.
PLUM PUDDING DOG	The Dalmatian was called this because of his spots.
POWDER PUFF	An American Cocker Spaniel.
PRINCE OF CAMOUFLAGE	K. name for a Dalmatian.
PYE	"the spotted."
RADAR	K. name for a Ch. Wire-haired Fox Terrier.
RAFFLES	K. name for a Boston Terrier.
RAJAH	"king." K. name for a Cocker Spaniel.

RAMBLER	K. name for a Beagle Hound.
READ	"red haired."
RATTLER	K. name for a Beagle Hound.
RING	"to sound clearly." K. name for a Cocker Spaniel.
RIP RAP	K. name for a Pointer.
ROADSTER	K. name for a Dalmatian.
ROLAND	"fame of the land." Name given to a Chesapeake Retriever. It was the name of Charlemagne's paladine.
ROVER	a white bull Terrier, that acted on the stage with Arnold Daly when he played in Shaw's "General John Regan."
SADDLER	K. name for a Smooth-haired Fox Terrier.
SATIN	K. name for a Retriever.
SALVADOR	"to save."
SCRAPPY	K. name for a Retriever.
SHED	K. name for a Retriever.
SHOT	K. name for a Pointer, a Springer Spaniel.
SHOWOFF	K. name for a Cocker Spaniel.
SIR BOLIVAR	Name given to a Boykin Spaniel, which is a water dog, strong swimmer, duck and dove retriever.
SIRIUS	dog star. Name given to a Dalmatian. Brightest star in the heavens.
SKIMMER	K. name given to a Beagle Hound.
SLUMBER	Name for an Old English Sheepdog.
SMART TONE	Name given an Australian Silky Haired Terrier.
SNAPBACK	K. name for a Beagle Hound.
SQUIRE	"shield-bearer." Name given to a Retriever.

TABS	Name of a British sentry sheep dog.
TITI	Name given to an English Toy Spaniel, which means, the seventh, for ti-ti is the seventh note of the diatonic scale.
TOP HAT	Name given a Bull Terrier.
TROJAN	Name given a Bull Mastiff. "pertains to ancient Troy, its inhabitants.
TURK	Name of a Mastiff owned by Charles Dickens.
TWEED	a Bob-tailed sheep dog that was a messenger.
UP FRONT	Name given to a Bull Terrier.
WILLOUGHBY	"from the place of the willows." Name given to a sheep dog.
WRINKLES	Name given to a Beagle Hound.
ZAPPEL	Name given to a Boston Terrier.

Female

ADA	K. name given to a Boxer. Means "happy."
ADELLE	K. name given to a Cocker Spaniel. Means, "noble."
ADORATION	K. name given to an English Springer Spaniel.
ALABAMA LADY	K. name given to a Boxer.
ALICE	"cheerful." K. name given to a Boxer.
ALVA	"fair." K. name given to a Boxer.
AMAZEMENT	K. name given to a Cocker Spaniel.

ANEMONE   K. name given to a Cocker Spaniel,
                           meaning, "a breath." A flower.

ANITRA   K. name given to a Boxer, meaning,
                           "graceful."

ARTEMIS   K. name for a Boxer, meaning, in
                           Greek Mythology, a goddess, sister
                           of Apollo, who was huntress and
                           goddess of the moon. Also, "vig-
                           orous."

AUDACIOUS LADY   K. name for a Cocker Spaniel.

AURELIA   "golden girl."

AURORA   "the dawn."

AVA   "the bird; busybody schemer."
                           Also: AVIS

AZALEA   flower name.

BABETTE   "God's oath." Name given to a
                           Cocker Spaniel.

BALLERINA   Name given to an English Springer
                           Spaniel.

BEATA   "blessed; happy."

BELINDA   "a serpent." Name given to a
                           Boston Terrier.

BELLE   "beautiful." Name given an English
                           Springer Spaniel, a Beagle, a Dal-
                           matian, a Pointer, a Cocker Span-
                           iel.

BENITA   "to bless."

BLACKBIRD   Name given a Cocker Spaniel.

BLACK CINDER   Name given a Cocker Spaniel.

BLAZE AWAY   Name given a Cocker Spaniel.

BLISS   "perfect job."

BLOSSOM   "to flower." Name given a Cocker
                           Spaniel.

BLUE IRIS   name given a Cocker Spaniel.

BONITA   "the good." Name given a Boston
                           Terrier, a Cocker Spaniel.

BONNIE FLORA	"beautiful flower." Name for a Dalmatian.
BROWN BETTY	K. name for a Dalmatian.
BUNK	Name given a Boston Terrier.
BUTTERFLY	K. name for an English Springer Spaniel.
CAIA	"to rejoice in."
CARA	"dear one."
CAREER GIRL	K. name for a Boxer.
CARESSE	"to pet."
CARMA	"destiny."
CASSANDRA	"helper of mankind."
CEARA	"the ruddy."
CESARINA	"queen."
CHALLENGER	Name given a Dalmatian.
CHARA	"joy."
CHARITY	"grace." K. name for a Cocker Spaniel.
CHASER	K. name for a Cocker Spaniel.
CHERI	K. name for a Boston Terrier. Means, "sweetheart."
CHICKIE	Name given a Boston Terrier.
CHLOE	"blooming." Name given a Cocker Spaniel.
CHIT CHAT	Name given a Boston Terrier.
CRISTAL	"Christ bearer."
CHRISTMAS HOLLY	Name given to a Boxer.
CILLY	Name given a Boxer.
CIRCE	"dangerously fascinating." Name given a Cocker Spaniel.
CLARA	"famous." Name given an English Springer Spaniel.
CINNAMON STICK	K. name for a Boston Terrier.

CLAUDINA	"lame; graceful."
COCKADE	K. name for a Cocker Spaniel.
CORNFLOWER	K. name for a Cocker Spaniel.
CREAM PUFF	K. name for a Cocker Spaniel.

DALLAS	"the playful."
DAPHNE	"bay tree." K. name for a Springer Spaniel, a Cocker Spaniel.
DAPPLE	K. name for a Cocker Spaniel.
DARE ME	K. name for a Cocker Spaniel.
DARK SECRET	K. name for a Cocker Spaniel.
DEUCE	K. name for a Pointer.
DEVNET	"white wave."
DIELLA	"the worshipper."
DOLL, DOLLY, DOLLIE	"a sweetheart." K. names for a Beagle Hound, a Boston Terrier, a Cocker Spaniel.
DORA	"a gift."
DORINDA	"the beautiful."
DUETT	"two."

EBONY QUEEN	K. name for a Ch. Beagle Hound.
EDANA	"the firey."
EDITH	"rich; prosperous."
ELEGANCE	K. name given to an English Springer Spaniel.
ENCHANTRESS	K. name for a Cocker Spaniel.
ESCORT	K. name for a Boston Terrier.
EVER TRUE	K. name for a Cocker Spaniel.

FAITH	"to trust."
FANTASY	K. name for a Springer Spaniel.
FASHION LADY	K. name for a Cocker Spaniel.

FASHION PLATE	K. name for a Boxer.
FELICITY	K. name for a Cocker Spaniel, meaning, "happy." Also: FELICITA Pop.: Felicia
FENELLA	"the white-shouldered." K. name for a Mastiff.
FIONA	K. name for an Airedale Terrier, meaning, "white and fair."
FLIRT	K. name for an English Springer Spaniel.
FLORIZEL	K. name for a Cocker Spaniel. Probably meaning, "to flower."
FLURRY	K. name for a Cocker Spaniel.
FLUSH	A Cocker Spaniel belonging to Elizabeth Barrett Browning.
FUSSY	Name given a Fox Terrier belonging to Ellen Terry, the actress.
GELGES	"swan-white."
GETAWAY	K. name for a Cocker Spaniel.
GINGER SNAP	Name given to a Cocker Spaniel.
GLYKERA	"the sweet."
GOLDEN DAWN	Name given to a Ch. Dalmatian.
GRETA	"pearl." K. name for a Cocker Spaniel.
GYP	"a gypsy." Name given to a Boston Terrier. Pop.: Gypsy.
GYTHA	"gift." Pop.: Agatha
HERITAGE	K. name for a Springer Spaniel.
HILDA	"battle." K. name for a Beagle Hound. Also: HILDY, HYLDA.
HOLDA	"gentle."

HOMESPUN	K. name for an English Springer Spaniel.
HONEY CLOUD	K. name for a Cocker Spaniel.
HONORA	"honor." Also: HONORIA, ONORE, NORAH, NORA. Pop.: Honor
HORTENSE	"a gardener."
INNOCENT	"harmless."
INDIGO	K. name for a Cocker Spaniel.
IROLITA	Name given a Cocker Spaniel.
ISOLDE	"the fair."
JACQUELINE	"take the place of." Also: JACOBINA, JACQUETTA. An English Springer Spaniel was given this name.
JADA	"the jade." Jewel name for 'love.'
JANE	"gracious." K. name for an English Springer Spaniel.
JEAN	"gracious." K. name for an English Springer Spaniel.
JUNO	"the heavenly."
JYNX	"charm."
KEITH	"of the wind." Either masc. or fem.
KOLFINNA	"cool, white one."
LADY ARGYLE	K. name for a Cocker Spaniel.
LADY BUG	K. name for a Beagle Hound, a Boston Terrier.
LARK	"bird name."
LASS	"little maid." K. name for an English Springer Spaniel.

LAURA	"laurel." K. name for a Cocker Spaniel.
LEILANI	"heavenly flower."
LEADING LADY	K. name for a Cocker Spaniel.
LEAVE IT TO ME	K. name for a Boston Terrier.
LIBUSA	"darling."
LIMELIGHT	K. name for a Springer Spaniel.
LOTUS	"the dream like."
LOVE	"to hold dear."
LUNETTA	"shapely."
MABEL	"beloved."
MACAROON	K. name for a Cocker Spaniel.
MADAME POMPADOUR	K. name given to a Ch. Bull Terrier.
MAIDA	"in honor of battles."
MALVINA	"chief handmaid." Also: MELVINE, MELVA
MARCHETA	K. name for a Cocker Spaniel.
MELANIE	"the dark, or black." Also: MELANY. Name given a Ch. Cocker Spaniel.
MISTLETOE	K. name for a Cocker Spaniel.
NUTCRACKER	K. name for a Cocker Spaniel.
ODD SOCKS	K. name for a Cocker Spaniel.
OH SHUCKS	K. name given to an English Springer Spaniel.
ORANGE QUEEN	K. name for a Whippet.
PANDORA	"all gifted." Pandora opened the sealed box from Zeus, and out flew all the ills of mankind. K. name given to a Boston Terrier, a

	Cocker Spaniel, a Dalmatian.
PAULA	"little."
PERIWINKLE	K. name for a Cocker Spaniel.
PIN UP GIRL	K. name for a Cocker Spaniel.
PRIMROSE	"the first rose." K. name for a Dalmatian.
PROPHECY	K. name for a Cocker Spaniel.
QUEEN OF SHEEBA	K. name for a Cocker Spaniel.
REDBEARD	K. name given to a Cocker Spaniel.
RINGLEADER	K. name given to a Cocker Spaniel.
ROWENA	"the white maned."
ROWDY	K. name for a Cocker Spaniel.
ROYALTY	K. name for a Pointer.
RUTH	"beauty."
SAILOR	K. name for a Chesapeake Bay Retriever.
SAPPHO	K. name for a Bloodhound, a Cocker Spaniel, meaning, the Greek Lyric Poetess.
SARAH	"princess." SARAH JANE is name for a Gordon Setter, meaning, princess Jane, or "Princess Gracious."
SASSY	K. name for a Chesapeake Bay Retriever.
SEDUCTIVE	K. name given to a Cocker Spaniel.
SILVER	whitemetal.
SORCERESS	K. name for an Airedale Terrier.
SPARERIBS	K. name given to a war dog, that was a parachutist.
SUGAR CANDY	K. name for a Cocker Spaniel.
SUSY SOFT PAWS	K. name for a Cocker Spaniel. Susy means, 'lily.'

SWEET PEA   K. name for a Beagle Hound.

TALITHA   "star; maiden."

TANDY   K. name for an English Springer Spaniel.

TATE   "the cheerful."

TELENA   Name given to a St. Bernard mongrel type. A messenger dog.

TESTY   K. name for a Dalmatian.

TIBETDA   "people's princess."

TITA   "the titled; safe."

TINKER BELLE   K. name for a Cocker Spaniel.

TOKEN   K. name for a Cocker Spaniel.

TRACY   "carrying ears of corn."

TRANQUIL   K. name for an English Springer Spaniel.

TRINKET   K. name for a Cocker Spaniel.

TWINKLE   K. name for a Cocker Spaniel.

TWINKLE TOES   K. name for an English Springer Spaniel.

TWINKLES   K. name for a Boston Terrier.

VALESKA   "ruling glory."

VEGA   "the falling." The brightest star in the Lyra constellation. K. name for a Beagle Hound.

VELVET   K. name for an English Springer Spaniel.

VELVET TOUCH   K. name given to a Cocker Spaniel.

VERA   "faith."

VENUS   "the star." K. name given to a Beagle Hound.

VICTORIA   "victory."

VIDA   "life."

VINGY   "a virgin."
                         Pop.: <u>Virginia</u>

WHIZETTE   K. name given to a Boston Terrier.

WILDA   "not tame." K. name given to a
                         Cocker Spaniel.

WITCH   K. name given to a Boston Terrier.

ZOE   "life." K. name for a Cocker
                         Spaniel.

DOGS OF THE NORTH and THE COLD COUNTRIES

Alaskan Malamute
Bernese Mountain Dog
Labrador Retriever
Newfoundland
Norwegian Elkhound
Saint Bernard
Samoyed
Siberian Husky

Names

Male

AEGIR
"god of the sea." Name given to a Newfoundland.

ALARICK
"noble ruler" Pop.: Alaric

ATU
K. name given to a Siberian Husky.

AMAGHUK
"wolf."

ARTIC REBEL
K. name given to an Alaskan Malamute.

ARI
"eagle." An Icelandic name.

ARVID
Arvid August Afzelius, author who edited folk songs in Sweden.

BALDWIN
"bold, courageous friend."

BANQUO
"white." Scottish warrior immortalized in Macbeth.

BALTO
Sled dog leader, Siberian Husky, who brought diptheria serum into Nome.

BALDY
K. name for a Siberian Husky.

BARDOLPH
"distinguished helper."

BARON
"strong man." K. name for a Retriever.

91

BARZAILAI	"firm; true."
BELISARIUS	"white prince."
BEN	"son of the right hand." A Labrador Retriever that was a canine Sherlock Holmes.
BENONI	"son of trouble."
BERN	"strong as a bear."
BLADE	"sharpwitted, wild."
BLAZE	"brand." K. name for a Mastiff owned by Elliot Roosevelt.
BIG ENOUGH	K. name for a St. Bernard.
BLITZEN	K. name for a Samoyed.
BLIZZARD	"furious blast." K. name for a bull dog.
BREVIE	K. name for a Norwegian Elkhound.
BRIAN	"strong."
BRUNO	"brown."
BOATSWAIN	Lord Byron's Newfoundland dog.
BOBO	Name given to a Siberian Husky.
BRIN	Sir Wilfred Grenfel's sled dog. From Brian, meaning, "the strong."
BRUTUS	"enslaved."
BUCKLE	K. name given to a Newfoundland dog.
CAPTAIN THUNDER	K. name for an Alaskan Malamute.
CARKA	K. name given to a Siberian Husky.
COURT JESTER	K. name for a St. Bernard.
CAESAR	"hairy; blue-eyed."
CAMP	A mongrel, part bulldog, part rat terrier belonging to Sir Walter Scott.
CARRO	K. name given to a Norwegian Elkhound. From Carrol? Meaning, "strong."

CHILDE	"young knight." Prefixed to name of eldest son until succeeded to his ancestral titles or was knighted.
CHINOOK	Bryd's expedition 'lead' dog, meaning, "ocean wind."
CHRISTOFFER	an early Danish king. "the Christ bearer."
CLEMENT	"merciful."
CONAN	"chief; wisdom."
CORAGGIO	St. Bernard type of mongrel. "courageous?"
CURRAN	"hero." A Danish prince who disguished himself to woo Argentile, then became King.
CZAR	K. name for a Samoyed, meaning, "emperor."
DANTE	"the everlasting."
DEAN	"a chief."
DUKE	K. name for a Newfoundland dog.
EBENEZER	"stone of help."
EDAN	"fire."
EDVARD	"guardian of property." Edvard Grieg was a Norwegian composer.
ELDRED	"the terrible."
ELI	"foster son."
ENOCH	"dedicated."
ERLAND	"outlander, stranger."
ERIK	an Early Danish King.
EROK	Ch. Alaskan Malamute.
ESAU	"covered with hair."
ETHAN	"firm; strong."
EXCALIBUR	"magic sword of King Arthur. Name given a mongrel.

EYVINDUR	"an Icelandic name."
EYVIND	Eyvind Johnson was a Swedish novelist.
FANTABULOUS	K. name for a St. Bernard.
FINNUR	Icelandic name.
FLUTE	K. name for Labrador Retriever.
FERGUS	"the choice."
FERNANDL	"from the far land."
GALAHAD	Sir Galahad, Knight of the Round Table, surnamed "the Chaste."
GARM	Mythological watch dog.
GARRETT	"firm spear."
GASTON	"the hospitable."
GENGISK	Mongolian conqueror of Asia. Name given to a giant hound belonging to Frederick, the Great, a constant companion of his military campaigns, and at home.
GENERAL BEAUREGARD	K. name for an Alaskan Husky.
GIH	"go." Name given to an Alaskan sled dog.
GREGORY	"watchful."
GRIFFITH	"ruddy."
GRIZZLY	K. name for a Retriever.
GUSTAFUS	"warrior."

GULLIVER   K. name for a St. Bernard.

HAAKON   "high kin."
HABOR   "dexterous."
HALLGRIMUR   Icelandic name.
HALVOR   "prudent."
HARALD   "powerful warrior."
HARDEKNUD   Danish king.
HELP & HOLD   Hounds that caught the white deer
                            that Robert the Bruce, said was a
                            demon in disguise.
HERCULES   "strong; fame."
HASSO   K. name for a St. Bernard.
HUMPHREY   "protector of the house."
HYPERION   K. name for a St. Bernard.   A
                            Titan in Mythology.

INTEGRITY   K. name for St. Bernard.
IVAR   A Swedish composer's name.

JUMBO   Name given to a Newfoundland dog
                            meaning, "large."

KAZAN   K. name for a Samoyed.
KENI   K. name for a Siberian Husky.
KIJE   K. name for a Siberian Husky.
KENELM   "defender of his kindred."
KENNETH   "leader."
KIM   Name given an Alaska wolf meaning,
                            "chief."
KINGMIK   Name given to an Eskimo sled dog,
                            meaning, "little chief."
KONGE   "king."
KOLA   K. name given a Siberian Husky.

LACHLAN	"war-like."
LANCER	"one who serves."
LEAR	"to learn." A sea-god and king of ancient Britian.
LINUS	"flaxon-haired."
LIVGARDE	"life guard."
LUBIN	"beloved friend."
MADOC	"good; beneficient."
MALACHI	"messenger."
MALAKOFF	Name given to a Newfoundland dog.
MANASSEH	"forgetfulness."
MARCUS	"a hammer."
MING	Name given to a yellow Labrador Retriever, means, "yellow."
MILES	a soldier.
MOODY	Name given an Eskimo Sled dog meaning, "gloomy."
NANOOK	"bear." Name given an Eskimo sled dog.
NIELS	A Danish king, meaning, "chief."
ODIN	"god of wisdom." Patron of the wild hund in Teutonic Mythology.
OLAF	"bearing the olive."
OLUF	Danish king.
ORESTES	"mountaineer."
PANDO	Name given to a Ch. Siberian Husky.
PAR	Par Lagerkvist, a Swedish dramatist.
PEDER	"rock."
PINNA	"blessed."

PRINCE KOFSKI   Name given to a Samoyed.

ROWDY   "rough." Name given to an Alas-
                     kan Malamute.

SATAN   Name given an Alaskan Malamute.
SEBASTIAN   "reverent."
SILVER LANCER   Name given to a Samoyed.
SHEPHERD   "tend sheep."
SIMSON   "strength."
SKIDOO   K. name for a Siberian Husky.
SPY   Name of an Eskimo sled dog in the
                     Little America Expedition.
STARCHAK   Name of an Eskimo sled dog.
STORMWIND   K. name for a Samoyed.
SVEND   an ancient Danish king.

THERON   "a hunter."
THOMAS   "a twin."
TOLLEF   K. name for a Ch. Norwegian Elk-
                     hound.
TRAHER   "the iron; strong."
TROL   K. name given a Norwegian Elk-
                     hound.
TINY TIM   Eskimo dog that belonged to Calvin
                     Coolidge.
TUNERAK   A Siberian Malamute.

ULICK   "mind reward."
URBAN   "courteous."

VIC   "a conqueror."
VIGI   King Olaf's iron gray shaggy giant
                     hound that died of grief at his

	master's death.
VALDEMAR	an early Danish king.
VILHELM	Vilhelm Svedbom, a Swedish writer of songs, ballads, means, "resolute."
VRAI	Name given to a Samoyed, meaning, "true."
VULPES	"a fox."
WADE	demon of the storm in Mythology.
WARREN	"protecting friend."
WENDELL	"wanderer."
WEEJE	name given to a Norwegian Elkhound.
WILLIWAW	K. name for a Samoyed.
WHITE DIAMOND	K. name for a Samoyed.
WHITE FANG	K. name for a Samoyed. Also a dog in WHITE FANG, by Jack London.
YEOMAN	K. name for a Labrador Retriever, meaning, "servant."
ZIRCON	K. name for a St. Bernard.

Female

ADELINE	"princess."
AEGIS	"protective cloak worn by Athena."
AGATHE	"good; kind." A character in Von Weber's "Der Freisch."
AGNES	"chaste."
AKKA	wife of Ukko, god of the sky and water in Finno-Ugric Mythology.

AMALIE	"beloved." Amalie Skram is a Norwegian naturalist.
ANNA	"gracious."
APHRODITE	goddess that was loved by Adonis.
ASTRID	"starry."
AUGUSTE	"venerable."
AURORA	"fresh."
AVIS	"a bird."
BEL	pet name for Isabel, meaning, worshipper of God.
BELKA	K. name given to a Ch. Siberian Husky.
BEATRIX	"making happy."
BEORHTWULF	"bright wolf."
BI	"a bee" (beeh).
BIRGITTA	"shining bright." St. Bridget was a religious writer in Swedish literature.
BLANKA	"white." Pop.: Blanch
BLOSSOM	"a bloom; to flourish."
BONAR	"the good."
BOREAS	"north wind."
BORNASTAR	K. name given to a St. Bernard.
BRAGANE	"servant of Isolde."
BROWN SUGAR	K. name given to a Ch. St. Bernard.
BROJIT	"motley."
BUTO	"goddess of the North."
BRUNNHILDE	maiden who slept surrounded by fire in "Siegfried," by Wagner.
CAMILE	K. name for a Ch. Newfoundland dog, meaning, "attendant at a

sacrifice."

CAMILLA | "attendant at a sacrifice." Camilla Collett, Norway's first woman novelist.

CANDIDE | "glowing white."

CANDY | K. name for a Labrador Retriever.

CASSANDRA | "prophetress whom no one believed.

CHARLOTTA | "noble spirited."   Pop.: Charlotte

CHITNA | K. name given to an Alaskan Malamute.

CHRISTINA | belonging to Christ." Name of an early Queen of Sweden.

CISSIE | K. name given to a Ch. Siberian Husky.

CLEMENTINE | "mild; gentle."

CLUNY BROWN | K. name given to a St. Bernard.

CHLORIS | "goddess of flowers."

CORDULA | "warm hearted."

CORINNA | "maiden." Dim. of Cora. Pop.: Cora

CYTHINA | "of the moon."

DAFFODIL | K. name given to a St. Bernard.

DAY | "of the day."

DAWN | A Scandinavian name.

DARE | "to dare."

DIANA | "goddess of the hunt."

DOROTHEA | "gift of God." (do-ro-tá-a)

DORKA | K. name given to a Samoyed, meaning, "gift of God."

DEBORA | "a bee." Pop.: Deborah

ETH | "fire."

EBONY SUE | K. name given to an Alaskan

	Malamute.
ECHO	a nymph loved by Narcissus.
ELIN	Elin Vagner wrote Swedish novels.
ELSA	was in love with Lohengrin.
ELISA	"consecrated to God." Pop.: Elizabeth
ENGEL	"angel."
ELSE	"noble." Pop.: Alice
EMMELINE	"industrious."
EPONA	"goddess in Celtic Mythology."
EROS	goddess of strife.
ERGON	"work."
ERNESTINE	"ernest." Fem. of Earnest
ETHEL	"noble."
EURUS	"East wind."
EVA	"life."
FAERDIG	"ready."
FILLIPPINA	"loving horses." Pop.: Phillipa
FIDELIA	"faithful."
FLORERE	"flower, flourish."
FLAPPER	K. name given to a Labrador Retriever.
FRANCISCA	"free." Pop.: Frances
FREIA	"goddess of love," in the opera "Das Rheingold" by Wagner.
FROLENE	Name given to a Ch. Samoyed.
FROSTY PRINCESS	K. name given to a Samoyed.
FRIJA	"well beloved."

GEFJON	"the giver."
GERTRUD	"true spear."
GILDA	Rigoletto's daughter in "Das Rhine-gold," Wagner's opera.
GULLFOS	"golden fall."
GRATIA	"gratious."
GRISELDA	"stone heroine."
GYPSY GIRL	K. name for a St. Bernard.
HANNE	"gracious." Pop.: <u>Hannah</u>
HENRIETTA	"rich." Pop.: <u>Harriet</u>
HEPHZIBAH	"my delight is in her."
HILLEL	"praise."
HONORA	"honorable." Pop.: <u>Honor</u>
HOPE	"hope."
HELENA	"brightness; light." Pop.: <u>Helen</u>
HILDEGARD	"war maiden." Pop.: <u>Hildegarde</u>
HELGA	K. name for a St. Bernard.
IDA	"god-like."
IDUN	wife of Brage; goddess of eternal youth.
INGRID	K. name for a Norwegian Elkhound.
ISABELLA	"worshipper of God." Pop.: <u>Isabel</u>
ISOLDE	in the opera "Tristram and Isolde" "lovers."
ISTAR	"star."
JERUSHA	"possessed."

JOHANNA	"gracious gift of God."
JOLEDAY	"Christmas Day."
JULIANA	"soft-haired." Pop.: Julia
JUSTINA	"just." Fem. of Justin.
KENDA	K. name for a St. Bernard.
KLARA	"bright; illustrious."
KAROLINA	"strong; noble spirited." Pop.: Caroline
KATARINA	"pure." Pop.: Catherine
KNASKE	"to grind the teeth."
KUUTAR	"daughter of the Moon," in Finno-Ugric Mythology.
KRIS	K. name for a Samoyed.
LADY	K. name for a Siberian Husky, also a German Shepherd.
LAIKA	shaggy dog that orbited the earth for over a week in 1957 in the second Soviet Sputnik.
LAETITIA	"joy." Pop.: Lettice
LINDA	A Newfoundland owned by Charles Dickens meaning, "the pretty, or the beautiful."
LORINDA	"a laurel." Pop.: Laura
LUCITA	"star of the sea." Pop.: Mary
LUDOVIKA	"fortress; defense."
LYDIA	"native of Lydia."
LUPA	K. name for a Siberian Husky.
MARA	"bitter." Pop.: Mary
MAHETABLE	"benefited of God."

MACHA	"duty." In Celtic Mythology a goddess.
MALCA	"the worker."
MARIKA	Marika Stiernstedt, swedish writer.
MAUNA	"great."
MINERVA	"goddess of wisdom, war."
MARGRETHE	"pearl." Name of a Danish queen. Pop.: Margaret.
MATHILDE	"heroine." Pop.: Matilda
MARIA	"star of the sea." Pop.: Mary
MARTA	"ruler of the house." Pop.: Martha
MYRA	"she who weeps."
NAAMAN	"pleasant." Pop.: Naomi (?)
NANA	The Newfoundland dog, a nurse, of the Darling children in Peter Pan.
NAHUM	"consolation."
NARCISSUS	"a daffodil" in love with Echo.
NADA	"hope."
NYAL	"champion."
NAKKE	genie of water in Finnish Mythology.
NOTUS	"south wind."
NOX	"night."
OLEA	Olea Styhr Croger is a Norwegian collector of folk music.
OLYMPIA	"heavenly." Suggests size.
OLIVIA	"an olive."
PAVILINA	"little." Pop.: Pauline

PRINCESS MOAH	K. name for a Norwegian Elk-hound.
PATIENCE	"patient."
PENELOPE	"weaver."
PHEBE	"shining." Pop.: <u>Phoebe</u>
RAHEL	"ewe."
RAG DOLL	K. name for a Ch. St. Bernard.
RAN	wife of Aegir, God of the Sea.
REDE	"ready." (rether)
RAKEL	"sheep, or lamb."
REBECCA	"of enchanting beauty."
SABEENA	"a Sabine woman."
SAGITTA	"white, or silver sleet." Name given to an Alaskan Malamute.
SEASPRITE	Name given a Newfoundland.
SELENE	"moon goddess."
SELMA	Selma Lagerlof, writer of Swedish novels.
SEKHMET	"powerful." A terrible goddess in war and battle in Egyptian Mythology.
SARA	"princess."
SILENUS	nurse of Dionysus.
SOFEEA	"Wisdom." Pop.: <u>Sophie</u>
SILVA	"a wood."
SILVER CHARM	K. name for a Samoyed.
SIF	"wife of Thor."
SNOW FIRE	K. name for a Samoyed.
SNOW LASSIE	K. name for a Samoyed.
SNOW MOON	K. name for a Samoyed.

STORM	"a storm."
SWEEP	Name given to a Labrador Retriever.
SIBYL	"a prophetess."
TALTIA	earth goddess in Celtic Mythology
TASKA	Name given a Norwegian Elkhound.
THAL	"valley."
THOMASINE	"a twin." Fem. of Thomas.
TEMPEST	K. name for a Samoyed.
TRYPHENA	"delicate."
TRUDY	"spear maiden." Pop.: Gertrude
ULRIKA	Sister of a King of Sweden, meaning, "rich." Pop.: Ulrica
URANIA	"heavenly."
URSULA	"female bear."
VANKA	name given to a Ch. Siberian Husky.
VESPER	"the evening star."
WEE TROUSERS	Name given to a St. Bernard.
WILMETT	"protector."
ZEPHYRUS	"west wind."
ZOYA	K. name for a Siberian Husky.

FRENCH, BELGIUM, HOLLAND DOGS

Basset Hound
Belgian Sheepdog
Belgian Tervuren
Bouviers des Flandres
Briard
Brittany Spaniel
French Bulldog
Great Pyrenees
Brussels Griffen
Keeshond
Papillon
Schipperke
Wirehaired Pointing Griffon
Belgian Malinois

Names

Male

AARDIG	"charming, pretty."
ACROBAAT	"acrobat."
ALEARD	"bold; firm." Pop.: Abelard
ACHILLE	"silent; valorous." Pop.: Achilles
ADRIEN	"the black; black earth." Pop.: Adrian
ALARIC	"ruler of all." Also: ULRIC Pop.: Albert
ALBRET	"noble bright; illustrious." Also: AUBERT Pop.: Albert
ALERON	"winged." An Old French chivalry name implying knighthood.
ALEXE	"aid to men; protector." Also: ALEXANDRE, ALEXIS. Pop.: Alexander.

ALFRED	"wise counsel." Pop.: Alfred
ALGERNON	"with the mustache." An Old French word that comes from the warrior's "the whiskered man."
ALPHONSE	"noble; battle keen." Pop.: Alphonso
ALUIN	"noble friend." Pop.: Alvin
AMAND	"worthy of love." Pop.: Amandus
ANATOL	"sunrise." Pop.: Anatol
ANDRÉ	"manly; strong." Pop.: Andrew
ANGE	"angelic; messenger." Pop.: Angell
ANICET	"unconquered." Pop.: Anicet
ANSELME	"warrior; with divine protection." Pop.: Anselm
ANTOINE	"flourishing; inestimable." Also: ANTONI Pop.: Anthony
ARISTIDE	"son of the best." Pop.: Aristides
ARNAULT	"Eagle strength; lit. eagle rule." Also: ARNAUD Pop.: Arnold
ARSÈNE	"virile." Pop.: Arsen
ARTUS	"noble or high." Pop.: Arthur
AUBRI	"fair-haired leader." Pop.: Aubrey
AVELIN	"life; pleasant." Old French name. Pop.: Evelyn

BANCO	K. name for a Brussels Griffin.
BAUDOUIN	"bold and courageous friend; royal friend." Pop.: Baldwin
BIEN-AIME	"beloved."
BENOÎT	"blessed." Pop.: Benedict
BON MICHEL	Name given to a Ch. French Bulldog, meaning, "good leader; good warrior." Pop.: Michael
BEAUFORT	"fair and strong." Old French.
BEAUMONT	"fair height; beautiful mountain." Old French.
BLACK DOMINO	Name given to a Schipperke.
BERTRAN	"bright raven." Also: BERTRAND, BERTRAM Pop.: Bertram
BOLD AS BRASS	K. name for a Basset Hound.
BLAISE	"a blaze or brand." Also: BLAISOT Pop.: Blaze
BOURNE	"destiny." Old French.
BUBBLES	Name given to a K. poodle, meaning, "eager, happy."
BUEVE	"bowman; archer." Also: BUEVES Pop.: Bogart
BURNETT	Old French, meaning "brown." Pop.: Brown
BUTCH	Name given to a Belgian Shepherd War-dog.
BRAZIL	"the glowing." Old French.
BRIAR	"strong." Pop.: Brier
BRIT	Dual Ch. Brittany Spaniel name.

CADEAU DE NOEL	"Christmas gift." Name given to a Ch. Standard Poodle.
CADICHON	"little cadet."
CALYPSO	"a musical style with improvised lyrics." Name given to a Briard.
CÉSAR	"king." Pop.: Caesar
CASIMIR	"desire for peace; high prince." Pop.: Casimir
CATON	"cautious." Pop.: Cato
CHARLOT	"strong." Pop.: Charles
CHARLTON	"Old French, "from the man's farm."
CHASE	"of the chase; a hunter."
CHRÉTIEN	"follower." Pop.: Christian
CLAUDE	"lame." Pop.: Claude
CLÉMENT	"mild; merciful." Pop.: Clement
COCOA	Name given a Brussels Griffon.
CONRAD	"wise counsel; able." Pop.: Conrad
CORBIN	Old French, meaning, "raven; black."
CORDELLE	"rope." Pop.: Cordell
CORNELIUS	"crowned." A war horm is the symbol of kingship.
CRÉPIN	"having curly hair." Also: CREPET Pop.: Crispin
CURTISE	"courteous." Pop.: Curtis
CYPRIEN	"sun; sunny." Pop.: Cyprian

DAMIEN	"conquering." Pop.: Damon
DAVID	"beloved." Pop.: David
DE LA NOY	"healthy; dark." Pop.: Delano
DENYS	"gay; god of wine." Also: DIONE Pop.: Dennis
DOMINIQUE	"Sunday." Pop.: Dominic
D'OYLE	"black stranger." Pop.: Doyle
DUC	"duke." Name given to a Ch. Standard Poodle.
DUDON	"God given."
DRAGON	K. name for a Bouvier de Flandres.
EDMOND	"defender of property." Pop.: Edgar
EDOUARD	"guard of goods." Pop.: Edmund
EDGARD	"protector of property." Pop.: Edgar
EMERI	"leader at work." Also: EMERU, AIMERI
EMILE	"the industrious." Pop.: Emil
ENEE	"praised." Pop.: Eneas
ENOCH	"dedicated." Pop.: Enoch
ERASTE	"beloved." Pop.: Erastus
ERIC	"kingly." Pop.: Eric
ESDRAS	"helper." Pop.: Ezra
ESTAGEL	K. name given to a Great Pyrenes.
EUSTACHE	"well put together." Pop.: Eustace
EVRAUD	"strong; always bold." Also: EVRART, EVERART, EVRE Pop.: Everard
EXCALIBUR	The magic sword of King Arthur. Name given to a Briard.

FALSTAFF	Name of a Ch. Bassett Hound.
FELIX	"happy; prosperous." Pop.: Felix
FERRAND	"to make peace; to be bold." Pop.: Ferdinand
FONTAINE	"a spring." Pop.: Fountain
FRANÇOIS	"the free." Also: FRANCHOT Pop.: Francis
FRASER	"the curly haired."
FRÉDERIC	"peaceful ruler." Pop.: Frederic
FREMONT	"peace protection."
GABRIEL	"strength."
GAGE	"Old French meaning "security."
GASPARD	"treasure holder." Pop.: Gaspar
GASTON	"hospitable."
GEORGES	"farmer." Pop.: George
GILLES	"shield bearer." Pop.: Giles
GIRAUT	"ruler." Pop.: Gerald
GLISSON	"glittering." Old French.
GODARD	"super-strength."
GOLIATH	"a giant." Name given to a Bouvier de Flandres.
GRÉGOIRE	"to awaken; be vigilent."
GROSVENOR	"great hunter."
GUI	"to steady; guide." Also: GUY Pop.: Guy
HANS	K. name of a Ch. Keeshond. meaning, "gracious."
HARCOURT	"armed; fortified." Old French.
HARO	Name for a Ch. Briard.
HAROLD	"leader."
HAVIOUS	Old French "to have."

HENRI	"ruler of private property." Also: HERRIOT Pop.: <u>Henry</u>
HERCULE	"chosen one." Pop.: <u>Hercules</u>
HERVE	"noble warrior." Pop.: <u>Harvey</u>
HILAIRE	"cheerful; merry; hilarious." Pop.: <u>Hilary</u>
HUBERT	"bright of mind." Pop.: <u>Hubert</u>
HUE	"mind." Also: HUON, HUES, HUET, HUGUES Pop.: <u>Hugh</u>
HUMBERT	"steadfast."
HUNTSMAN	K. name of Bassett Hound.
HUZAAR	Name of a Brussels Griffon.
IGNACE	"firey; ardent." Pop.: <u>Ignatius</u>
INTREPIDE	"fearless; valorous." Pop.: <u>Intrepid</u>
ISAAC	"laughter."
JACQUES	"one who replaces." Pop.: <u>James</u>
JEAN	"gracious." Also: JEHAN, JO-HANNOT, JEANNOT, JEANNO Pop.: <u>John</u>
JUSTIN	"the just; upright." Also: JUSTE Pop.: <u>Justin</u>
KIT	Name given to a Bouvier de Flandres.
LAURENT	"the laurel; crowned." Also: LORENZ Pop.: <u>Laurence</u>
LEO	Name given to a St. Bernard.
LÉON	Name given to a St. Bernard, meaning, 'lion-like.'
LEROY	Old French for 'the king.'

LEVANDER	Old French for 'rising of the sun.'
LICHTBRUIN	"light brown."
LOMBARD	"the long-bearded."
MALLORY	Old French for "ill-omened."
MARC	"a warrior." Pop.: Mark
MARSOUS	Name given to a Ch. Great Pyrenees.
MÂTIN	"mastiff."
MAURICE	"the dark one." Pop.: Maurice
MÉCHANT	"mischievous."
MORTIMER	"dweller by the still water."
(de) MUSKIET	"mosquito."
MOUCHE	Name given to a Brussels Griffon, meaning, "beauty patch?"
NAPOLÉON	Name for a Ch. French Bulldog.
NÈGRE	"blacky."
NIC	A victory name, short form of Nicholas. Name given to a Bouvier de Flandres.
NOEL	"Christmas, born on Christmas day."
NOIR	"black."
OCTAVE	"the eighth." Pop.: Octavius
OLIVIER	"the olive; peace; bearer of the olive branch." Pop.: Oliver
ONFROI	"home protector." Pop.: Humphrey
OTHO	"happy."
PAGET	Old French for "attendant on a noble."
PAPILLON	"butterfly."

PARAGON	Name given to a Basset Hound.
PARRY	Old French, "to ward off."
PATRASCHE	Name given to a Belgian Sheepdog in "Dog of Flanders," by Ouida.
PAULOT	"little." Pop.: <u>Paul</u>
PERCEVAL	"guard of the grail; stalwart; perceptive."
PICARD	Name for a Ch. Bouviers des Flandres, possibly from the word Picardy, a former province in France, or 'pikhaar,' a Flemish name meaning, 'hair which pricks.'
PRINCE D'OR	"Golden Prince," name given to a Bouvier des Flandres.
RAIMOND	"wise protector." Also: RAIMONT RAYMUND Pop.: <u>Raymond</u>
RENAUT	"strong ruler." Also: REGNAULT Pop.: <u>Reginald</u>
ROB ROY	Name given to a sheep dog belonging to Calvin Coolidge.
RODRIQUE	"rich in fame." Pop.: <u>Roderick</u>
ROI	"king." Pop.: <u>Roy</u>
ROMÉO	Name given to a Ch. Keeshond.
ROYCE	"son of a king."
RUMPELSTILTSKIN	Name given to a Poodle, which was nicknamed 'Curly.' The dwarf in the fairy tale.
SAD SACK	Name given to a Basset Hound.
SISKE	Name given to a Bouvier des Flandres.
SNOWMAN	Name given to a Toy Poodle.
SULTAN	Name given to a Bouvier des Flandres, meaning, "kingly."
SUMNER	Old French name for "one who summons."

TALBOT	Old French word for "the blood-hound."
TERRY	K. name for a Ch. Brussels Griffon.
TOMY	Name given for a Belgian Sheep dog in 1898.
TROUW	"faithful."
VANGABANG	Name for a Ch. Keeshond.
VIXEN	Name given to a Bouvier des Flandres.
WHITE ROLAND	Name given to a Great Pyrenees. One of Charlemagne's knights.
WHITE HOPE	K. name for a Great Pyrenees.
WHIZZER	K. name for a Brussels Griffon.
YWAIN	K. name for a Papillon.

Female

ACTIEF	"active."
ADELE	"noble maid; good cheer." Also: ADELAIDE, ADELINE, ADELAIS. Pop.: Adela
ADRIENNE	"black; bold." Pop.: Adria
AGATHE	"good; kind." Pop.: Agatha
AGLAE	"brightness." Pop.: Aglaia
AGNIES	"chaste; mild; lamb." Pop.: Agnes
ALAIN	"child; harmonious." Pop.: Alanna
ALEXANDRINE	"helper of men." Pop.: Alexandra
ALPHONSINE	"noble; eager to fight." Pop.: Alfonsine

ALIX	"truth; noble." Pop.: <u>Alice</u>
ALISTE	"turned aside; prejudiced." Pop.: <u>Alistair</u>
AMADEE	"worthy to be loved." Also: AMANDINE, AMANDIS Pop.: <u>Amanda</u>
AMBRE	"amber." Pop.: <u>Amber</u>
AME	"beloved." Also: AIMEE, AMICIE AMORET, AMORETTE Pop.: <u>Amy</u>
ANCILEE	"a handmaiden." Also: ANCELOT Pop.: <u>Ancelin</u>
ANDANTE	"Slow and even." K. name for a Ch. Keeshond.
AMI	"beloved." K. name for a French bulldog.
AMIC	K. name given to a Bouvier de Flandres, meaning, "friendly."
AMI AU PIED	"friend on foot."
ANDREE	"womanly." Pop.: <u>Andrea</u>
ANGÉLIQUE	"angelic; messenger." Also: ANGELE, ANGELINE Pop.: <u>Angela</u>
ANNETTE	"grace; merry; prayer." Also: ANNE, NANETTE, NANON, NINON, NINETTE, NICHON. Pop.: <u>Ann</u>
ANTOINETTE	"graceful; inestimable." The name for a Queen of France. Also: ANTONIE, TOINETTE, TOINON Pop.: <u>Antonia</u>
ARABELLE	"fair refuge; eagle heroine." Pop.: <u>Arabella</u>
ARIANE	"grace." Pop.: <u>Ariana</u>
ARMINE	"noble maid; high degree." Also: ARMANTINE, ARMANDE Pop.: <u>Armina</u>
ARTÉMISE	"flawless one." In Greek Mythology she was protector of women and children, the moon goddess.

This is a romance name in France. Pop.: Artemis

ARLETTE "pledge." A name given to a Ch. Great Pyranees. Pop.: Arlene

ATHALIE "innocent." Pop.: Athalia

ATHENAIS "wisdom." Pop.: Athena

AUDREE "noble helper." Pop.: Audrey

AURE "golden." Also: AURELIE Pop.: Aurelia

BELLA "beautiful." K. name for a Bouvier de Flandres.

BÉATRIX "she who blesses; makes happy." Pop.: Beatrice

BENOITE "the blessed." Pop.: Benedicta

BARIKA "little lamb."

BENIGNE "benign." Pop.: Benigna

BÉRÉNICE "bringer of victory." Also: VERONIQUE Pop.: Berenice

BERNADETTE "strong as a little bear." Name of the maid who saw the vision at Lourdes. Also: BERNARDINE Pop.: Bernardine - f. of Bernard.

BERTHE "the bright." Pop.: Bertha

BLACK VAMP K. name for a Schipperke.

BLANCHE "white; pure." Pop.: Blanche

BLAUW "blue."

BONNE ET BELLE "good and handsone."

BONNE "sweet; fair little good one." Pop.: Bonnie

BRIGITTE "firey dart; mighty; high." Also: BRIGIDE Pop.: Bridget

BURNETTA "Old French meaning "little brunette."

BUNNY Name given to a Brussels Griffon.

CAMILLE	"temple maiden." Pop.: <u>Camilla</u>
CANDIDE	"fire-white; shining white." Pop.: <u>Candace</u>
CANDY	American dim. of Candace. A K. name for a White Toy Poodle; meaning, "shining white."
CAROL	"to sing joyfully." Old French.
CARON	"pure." Also: CATANT, TRINETTE Pop.: <u>Catherine</u>
CASQUE	"great coat."
CASSANDRE	"winning love; helper." A true prophetess whom no one believed.
CÉCILE	"blind; dim-sighted." Pop.: <u>Cecilia</u>.
CÉLESTE	"heavenly." Also: CELESTINE, CELIE Pop.: <u>Celia</u>
CELINE	"radiant one." Also: CELINETTE Pop.: <u>Selena</u>
CENDREE	"small shot."
CHERI	"sweetheart." Pop.: <u>Pulcheria</u>
CHOCOLATE	K. name for a Wire-haired pointing Griffon.
CHRISSANTH	"gold flower."
CLARETTE	"bright; clear; illustrious." Also: CLARE, CLAIRE, CLAIRETTE, CLARICE. Pop.: <u>Clara</u>
CLÉANTHE	"glory flower; sweet pea." Pop.: <u>Cleantha</u>
CLÉMENTINE	"merciful." Pop.: <u>Clemency</u>
COCOA	K. name of a Brussels Griffon.
CONSTANCE	"steadfast." Pop.: <u>Constance</u>
CORALIE	"coral-pink." A charm name. Coral was used in amulets to protect from harm. Pop.: <u>Coral</u>
CORDELIE	"sea jewel." Pop.: <u>Cordelia</u>
CORNÉLIE	"sea jewel." Pop.: <u>Cornelia</u>

COSETTE	"a pet lamb."
CHOSETTE	"little thing."
CHOU	"dear; darling."
CLARINE	"a small bell."
COLETTE	"a collar; necklace; little winner."

DEANA	Name given to a Papillon, meaning, "bright as day.
DARRIELLE	"darling; dearly beloved." Pop.: Daryl
DELICE	"pleasurable." Pop.: Delight
DENICE	"serving." Name for a Ch. Schipperke. Also: DENYS Pop.: Denise
DESTA	Old French, "destiny."
DESIRÉE	"desired; beloved." Pop.: Desire
DIANE	"divine; goddess of the moon." K. name given to a Brittany Spaniel. Pop.: Diana
DOREEN	"gold colored." Old French. Also: DORINE
DORETTE	"gift." Also: DOROTHEE, DORALICE Pop.: Dorothy
DREAM	Name given to a Papillon.

EBONETA	Name given to a Schipperke.
EDMEE	"protector." Pop.: Edmonda
EGIDE	"shield bearer." Pop.: Egidia
EMERENCE	"the deserving." Pop.: Emera
ÉMILIE	"industrious; worker." Pop.: Emily
ESTELLE	"star." Pop.: Esther
ÉTIENNE	Name of a Ch. Briard.
EUPHRASIE	"to delight the heart or mind." Pop.: Euphrasia

FAMEUSE	"famous." Pop.: Fayme
FANCHON	"the free." Also: FRANCHETTE, FRANCOISE, FANCHETTE Pop.: Frances
FAY	"faith; fairy." Old French.
FEALA	"faithful." Old French.
FÉLISE	"happy." Also: FÉLICITÉ Pop.: Felicia
FLEUR	"to flower; flourish." Also: FLORE, FLEURETTE Pop.: Florence
FORT	"mighty."
FRASQUE	"mischief."
FREDERIQUE	"peaceful ruler." Pop.: Frederica
FRESA	"curly haired."
GABRIELLE	"strength of God."
GAI	"joyful."
GAITE DE COEUR	"gay heart."
GAMIN	"urchin." Name given to a French bulldog.
GARDE	"protected."
GEMOEVRE	"white." Also: GENIEVRE, JAVOTTE Pop.: Guinevere
GITANE	"gypsy."
GLYCERE	"sweet."
GOGO	"pearl." Also: MARGARETE, MARGOT, MARGUERITE Pop.: Margaret
GRAZIELLE	"loved; favored." Pop.: Grace
HADJI	"a pilgrim." A name given to a Belgian Shepherd.
HEDVIGE	"fighting lady guard." Pop.: Hedwig

HENRIETTE	"ruler of private property." Pop.: <u>Henriette</u>
HILARIA	"jolly." Pop.: <u>Hilary</u>
HUETTE	"mind." Pop.: Huette, f. of Hugh.
HYACINTHE	"color, flower, jewel." Also: HYAZINTHE Pop.: <u>Hyacinth</u>
IDA	"happy." Also: IDE Pop.: <u>Ida</u>
IPHIGÉNIE	"of royal birth."
ISEUT	"fair." Also: ISOLDE, ISOLT Pop.: <u>Isolde</u>
JASMIN	"flower." K. name for a Schipperke.
JEANNE	"gracious." Also: JEANNETTE, JEHAN, JEHANNE Pop.: <u>Jane</u>
JEWELL	"a toy, or trinket; jest." Pop.: <u>Jewel</u>
JOLI	"pretty."
LAURE	"laurel; crowned." Also: LAURETTE Pop.: <u>Laura</u>
LAUREL	Name given to a Ch. Belgian Sheepdog.
LEALA	Old French, meaning "faithful."
LÉONIE	"lioness; like a lioness." Also: LEONCIE Pop.: <u>Leona</u>
LISA	Name given to a Ch. Belgian Sheepdog, meaning "God is my oath." Pop.: <u>Elizabeth</u>
LISETTE	"famous fighter." Also: ALOYSE, HELOISE, LOUISE Pop.: <u>Louise</u>
LOLA	Name given to a Ch. Belgian Sheepdog, meaning, "manly."
LUCRÈCE	"lucky one." Pop.: <u>Lucretia</u>

LOUVETTE	Name given to a Ch. Belgian Sheepdog.
LUCIENNE	"light; bright." Also: LUCIE, LUCILLE, LUCE Pop.: <u>Lucy</u>
LYCA	Name given to a Bouvier de Flandres.

MALVINE	"chieftainess; handmaid." Pop.: <u>Malvina</u>
MARTINE	"warlike."
MAVIS	"joy." Pop.: <u>Mab</u>
MAXIME	"the greatest." Pop.: <u>Maxine</u>
MÉLANIE	"black one."
MÉTISSE	"wisdom; skill." Pop.: <u>Meta</u>
MIGNON	"delicate; dainty; petite; graceful." Also: MIGNONNE, MIGNONETTE Pop.: <u>Mignon</u>
MINETTE	"purpose; force." Pop.: <u>Minerva</u>
MIMI	Name given to a Papillon owned by Madame de Pompadour, meaning "chosen protection." Pop.: <u>Wilheminia</u>
MIRABELLE	"she looks beautiful." Pop.: <u>Mirabel</u>
MISSIE	Name given to a Ch. Basset Hound.
MODESTINE	"modest; virtue name." Pop.: <u>Modesty</u>
MORGANCE	"sea woman." Pop.: <u>Morgan</u>

NADINE	"hope." Pop.: <u>Nada</u>
NATALIE	"born on Christmas day." Also: NOELLE Pop.: <u>Natalie</u>
NICOLETTE	"victory; conqueror." Also: COLETTE Pop.: <u>Nicola</u>

NINETTE	"little one." Also: NINON, NANON, NICHON, ANNE, AN-NETTE, NANETTE Pop.: Ann
NOIRE DE RAPEAU	"black banner."
ODETTE	"noble." Pop.: Odelia
ORABEL	"of golden beauty."
OUIDA	"yes." Pet name for Louise. Also pen name of Louisa de la Ramee. Also: OUIDETTE
PAMALIE	A name given to a Brittany Spaniel, meaning "all-sweetness; all honey."
PAULETTE	"little." Also: PAULINE Pop.: Paula
PERETTE	"adamant." Also: PETRINE, PERRINE, PIERETTE Pop.: Petra
PHILOXENE	"loving stranger." Pop.: Philoxia
PITTER PATTER	Name for a Ch. Miniature Poodle.
PROMISE	Name given to a Standard Poodle.
REINE	"a queen." Also: REINETTE Pop.: Regina
RIVA	Old French, "of the river."
ROCHETTE	"adamant; rock-like."
ROOD	"red."
ROSINE	"the rose." Also: ROSETTE Pop.: Rhoda
ROXANE	"the brilliant; the dawn." Pop.: Roxana
RUFINE	"red-haired." Pop.: Rubina
RUSE	"slyness."
SABINE	"a little holy one." Pop.: Sabina

SARA	"princess." Also: SAROTTE, ZAIDEE Pop.: Sarah
SCHUW	"shy."
SIMONE	"she who listens." Also: SIMON-ETTE Pop.: Simone
SLOW POKE	Name given to a Basset Hound.
SNEL	"fast."
SWAN	Name given to a Toy Poodle.
STERK	"strong."
SPRING SONG	Name for a Brussels Griffon.
TETU	"stubborn."
TECLA	"divine fame." Pop.: Thecla
TRAMPS	Name given to a Miniature Poodle.
VIOLETTE	"violet; shy." Pop.: Violet
VIVIANE	"vitality; lively." Pop.: Vita
VREEMD	"strange; foreign."
WHIZZER	Name given to a Brussels Griffon.
WIT	"white."
YVONNE	Popular French name commemorating the famous St. Yves or Ivo of Brittany. Also: YVETTE Pop.: Yvelte
ZA	Name given to an Alsatian Sheepdog, a French war dog, possibly from Zada, meaning "prosperous."
ZAMPA	Name given to a Brussels Griffon.
ZOÉ	"life; vitality." Pop.: Zoe

GERMAN DOGS

Affenpinscher (monkey dog)
Boxer
Dachshund (Long haired, Smooth, Wire- haired)
Doberman Pinscher
German Shorthaired Pointer
German Shepherd
German Wirehaired Pointer

Giant Schnauzer
Great Dane
Miniature Pinscher
Miniature Poodle
Miniature Schnauzer
Pomeranian
Rottweiler
Standard Schnauzer
Standard Poodle
Toy Poodle
Weimaraner

Names

Male

ACE   "first!"   K. name given to a German Shepherd.

ACHILL   "quiet; silent; valorous." Pop.: Achilles

ALBRECHT   "illustrious." Also: ADELBRECHT ULBRECHT Pop.: Albert

AHRENT   "strong as an eagle." Also: AROLD Pop.: Arnold

AFFE, der   "monkey."

AFFENPINSCHER   "monkey, rough-haired terrier."

ALFONS   "ready; eager; willing." Pop.: Alphonso

AJAX   "mighty warrior." K. name given to a Dachshund.

ALWIN   "noble friend; beloved." Pop.: Alvin

ANDREAS   "strong." Pop.: Andrew

ANDY   Name given to a Doberman Pinscher, a scout dog during the war.

ANTON	"the inestimable." Also: ANTONIUS, ANTOLIN Pop.: <u>Anthony</u>
APELGRAU	"dapple grey."
ARCHIMBALD	"nobility; bold; very valiant." Also: ERCHANPALD Pop.: <u>Archibald</u>
AROLD	"eagle strength." Also: ARANOLD, AHRENT Pop.: <u>Arnold</u>
ARNO	"eagle." K. name given to a Ch. Standard Schnauzer.
ATILLA	K. name for a Dachshund, meaning, 'King of Huns.'
BALDUIN	"bold; courageous; royal friend." Pop.: <u>Baldwin</u>
BARRON	"noble warrior; freeman." Name given to a Doberman Pinscher during the war.
BART, der	"beard."
BÄRTIG	"bearded; whiskered."
BENGAZE	Name given to a Ch. Boxer.
BENNO	"bold; strong." Name given to a Giant Schnauzer.
BERNHARD	"bold as a bear." Also: BEREND, BAREND, BENNO Pop.: <u>Bernard</u>
BERNSTEIN	"amber."
BIT O'BLACK	K. name for a Dachshund.
BITTERSWEET	K. name for a German Pinscher.
BLACKBEARD	K. name for an Affenpinscher.
BLAUÄUGIG	"blue-eyed."
BLAUJACKE	"blue-jacket."
BLAÜLICH	"bluish."
BLITZ	"by storm." K. name for a Doberman Pinscher.
BOUNCE	Name of the Great Dane that belonged to Alexander Pope.

BOY   Name of a Doberman Pinscher.

BRASS   "the color; forward." K. name for
                             a Doberman Pinscher.

BROWNY   K. name for a German Shepherd.

BRUTUS   K. name for a Dachshund, meaning,
                             "heavy." Brutus killed Caesar in
                             Shakespeare's play.

BULLITT   K. name given to a German Shep-
                             herd.

BUNT   "parti-colored."

BUTCH   K. name given to a German Shep-
                             herd, meaning "bungler."

CAESAR   "king." Name given to a German
                             Shepherd on Bougainville Island dur-
                             ing the war where he achieved out-
                             standing success against the enemy.

CAPTAIN   Name given to a Doberman Pinscher.

CAVALIER   K. name for a Dachshund, mean-
                             ing, 'courtly; gallant; knight.'

CHIPS   A German Shepherd's name.

COUNT SILVER   A K. name for a Ch. Weimaraner.

CRUSADER   K. name for a Ch. Great Dane.

DAAG   Name given to a Doberman Pinscher.
                             Dutch daags means, 'daily.'

DEREK   "ruler." Name given to a Dober-
                             man Pinscher, a Dachshund.

DICK   "dense."

DICTATOR   Name given a Ch. Doberman Pin-
                             scher, a Dachshund.

DIETRICH   "ruler." Pop.: Theodoric

DIPLOMAT   K. name for a Dachshund.

DRAHTEN   "wirey."

DRAHTHAARIG   "wire-haired."

DUKE   Name given to a Doberman Pinscher.

DUNKLEBLAU	"blue-black."
EBERT	"always bold." Also: EBERHARD, EWART, EPPO, EBBO Pop.: Everard
ECHO	K. name for a Ch. Dachshund.
EDELWEISS	K. name for a Dachshund.
EDRA	"mighty prosperous." K. name given to a Boxer.
EGON	"ardent; formidable." K. name given to a Boxer.
EMIL	"industrious." Pop.: Emile
ENDYMION	a beautiful youth, in Greek Mythology, who the poets say, was a king, a shepherd, whom the moon loved. Name given to a German Shepherd.
ENGEL	"an angel; angelic; messenger." Pop.: Angell
ERNST	"to be earnest; zealous." Also: ERNOST, ERNUST Pop.: Ernest
ERIK	"kingly; power." Name given to a Boxer.
ESRA	"helper." Pop.: Ezra
EUGEN	"well-born." Also: EUGENIUS Pop.: Eugene
FAR AWAY	Name given to a Dachshund.
FAROLD	"power that travels far."
FAUST	Name given to a Dachshund, meaning, "the fortunate."
FELIX	"happy." Pop.: Felix
FERDINAND	"peace; bold; brave; valiant." Pop.: Ferdinand
FERRY	Name given to a Ch. Doberman Pinscher, meaning, 'transporting.'

FESTUS	"joyous; gay."
FEURING	"high-spirited."
FLAME	Name given to a German Shepherd.
FLASH	Name given to a German Short-haired Pointer.
FLINK	"brisk; nimble; alert." Name given to a Dachshund.
FLOTT	"lively; gay; chic." K. name given to a Dachshund.
FLUG	"pom-pom." Pop.: Flugabwehrmaschienenkanone
FOGAL	"a deeper or catcher of birds." Also: VOGLER, VOGEL Pop.: Fowler
FRANZ	"free." Also: FRANZISCUS, FRANC Pop.: Francis
FREDERIC	"peaceful ruler." Also: FRIEDRICH, FRIEDEL, FRITZ. Pop.: Frederick
FRISIEREN	"curly" (hair)
FUCHS	"fox."
FURCHTLOS	"fearless."
GARDELL	"guard; high protector."
GEHORSAM	"obedient."
GEIST	"spirit; ghost." Matthew Arnold wrote a poem about Geist's Grave. A Dachshund.
GELB	"yellow."
GELEHRIG	"docile."
GELBLICH-GRAUWEISS	"pepper and salt."
GERHARD	"bold spearsman." Pop.: Gerard
GINGER SNAP	Name given to a Boxer.
GIRALT	"ruler; bold." Also: GERWALD Pop.: Gerald
GISELBERT	"bright servant." Pop.: Gilbert

GLÄTT	"glossy."
GLOBE TROTTER	K. name for a Boxer.
GOLDARTIG	"golden."
GOTTHART	"strong." Also: GODDHARD, GOTTHARD Pop.: Goddard
GRAUBART, der	"graybeard."
GRAY GHOST	Name given to a German Shepherd.
GREY SHADOW	Name given to a German Shepherd.
GREGOR	"watchful; to awaken." Also: GREGORIUS Pop.: Gregory
GUT	"kind."
GUSTAV	"staff." Pop.: Gustavus
HAAKON	"a king of Norway." given to a K. Dachshund.
HANS	"gracious." Pop.: John
HÄNSE	K. name for a German Shepherd, meaning, "gracious." Pop.: John
HANSWURST	"harlequin."
HARLEQUIN	K. name for a German Shepherd.
HECTOR	Name given to a German Wire-haired Pointer, meaning, 'support.'
HEINE	"home lord; ruler of private property." Also: HEINTZ, HEINIE, HAGEN, HEINRICH Pop.: Henry
HERCULES	"strength; chosen one." K. name given to a police dog.
HERMANN	"army man; noble." Pop.: Herman
HERMES	K. name given to a Boxer, meaning, "messenger of the gods."
HERR, der	"Master."
HIGH TEST	K. name given to a Standard Schnauzer.
HILARIUS	"cheerful; merry; hilarious." Pop.: Hilary

HISKIA	"strength." Pop.: <u>Hezekiah</u>
HOFHUND	"watch dog."
HUGIBERT	"bright." Pop.: <u>Hubert</u>
HUMFRIED	"home protector." Pop.: <u>Humphrey</u>
I-GO-FORTH	K. name for a Dachshund.
IGNAZ	"ardent; fiery." Pop.: <u>Ignatius</u>
ISAAK	"laughter." Pop.: <u>Isaac</u>
ISIDOR	"gift."
JACK O'DANDY	K. name for a Dachshund.
JACK OF HEARTS	Ch. name for a Boxer.
JACKEL	"take the place of." Also: JAKOB, JOCKEL. Pop.: <u>Jacob</u>
JAGDHUND, der	"the hunter."
JULIANUS	"soft-haired; light-bearded." Pop.: <u>Julian</u>
JURGEN	"earth worker."
JUSTUS	"upright; just." Also: JUST Pop.: <u>Justin</u>
KARAL	"strong."
KETTENHUND, der	"watch dog."
KING	Name given to a German Shepherd Scout dog in the war.
KING ERIC	Name given to a Miniature Pinscher, meaning, 'king heoric.'
KING TUT	A German Shepherd belonging to Herbert Hoover that could open doors. Tut is an abbreviation for Tutankhamen, a king of Egypt in the 14th century B. C.
KLEIN	"little."
KLEMENS	"mild; merciful." Also: MENZ Pop.: <u>Clement</u>

KÖNIG	"king."
KONRAD	"wise counsel." Also: KURT Pop.: Conrad
KRISPEIN	"curly; crinkle."
KRISS	"Christ-bearer." Also: CHRISTOPHORUS, STOFFEL Pop.: Christopher
KURZ	"short."
LAD	Name of a German Shepherd.
LAURIN	K. name for a Miniature Dachshund, meaning, "laurel."
LÄUFER	"the runner."
LEOPOLD	"bold and beloved." Also: LUITPOLD, LUITBALD, LEUTPALD Pop.: Leopold.
LIEBWACHE	"bodyguard."
LIENL	"lion-like." Pop.: Leon
LITTLE EMIR	K. name for a Pomeranian.
LOBO	Name given to a German Shepherd war dog; meaning, 'large grey wolf.'
LUBIN	"love; friend; defender."
LUDWIG	"Famed fighter." Also: LUDOWICK, LUDOVIC, LOTZE, HLUTHAWIG, HLUDWIG. Pop.: Lewis
LUGAR	Name given to a Schnauzer.
LUMPENKERL	"ragamuffin."
MAGNET	Name given to a Boxer.
MAJESTAT	"majesty."
MAJOR	K. name for a German Shepherd belonging to F. D. Roosevelt.
MARCO	"hammer." K. name given to a Pomeranian that belonged to Queen Victoria.

MARKUS	"bright defender." Also: MARTEL, MARTIN Pop.: <u>Mark</u>
MARMADUKE	K. name for a Ch. German Short-haired Pointer.
MEIN TRAUM	"my dream." D. name for a Dachshund.
MOPS	K. name for a Dachshund.
MORTIZ	"dark in color."
MOSES	"drawn from the water."
MUCK	"makes no sound." Name given to a Dachshund.
NIEMAND	"nobody."
OTTO	Name of a Doberman Pinscher war dog, meaning, "mountain; happy."
OZONE	"invigorating fresh air." Name given to a Dachshund.
PASCH	"of the Passover; Easter." Pop.: <u>Pascal</u>
PEPPER POT	Name given to a Miniature Schnauzer.
PEPPER & SALT	Name given to a Schnauzer.
PEPPY	Name of a Doberman Pinscher war dog on Guam.
PERSIMMON	"rich, red orange." Name of a Dachshund.
PRINCE	"high-born." Name of a German Shepherd.
PRINCE VALIANT	Name given to a Great Dane in the movies.
PRINZ	Name given to a K. Dachshund.
RAJAH	Name given to a Ch. Miniature Pinscher.

RAP	Name of a German Short-haired Pointer.
RATTENFÄNGER, der	"a ratter."
RECALL	A German Shepherd captured from the Germans at St. Malo.
REITAL	Name given to a Ch. Standard Schnauzer.
RENNIE	Name of a German Shepherd in "Rennie, the Rescuer," by Felix Salten.
REX	Name of a Doberman Pinscher meaning, "king."
RIN-TIN-TIN	Name given to a German Shepherd, famous movie star.
ROLLO	"famed wolf." Name given to a Miniature Schnauzer.
ROMMEL	Name given to a Ch. Dachshund.
ROT	"red."
ROTROCK	"red coat."
RÖTLICH GELB	"orange."
ROSTFARBIG	"rusty."
ROTBARD	"barbarosso or red-bearded."
RUSTY	Name given to a Ch. German Short-haired Pointer.
SASSY LASSY	Name given to a Dachshund.
SCHAFER	"shepherd."
SCHLUPP	"bow." (of ribbon) Name given to a Dachshund.
SCHWARZ UND WEISS	"black & white."
SCHNAUZE	"muzzle."
SCOUT	Name given to a Doberman Pinscher.
SHAH	Name given to a Great Dane.
SIEGFRIED	"peace conquers." Name given to a Miniature Schnauzer.

SKAL	"drinking a toast." Name given to a Boxer.
SILVER	Name given to a Ch. Weimaraner.
SIMON	"hearkening." Also: SIMEON
STÄTTLICH	"proud."
STARK	"strong."
STEPHAN	"fitly crowned." Also: STEFFEL Pop.: Stephen
STORM	"excitable; energetic." Name given to a Ch. German Shepherd. Also: STURM
STORM CLOUD	"brewing energy." Name of a Weimaraner.
STORMY	"energetic." Name given to a Doberman Pinscher.
SWIFT	Name given to a German Shepherd.
TASSO	Name given to a Dachshund. "An Italian epic poet."
THADDAUS	"fervent devotion." Pop.: Thaddeus
TIM	"honor." Name given to a German Shepherd.
TOP WIRE	Name given to a Ch. Dachshund.
TRIBUTE	Name given to a Standard Schnauzer.
VERMILLION	Name given to a Dachshund.
VICTOR	"a warrior; fighter; conqueror." Pop.: Victor
VIKING	"Scandinavian sea rover." Name given to a Ch. German Shepherd.
VIVIAN	"lively." Pop.: Vito
WALDO	"one who rule." Pop.: Waldemar
WERNER	"the protector." Pop.: Warner

WIGGER	"had a nose." Name given to a German Shepherd, a police dog.
WILDFIRE	Name given to a Ch. German Short-haired Pointer.
WILHELM	"protector." Also: WILM, WILLEHELM Pop.: William
WIZARD	"skilled." A Seeing Eye German Shepherd.
YONKER	"young fellow."
YORK	name given to a Rottweiler, meaning, "the yew."
ZEP	Name given to a Dachshund, meaning, the Lord hath treasured. Pop.: Zephaniah

Female

AACHEN	A city in Western Germany, taken by U.S. forces. K. name given to a Dachshund.
ADELICIA	"truth; noble." Pop.: Alice
ALWINE	"white." Pop.: Albina
AMALIE	"busy." Pop.: Emily
AMBER	"color of amber." K. name given to a Dachshund.
ASPIRANT	K. name given to a Dachshund.
ASCHGRAU	"ash colored."
ASTA	"star." K. name for a German Short Haired Pointer.
ASTRA	"the star; sensible." A name given to a Rottweiler.
BÄRBEL	"little stranger." Name given to a Ch. Miniature Pinscher.

BISTERBRAUN	"fawn, the color."
BLANCH	"white; bright; shining."
BLASIA	"a blaze."
BLAU	"blue."
BLESSE, die	"blaze."
BORSTIG	"wiry-haired."
CENZI	K. name for a Dachshund.
CHARLOTTE	"the strong; womanly." Also: LOTTCHEN, KARLA, LINE, CHERYL Pop.: Caroline
CHERRY BELL	K. name given to a Pomeranian.
CINNAMON	K. name for a Dachshund.
CLOTHILDE	"illustrious war-maid." Also: KLOTHILDE Pop.: Clothilda
COMET	K. name for a Dachshund.
DAME	Name given to a Ch. Doberman Pinscher.
DINA-MITE	K. name for a Boxer, meaning, lit. "the judged - little one." Or, "little judge," possibly.
DUNKEL	"dark."
DUNKELLÄUGIG	"dark-eyed."
EBONY	K. name for a Dachshund.
ELSBET	"God is my oath." Also: ELISE, LISE, BETTINE, BETTE, ELSE, ILSE, LISE; Pop.: Elizabeth
ELSE	"noble; good cheer." Also: ILSA, ILSE.
ERNESTINE	"the earnest; little zealous one." Pop.: Ernestine
EUGENIA	"well-born." Pop.: Eugenia

EUFEMIA	"well spoken of." Pop.: <u>Euphemia</u>
EWA	"life; lively." Pop.: <u>Eva</u>
FERDINANDA	"make peace boldly." Pop.: <u>Fernanda</u>
FAUSTINA	"fortunate; little lucky one." Pop.: <u>Faustine</u>
FLOTTENBERG	Name given to a Dachshund.
FLORENTIA	"flowering; flourish." Also: FLORENCITA Pop.: <u>Florence</u>
FLORA	Name given to a Boxer, meaning, 'goddess of flowers.'
FRANZE	"free." Also: FRANZISKA, SPRINZCHEN Pop.: <u>Frances</u>
FREIA	"free." Name given to a Dachshund.
FRIEDA	"peaceful." Pop.: <u>Freda</u>
FRISKY MISS	K. name for a Boxer.
FREDERICA	"peaceful ruler." Also: FRIEDERIKE, FRITZE, FRITZINN, RIKE Pop.: <u>Frederica</u>
FROMM	"gentle beast."
FROU FROU	K. name for a Dachshund, meaning, 'the rustling of silk.'
GABRIELE	"God is my strength." Pop.: <u>Gabrielle</u>
GALA	Name given to a seeing eye dog, a German Shepherd.
GARLAND	"to encircle; adorn."
GAVOTTE	Name given to a Boxer, meaning, an old French dance, in moderate- ly quick time.
GAY	"beautiful and good."
GAYETY	K. name for a Boxer.
GENOVEFA	"the white one." Also: VEVAY

	Pop.: <u>Guinevere</u>
GERHARDINE	"little one with the bold spear." Pop.: <u>Geraldine</u>
GEGLÄTTET	"smooth."
GERTRUT	"bold in truth." Also: GERTRUD, GERTRAUD Pop.: <u>Gertrude</u>
GIZZI	Name given to a Dachshund.
GINA	"queen." Also: REINHILD Pop.: <u>Regina</u>
GLATT	"glossy."
GLINT O'GOLD	Name given to a Boxer.
GOLDEN DOLL	Name given to a Great Dane.
GÖTTEN	"the goddess."
GRETHEL	"pearl." Also: MARGARETHE, MARGHET, GRETCHEN, GRETHE, GRETE, GRETTA, GRETEL, GREDEL, METE. Pop.: <u>Margaret</u>
GRAU	"grey."
GRISELDA	"grey-eyed one." Pop.: <u>Griselda</u>
GUNNA	Name given to a Boxer. Might come from Gunther, meaning, 'warrior.'
HAARE	"hair."
HEDDA	"lady guard." Also: HEDWIG Pop.: <u>Hedwig</u>
HEKA	Name given to a Dachshund.
HELLA	"dawn-bright." Pop.: <u>Helen</u>
HELLFARBIG	"light-colored."
HERRIN	"mistress."
HALLÄUGIG	"bright-eyed."
HETTEL	Name given to a German Shepherd.
HENRIETTE	"ruler of home; little head of the hearth." Also: HENNIKE Pop.: <u>Henrietta</u>

HEXE	"star."
HILDUR	"mighty in battle." Also: HILDR Pop.: _Hilda_
HOLLA	"to conceal." Pop.: _Holda_
HONEY	Name given to a Dachshund.
HILDGARD	"guardian in battle." Pop.: _Hildegarde_
HORTENSIA	"gardener." Pop.: _Hortense_
HYACINTHIE	"flower." Pop.: _Hyacinth_
IDA	"the happy." Also: IDELLE, IDETTE Pop.: _Ida_
IMAGINA	"born of love; an image." Pop.: _Imogene_
IMPUDENCE	Name given to a K. Dachshund.
INKA	Name given to a Dachshund, meaning, possibly, 'black.'
INNOCENZ	"pure of heart; innocent." Pop.: _Innocent_
ISABELLE	"oath of God." Pop.: _Isabel_
ISOLANI	Name given to a Dachshund.
JAKOBINE	"in the place of." Pop.: _Jacqueline_
JEZABEL	"consecrated." Name of a K. Dachshund.
JOACHIME	"judge." Pop.: _Joakima_
JOHANNE	"gracious." Also: JOHANNA, HANNE Pop.: _Jane_
JUSTINE	"upright; the just." Also: JUSTE Pop.: _Jocelyn_
JOSEPHA	"he shall add." Pop.: _Josephine_
JULIANO	"soft-haired." Also: JULIE Pop.: _Julia_
JUTTA	"the praised." Also: JUTHA, JUDITHA

KARLA	"womanly." Name of a Ch. German Shepherd.
KATCHEN	"pure one." Also: KATRINA, KATHE Pop.: Catherine
KATYDID	Name given to a Ch. Miniature Schnauzer.
KEPHEN	"drone bee."
KETURAH	"incense." Name given to a Boxer.
KINDA	"child." Name given to a German short-haired Pointer.
KISS	Name given to a seeing eye German Shepherd.
KÖNIGIN	"queen."
KLEINES	"little." Name given to a Dachshund.
KURZ	"short."
KRÄFTIG	"sturdy."
KRÄUSELN	"fuzzy hair."
KLUG	"intelligent; smart; cunning."
LAURA	"sign of triumph; laurel." Pop.: Laura
LEICHT	"buoyant; nimble; light."
LENZLEIN	"little bloom." Name given to a Dachshund.
LEONARDA	"lioness-like." Pop.: Leontine
LIEBCHEN	"sweetheart." Also: LIEBE, LIUBA, LIEVINA Pop.: Love
LITTLE TERRIFIC	K. name for a Poodle.
LOCKEN	"curling."
LOHFARBEN	"tan color."
LORLE	Name given a Dachshund, meaning, possibly Little Laura.
LUCIA	"light; bright." Also: LUCIANA, LUCINA, LUZIA Pop.: Lucy

LUDOVIKA	"famed fighter." Also: ALOISIA, LUISE Pop.: Louise
LUDMILA	"love of the people." Also: LUDOMILLA Pop.: Ludmilla
LURLINE	"the alluring." Also: LORELEI Pop.: Lurline
MAJESTÄT, die	"majesty."
MARCA	"warlike." Pop.: Marcia
MARLENE	"watchtower; rebellion." Also: MADLEN, LENCHEN, LENE, MAGDALENE Pop.: Madeline
MARTHE	"sorrowful; mistress." Pop.: Martha
MATHILDE	"mighty battle maid." Pop.: Mathilde
MATTGELB	"cream color."
MÄUSERL	Name given to a Dachshund, meaning, "little darling. lit. "mouse."
MAXA	"little great one." Pop.: Maxine
MENA	German Shepherd K. name.
MICHAELINE	"divine." Pop.: Michaela
MIGNONNE	K. name for a Dachshund, meaning, 'dainty; graceful; petite.'
MINNE	"love; memory." Also: MINETTE Pop.: Minna
MISCHIEF	Name given to a Ch. Pomeranian.
MONA LISA	Name given to a Pomeranian.
MUTIG	"courageous; spirited."
NOCTURNE	"evening." Name given to a Boxer.
NORA	"honor-bright." Name given to the first Ch. in the German Studbooks for a Boxer.
OCTAVIA	"the eighth." Pop.: Octavia

ODELIA	"noble." Also: ODILE Pop.: <u>Oelrich</u>, m.
OLIVIA	"sign of peace." Pop.: <u>Olga</u>
OLYMPIE	"heavenly." Pop.: <u>Olympia</u>
OTTILIE	"happy; rich." Pop.: <u>Otho</u>
PAINTED DOLL	K. name for a Boxer.
PAULA	"little." Also: PAULINE Pop.: <u>Paula</u>
PEEFKA	Name given to a German Shepherd.
PEPITA	Name given to a Dachshund, meaning, "small one."
PERSIS	"commended." Pop.: <u>Persis</u>
PETRACA	"adamant." Also: PETRONILLE, NILLEL, PETRISSE Pop.: <u>Petra</u>
PICCOLO	"small flute." Name given to a Dachshund.
PINE	"lover of horses." Also: PHILIPPINE Pop.: <u>Philippa</u>
PIXIE	'faylike.' Name given to a Ch. Pomeranian.
PRETZEL	Name given to a Dachshund, meaning, a 'crisp, dry biscuit, formed into a salted knot.'
PRIMROSE	Name given to a Ch. Pomeranian, meaning, "the first rose."
PRINCESS	K. name for a Dachshund.
PRINCESS ANNA	Name given to a German Short-haired Pointer, meaning, "Princess Gracious."
PRISKE	"old-fashioned." Pop.: <u>Priscilla</u>
RAGTIME	Name given a Ch. German Short-haired Pointer.
RAUG	"ragged."
RAUHAARIG	"wire-haired dog."

RAHEL	"lamb; love." Pop.: <u>Rachel</u>
RAMME, de	"monkey."
REBEKKE	"to bind; snare of beauty."
RICCADONNA	"firm; good character."
RICARDA	"firm and good character."
RINKY	K. name for a Dachshund.
ROSAMUNDA	"famous guard." Pop.: <u>Rosamond</u>
ROSALIE	"rose." Pop.: <u>Rhoda</u>
RÖTLICH BRAU	"liver color."
RÖTLICH GELB	"orange."
ROSTFARBIG	"rusty."
ROTHAARIG	"red haired."
RUDELLE	"the famed."
RUDOLPHINE	"guarded by the wolf."
SABINE	"little holy one." Pop.: <u>Sabina</u>
SACHT	"soft."
SANFT	"gentle."
SANFTÄUGUG	"soft-eyed."
SARA	"high-born." Pop.: <u>Sarah</u>
SCHARF	"sharp."
SCHARP NOTE	Name of a Ch. Dachshund.
SCHECKIG	"brindle."
SCHNEEWEISS	"white as snow."
SCHNELL	"fast; quick."
SCHNIPPISCH	"pert."
SCHWARZÄUGIG	"dark eyed."
SCHWARZBLEVH	"very dark blue."
SCHWARZGELB	"tawny; dark yellow."
SCHWARZGRAU	"dark grey."
SEBASTIANE	"reverenced." Pop.: <u>Sebastiana</u>

SIBYLLE	"sibyl; prophetess." Pop.: Sibyl
SIDONIE	"the enchantress." Pop.: Sidonia
SIGRADA	"impulse; winning wisdom." Pop.: Sigrid
SILBERGRAU	"silver grey."
SILBERHAARE	"silver-haired."
STELLA	"star." K. name for a German Shepherd.
STEPHANINE	"crown; fitly crowned." Pop.: Stephana
STOFFPUPPE	"rag doll."
SUE	"lily; white." Name given to a German Short-haired Pointer. Also, to a Weimaraner.
SUGAR 'N SPICE	Name given to a Boxer.
SUSCHEN	"lily." Also: SUSANNE, SUSE Pop.: Susan
SWANHILDA	"swan battle maid." Pop.: Susan
TIA MARIA	Name given to a Ch. Dachshund, meaning, 'aunt Maria, or sweet fragrance.'
TRICOLOR	"three colors."
THEOBALDA	"the people's princess." Also: TIBELDA Pop.: Theobald.m.
THOMASIA	"a twin." Pop.: Thomasa
THYRZA	"the pleasant." Pop.: Thirza
TRESA	"bearing the harvest." Also: THERESE, THERESIA, TRESCHA Pop.: Theresa
TWINKLE TOES	"little miss light on her feet." Name given to a Pomeranian.
ULRIKE	"noble ruler." Pop.: Alarice
UTSI	"little bear, strong little one." Pop.: Ursula

VELEDA	"of inspired wisdom." Pop.: <u>Velda</u>
VIRGINIA	"twig; chaste." Pop.: <u>Virginia</u>
VITALIANA	"vitality; lively." Pop.: <u>Vita</u>
VOLLBART	"beard."
VORLAUT	"pert."
WALDA	"to rule, or wield." F. of Waldo.
WALLIS	lit. "a Welsh girl."
WENDELA	"the wanderer." Also: WENDELIN, WENDELINE Pop.: <u>Wandis</u>
WHITE BLAZE	K. name for a Weimaraner.
WILHELMINA	"chosen protection; little guard of the host." Also: HELMINE, MINCHEN, MINNA, MINA; Pop.: <u>Wilhelmina</u>
WACHSAM	"alert."
WEISS	"white."
WEISSLICH	"whitish."
WEISSFUSS	"white foot."
ZACHIG	"ragged."
ZANZIBAR	K. name for a Dachshund.
ZEPHANJA	"treasure." F. of Zephaniah.
ZINNIA	K. name for a Dachshund.
ZITA	Name given to a Dachshund.
ZOLESTINE	"little heavenly one." Pop.: <u>Celestine</u>
ZOPFE	"tuft."
ZUCKERPLÄTZCHEN	"sugar plum."
ZULETTE	K. name for a Dachshund.
ZYKLONE	"cyclone."
ZYKLOPEN	"cycloptic; gigantic."

IRISH DOGS

Irish Setter
Irish Terrier
Irish Water Spaniel
Irish Wolfhound
Kerry Blue Terrier

Names

Male

AONGHUS	"choice; exceptionally strong." Pop.: Angus
ART	"valorous; brave; firm." Pop.: Arthur
AYMAR	"ruler of work."
BANSHEE	In Gaelic folklore, a fairy visitant whose wailing foretold death. K. name given to an Irish Wolfhound.
BARNEY	"brave; bold; strong." Pop.: Bernard
BARTLEY	"plowman." Patriarchal name of the Bible. Pop.: Bartholomew
BAYARD	"intellectual; the ruddy-haired; without fear."
BIG RED	Name given to an Irish Setter in Jim Kjelgaard's story, "Big Red."
BLUE DIAMOND	K. name given to a Kerry Blue Terrier.
BLUE LIGHTNING	K. name given to a Kerry Blue Terrier.
BRIAN	"strong; glowing." Brian Boru was a glowing figure in early Ireland;

148

	he led his warriors against the Danes and became a heroic figure in legends and ballads.
BRIAN BORU	"high king of all Ireland."
BRIAR	"strong; the heath." Briarcus was a mythological monster with a hundred hands, fifty heads; thus possessed uncommon strength."
BRICK	"a yellowish, or brownish red."
BURKE	"of the castle." K. name given to an Irish Wolfhound.
CADWALLADER	"valiant in war."
CAMERON	"bravery."
CONN-OF-A-HUNDRED BATTLES	"for a scrappy dog."
COPPER	"a metallic, reddish brown."
COPPER TOPPER	"copper coat."
CORNEY	"war horn; a horn is the symbol of kingship." A pet name. Pop.: Cornelius
CRUSADER	K. name for an Irish Setter.
DELANEY	"dark one; healthy." Pop.: Delano
DENIS	"from Dionysos, the Greek god of wine." Frequently used Irish name. Also means, "joyful." Pop.: Dennis
DERMOT	"dear."
DONN	"proved chieftan; dark-haired stranger." Pop.: Dennis
DOMNECH	"born on Sunday." Pop.: Dominic
DONATH	"a gift; donation." Pop.: Donato
DUFFY	"black; dark-faced." Pop.: Duff
DUNCAN	"brown chief."

EIRE BROGUE	Irish brogue.
ELAIR	A Clan name, meaning, "borrowed."
EOGHAN	"young warrior." Pop.: <u>Evan</u>
FINLEY	"sunbeam."
FEARGUS	"Strong; choice." Feargus, the Eloquent in Irish legend was a fellow-warrior of the great Finn MacCool. Pop.: <u>Fergus</u>
FIN McCOUL	K. name given to an Irish Terrier. McCoul was the leader of the Fianna, the warrior hunters of the 2nd century Ireland.
FINGAL	"fair-haired foreigner." In Irish legend he was a Norseman.
FIONN	"the white." Comes from Finn MacCool. Also: FINN
FLAMING FEATHER	"red feather."
FLOBERT	"wise; splendid." Flaubert, famous French novelist's name is derived from this one.
GELERT	"given to an Irish Wolfhound belonging to King John of England in 1210.
GLENN	"from the place in the glen, in the dark, narrow valley." Pop.: <u>Glen</u>
GOLDEN CHANCE	K. name given to an Irish Terrier.
HIGH TIME	K. name given to an Irish Setter.
INIS	"from the island." Pop.: <u>Innis</u>
KENNETH	"leader; handsome." The Scottish St. Kennet became the patron saint of the city of Kilkenny in Ireland.

KILIAN	"well-tried." Pop.: Cecil
KILLINEY BOY	K. name for an Irish Terrier.
LACHLAN	"war-like."
LANCE	K. name for an Irish Wolfhound, meaning, "one who serves."
LANTY	"crowned with laurel." Also: LARRY, LAURISON, LARSON, LARRSON, LAWSON, LAWES Pop.: Laurence
LEIR	"of the sea." A sea god and king of ancient Britain.
LENNOX	"chieftan."
LOGAIRE	"an Irish King."
LUG	"of the long arm; many skilled; lightning." In Irish Mythology he was the god of Many Skills." Pop.: Llewellyn
MAC	"son." Mc or Mac placed before a name means, 'son of,' as Mac Flynn, 'son of Flynn.'
MACLEOD	"bold master."
MACMAHON	"son of the strong." A clan name. Pop.: Matheson
MAHONEY	"a strong chief." Father Mahoney was an Irish poet. K. name for an Irish Water Spaniel.
MAILMORA	"King of Ireland, brother of Brian Boru."
MARMADUKE	"sea leader."
MONTY	"from the mountain, or sharp peaked hill; lordly." Pop.: Montague
MURREY	"dark, deep red."
NIALL	"swarthy; courageous." King Neill was Ireland's last pagan King.

Also: NEAL   Pop.: <u>Neal</u>

NEMED   "leader." A leader in one of the
                    earlier invasions of Ireland.

OGMA   "the champion." He was a deity
                    of the Tuatha, a tribe inhabiting
                    mythical Ireland.

O'TOOLE   K. name for a Ch. Irish Water
                    Spaniel, meaning, "lordly." O'
                    stands for 'son of.'

PADDY   "name given to all Irishmen; noble;
                    patrician." Also: PAT, PATRICK,
                    PATRAIC   Pop.: <u>Patrick</u>

PRIDE   K. name given to an Irish Terrier.

QUINN   "chief; wise."   Pop.: <u>Cohan</u>

RED SAILS   K. name for an Irish Setter.

ROBIN ADAIR   "famous; from the oak-ford." A
                    famous Scotch ballad." K. name
                    for a Kerry Blue Terrier.

ROISE   K. name for Irish Wolfhound, mean-
                    ing, "noisy" or "boisterous?"

SEAMOS   K. name for Irish Wolfhound, mean-
                    ing, "one who takes place of."
                    Pop.: <u>James</u> or <u>John</u>

SILHOUETTE   K. name for Kerry Blue Terrier.

TANDY   K. name for Kerry Blue Terrier.

Female

AIDAN   "fire; the firey." Honors St.
                    Aidan, the great Irish Saint.

AINE	"joy." An Irish favorite in Celtic Mythology.
AISLINN	"a dream."
ALANNA	"harmonious; term of endearment; comely; fair."
ALBA	"the white." Pop.: Albinia
ANA	"graceful." In Irish Mythology Ana was the mother of the gods. Pop.: Ann
ANASTASIS	"lively." Two Christian martyrs made the name beloved in Ireland. Also: STACY, ANTY Pop.: Anastasia
AOIFFE	"pleasant." Beloved old Irish name, equivalent to Mother Eve. Pop.: Aoife
ASTHORE	"treasure; sweetheart." A pet name.
BIDDY	"mighty; strong." A beloved and most frequently used given-name in Ireland. Also: BRIGHID, BRIGITA, BRIETTA Pop.: Bridget
BRENNA	"raven; dark." In an Irish myth the raven was possessed of a supernatural power.
BRISCIA	"strength."
CAPRICE	"the fantastic, or humorous." K. name for a Ch. Kerry Blue Terrier.
CARA	"dear one; friend." A term of endearment beloved by all the Irish for centuries.
CATHLEEN	"pure; the beautiful-eyed." The ending 'een' is typically Irish. Also: CATHLIN, KATTY, KATHLEEN. Pop.: Catherine
CELIA	"little heavenly one." Also: SILE Pop.: Celia

CLARET	the wine of France; deep, purplish red. K. name for an Irish Setter.
COLEEN	"an Irish girl; little maiden." Colleen bawn is a "fair girl." Colleen daun is a "brunette."
COQUETTE	"a flirt." K. name for an Irish Setter.
DALLAS	"skilled."
DEIRDRE	"raging; sorrow." The Helen of Troy of pagan Ireland.
DEMMY	"white foam." The Patroness of lovers. Pop.: Dwynwen
DUBADEASA	Old Irish favorite, 'black beauty.'
ERIN	"peace." Poetic name for Ireland.
EVELEEN	"pleasant; little Eva." Also: AVELINE Pop.: Eva
FALA	"the faithful." Franklin D. Roosevelt's name for his dog. Pop.: Fealty
GRAINE	"love." The daughter of a King of Alster, popular in Gaelic folklore. Pop.: Grania
HELENA	"dawn-bright." Also: EILEEN, AILEEN, AILLEEN, NELLIS, ALLIE. Pop.: Helen
HONORA	"honorable." Also: ONORA Pop.: Honora
ISHBEL	"within Divine love." From: Isabel
JUDY	"praised." An Irish favorite. Pop.: Judith

KEELTA	K. name for an Irish Wolfhound.
KERRY	"dark." Irish place name for county Kerry. An Apron worn by Irish girls. A breed of cattle.
MAB	"joy." Queen of the Fairies in Irish and English folklore who is mischievous, tantalizing, who governs, produces the dreams of men. Also: MEAVE, MAEV Pop.: Mab
MACHA	"a warrior queen in Irish mythology.
MAIRGREG	"child of light." Also: MEGHAN Pop.: Margaret
MARCELLA	"little Marcie; belonging to Mars." Also: MARCHELL Pop.: Marcia
MAUREEN	"fate; dark; the sea." Also: MOYA, MAURA, MOIRA, MAURYA, MAIRE, MUIRE. Pop.: Mary
MEARA	"from the water, or mere."
MEGHAN	"great." Pop.: Margaret
MORNA	"the soft; or gentle; beloved." A name loved in Ireland and Scotland. Also: MOINA Pop.: Monica
MORRIGAN	"spirit queen." In Irish Mythology she was goddess of War.
MUIRNE	"beloved; affectionate." "A Celtic heroine of Ossianic legend, daughter of an ancient King of Ireland, whose name was loved in early Ireland."
NOLA	"noble."
NUALA	"the fair-shouldered." She was called Finghuala by the Irish; her name split in half, Nuala and Fenella, were used as well."

OONA   "born in famine; one."
                Pop.: <u>Una</u>

OSSIA   "a fawn." Honors the Irish hero-
                bard, Ossian.

O'STORM   K. name for an Irish Setter.

PATRICIA   "noble; high-born." "St. Patrick
                made this name a favorite in Ire-
                land."

ROISIN DUBH   "dark, little rose."

ROSALEEN   "a rose; rose-bush."   Ireland sang
                of 'Dark Rosaleen.'

SARAID   "princess; high-born." Pop.: <u>Sarah</u>

SELINA   "winner through artifice."
                Pop.: <u>Selinde</u>

SHANNON   "slow waters."   An Irish place
                name for the River Shannon.

SHEELAH   "dim-sighted; blind; a flame."
                Also: SHELAH, SHEILA, SHERAH
                Pop.: <u>Cecelia</u>

SHILLELAGH   "a cudgel of blachthorn, or oak."
                K. name of an Irish Wolfhound.

SIB   "a sibyl; wise; prophetess."
                Also: SIBBIE   Pop.: <u>Sibyl</u>

SORCHA   "the dazzling fair; high-born; prin-
                cess."   An Early Irish diminutive.
                Pop.: <u>Sarah</u>

STARDUST   K. name for a Kerry Blue Terrier.

STEP   Name given an Irish Water Spaniel.
                Might be shortened from either f.
                or m. meaning, "a crown."
                Pop.: <u>Stephana,</u> or m. <u>Stephen</u>

TARA   "adamant; fortified."   An Irish
                place name from the city of Tara.
                Ancient Irish kings lived in craglike

	towers. K. name of a Ch. Irish Wolfhound.
TARTAN	K. name of a Ch. Irish Wolfhound, meaning either the plaid worn by Scottish Highlanders, or, a sailing vessel.
VEFELE	"white wave." Pop.: <u>Vanora</u>
VEVILA	"the harmonious."
WENEFRIDE	"white wave, or stream; peace-maker; friend of peace." Pop.: <u>Winifred</u>
WILD HARP	"active."
WILD KITTY	"heroine of an 18th century novel. The Irish love this name more than any other country. The favorite form in Ireland is Kathleen.

ITALIAN DOGS

Italian Greyhound
Maltese

Names

Male

ADAMO	"red dust; first man." Pop.: Adam
ABITO	"coat."
ABRAMO	"born of famous parents." Pop.: Abraham
ADRIANO	"black." Pop.: Adrian
ALADIN	K. name given to a Maltese.
AMICO	"friend."
ALLEGRO	"merry."
ALLESIO	"defender of man." Pop.: Alexander
ANIMATI	"animated."
ALUINO	"noble friend; beloved." Pop.: Alvin
ARGENTO	"silver."
ANDREA	"strong." Pop.: Andrew
ARMONISO	"agreeable."
ANGELO	"angelic." Pop.: Angel
ALTORE	"actor."
ANSELMO	"protector." Pop.: Anselm
ALARICO	"ruler of all." Pop.: Alaric
ALFREDO	"small." Pop.: Alfred
ALFONSO	"ready, willing, eager." Pop.: Alphonso

ARANCIO	"orange." (color)
BARBA	"beard."
BEACH COMBER	K. name for an Italian Greyhound.
BIANCO	"white."
BLU	"blue."
BULL	K. name for a white Maltese.
BURLONE	"joker."
BASILIO	"kingly; royal." Pop.: Basil
BENEDETTO	"blessed." Pop.: Benedict
BERNARDINO	"devoted; strong." Also: BERNARDO Pop.: Bernard
BERTRANDO	"bright raven." Pop.: Bertram
BIAGIO	"blaze, or brand." Also: BACCIO Pop.: Blaze
BONIFACIO	"of good fate." Also: FACIO Pop.: Boniface
CALVINO	"the bald." Pop.: Calvin
CANDIDO	"pure white."
CAPELLI	"hair."
CAPPETTO	"overcoat."
CAP D'ANNO	"New Year's Day."
CARABINIERE	"policeman."
CARO	"dear."
CESARIO	"hairy."
CHIARO	"light (color)."
CIRILLO	"lordly." Pop.: Cyril
CLICK	K. name for an Italian Greyhound.
CLEMENTE	"mild-tempered; merciful."
COLOR CAFE	"tan."
COLUMBO	"the dove." Pop.: Colan

CONRADO	"wise; bold." Pop.: <u>Conrad</u>
CONSTANTINO	"firm; constant." Pop.: <u>Constantine</u>
CREMA	"cream (color)."
CRISPINO	"curly."
CUPID	K. name for a Ch. Maltese.
DAMIANO	"the tamed; taming." Pop.: <u>Damon</u>
DARBY	"free." K. name for a Ch. Italian Greyhound.
DAVIDDE	"beloved." Pop.: <u>David</u>
DIONISIO	"divinity; excellent." Pop.: <u>Dennis</u>
DOLPHIN	K. name given to an Italian Greyhound.
DONATI	"gift." Also: DONATO, DONATELLO Pop.: <u>Donato</u>
DRAGON	K. name for an Italian Greyhound.
EDGARDO	"protector of property." Pop.: <u>Edgar</u>
EDMONDO	"defender of property." Pop.: <u>Edmund</u>
EDUARDO	"defender; guardian." Also: EDOARDO, ODOARDO Pop.: <u>Edward</u>
ELMO	"the amiable." St. Elmo warns sailors of storms.
EMILIO	"worker." Also: AEMILIUS Pop.: <u>Emil</u>
ERASMO	"loveable." Pop.: <u>Erasmus</u>
ERNESTO	"earnest." Pop.: <u>Ernest</u>
EUSTAZIO	"healthy; standing firm." Also: EUSTACHIO Pop.: <u>Eustace</u>
EVERADO	"fierce." Also: EBERARDO, EBBO

EZECHIELLO   "strong." Also: EZECHIELE
                            Pop.: Ezra

FALCON CLAW   K. name for an Italian Greyhound.

FEDERICO   "powerful; peaceful." Also:
                            FEDERIGO   Pop.: Frederic

FELICE   "happy." Pop.: Felix

FERRANDO   "valiant; risking life."
                            Pop.: Ferdinand

FIERO FIGLIS   "proud son."

FLAVIO   "yellow, or blond."
                            Pop.: Flavius

FLINT   K. name for a Maltese.

FULVIO   "yellow-haired." Pop.: Fulvius

FURBO   "cunning."

GASPARE   "treasure master; wins for a mas-
                            ter." Also: CASPARO, GASPARDO
                            Pop.: Caspar

GEORGIO   "earth worker, farmer."
                            Pop.: George

GIALLO   "yellow."

GIOIELLO   "a jewel."

GIRALDO   "ruler." Also: GERARDO
                            Pop.: Gerald

GUISEPPE   "he shall add."

GREGORIO   "watchful."

GRIGIO   "gray (color)."

GUIDO   "sensible; to steady; guide."
                            Pop.: Guy

IGNAZIO   "ardent; firey." Pop.: Ignatius

ISACCO   "laughter." Also: SACCO
                            Pop.: Isaac

ISIDORO   "gift." Pop.: Isidore

JACOBO   "taking the place of." Also:
                          GIACOBBE, JACHIMO, GIACOMO,
                          GIACOPO, COMO, COPPO
                          Pop.: Jacob

LAMBERTO   "his country's glory."
                          Pop.: Lambert

LAUGHTER   K. name for Italian Greyhound.

LELAPS   The Greyhound of Procris, in
                          Mythology.

LOMBARDO   "the long bearded."
                          Also: LOMBARDI Pop.: Lombard

LUCKY PILOT   K. name for an Italian Greyhound.

LUIGI   "famous warrior; wise."
                          Pop.: Lewis

MANFREDI   "peaceful." Pop.: Manfred

MASSAMO   "the greatest." Pop.: Maximilian

MATTEO   "gift." Also: MAFFEO, FEO,
                          MATTIA   Pop.: Matthew

MAURO   "dark in color." Pop.: Maurice

MITE   "gentle; soft."

MODESTO   "the modest." Pop.: Modesto

MORE TAXES   K. name for an Italian Greyhound.

MOUNTAIN SIDE   K. name for an Italian Greyhound.

NAPOLEONE   "lion of the forest."
                          Pop.: Napoleon

NATALE   "Christmas Day."

NERO   "the black."

NEVE FIAMMA   "snow flame."

NICOLO   "victory."

NOBILI   "well-known." Pop.: Noble

OECHIO   "eye."

OSCURO	"dark."
OLVERO	"peace." Pop.: <u>Oliver</u>
PICCOLO	"small."
PALMA	"peaceful; peace bringer." Pop.: <u>Palmer</u>
PIERO	K. name for a Ch. Italian Grey- hound.
PASCOLI	"honors Good Friday." Name of an Italian poet. Pop.: <u>Pascal</u>
PATRIZIO	"noble; patrician." Pop.: <u>Patrick</u>
PAOLA	"little." Pop.: <u>Paul</u>
PIERO	Italian Greyhound Ch. "a stone."
PIPPO	"lover of horses." Pop.: <u>Philip</u>
PIO	"pious." Pop.: <u>Pius</u>
PODESTA	"powerful." Pop.: <u>Power</u>
PROSPERO	"successful." Pop.: <u>Prosper</u>
RAFFAELLO	"sublime." Pop.: <u>Raphael</u>
RE	"king."
REFLECTION	K. name for an Italian Greyhound.
ROSSO	"red."
RUBIO	"ruby."
RUFIO	"red-haired." Pop.: <u>Rufus</u>
SANSONE	"strong." Pop.: <u>Sampson</u>
SCIPIONE	"a staff." Pop.: <u>Scipio</u>
SECUNDO	"the second."
SERENO	"calm."
SERAFIO	lit. "one of the Rosy angels of God." Pop.: <u>Seraph</u>
SNAIL	"the fleetest greyhound in the world."

| STEFANO | "crowned."   Pop.: Stephen |

TAGLIERINI	"noodles."
TEMPESTO	"storm."
TESTO	"head."
TOE DANCE	K. name for an Italian Greyhound.
THADDEO	"fervent devotion." Pop.: Thaddeus
TOMASO	"twin." Pop.: Thomas

| UGO | "bright mind." |
| URBANO | "from the town; courteous."
Pop.: Urban |

VIAGGIATORE	"traveller."
VITTORIO	"conqueror." Pop.: Victor
VALERIO	"strong." Pop.: Valerian
VITO	"vitality; lively."

| WISE KING | K. name for an Italian Greyhound. |

Female

AIDA	"the first."
ADRIANA	"black." Pop.: Adria
ALBA	"the dawn."
ALBINIA	"white." Also: ELVIRA Pop.: Albinia
ALLEGRA	"merry and gay."
ALESSANDRA	"defender." Pop.: Alexandra
AMICA	"friend."
AMORETTA	"beloved." Pop.: Amy
ANGELICA	"angelic." Also: ANGIOLA, ANGIOLETTA, AGNOLA

	Pop.: Angela
ARGENTA	"silver."
ARANCIA	"orange color."
ARTEMISEA	"healthy." Pop.: Artemis
ARMONIA	"harmony."
AURELIA	"golden." Pop.: Aurelia
AZZURRA	"blue."
BEATRICE	"she who blesses; makes happy." Pop.: Beatrice
BELINDA	"a serpent." This signifies wisdom to the ancients.
BELLA	"beautiful." Equivalent to Beau in French. Name of an Italian Grey-hound.
BELLA DONNA	"beautiful one."
BELLEZZA	"beauty."
BENEDETTA	"little blessing." Also: BETTA Pop.: Benedicta
BIANCA	"white." Pop.: Blanch
BRIGIDA	"the mighty or high." Pop.: Bridget
CAIETA	"the rejoiced in." Pop.: Caia
CAMEO	"Italian 'jewel' name; a carving on a jewel or stone."
CAMPANELLA	"little bell."
CARA	"dear."
CARMIA	"fruitful." Also: CARMINE Pop.: Carmel
CELESTE	"pale blue; radiant."
CELESTINA	"heavenly." Pop.: Celia
CICALA	"cricket."
CODA	"tail."

CONSTANZA	"firm of purpose; devoted."
CREMA	"cream (color)."
CRISPINA	"curly."
CROCCOLATA	"chocolate."
CZARINA	K. name of an Italian Greyhound.
DARK EYES	K. name for a Maltese.
DESIRATA	"the longed for; desired." Pop.: Desire
DISCEPOLA	"follower."
DOMINIA	"lady." Honors St. Dominic.
EDITA	"prosperous and happy." Pop.: Edith
EMILIA	"the industrious." Pop.: Emily
ELENA	"light." Pop.: Helen
ELECTRA	K. name for a Maltese.
ENCHANTING	K. name for an Italian Greyhound.
ENRICHETTA	"home ruler." Pop.: Henrietta
ESTERRE	"star; bright." Also: ESTER Pop.: Esther
EUGENIA	"well-born." Pop.: Eugenia
EUFEMIA	"fair fame." Pop.: Euphemia
FANCIULLETTA	"little girl; little one."
FAUSTA	"Lucky; fortunate." Pop.: Faustine
FEDERICA	"peaceful ruler." Also: FERIGA Pop.: Frederica
FEVE	"bright." Pop.: Phoebe
FILOMINA	"daughter of light; loving." Pop.: Philomena
FIORE	"flower; flourishing." In honor of Flora, goddess of flowers. Pop.: Florence

GIRALDA	"battle maid." Pop.: Geraldine
GENEVRA	"white wave; ready for duty." Pop.: Guinevere
GIALLA	"yellow."
GREY - RUSSET	"coarse grey cloth."
GRIGIA	"grey."
GRISAILLE	"varied tones and shades of grey."
GUIDA	"guide."
GUIDITTA	"praised one."
IGNACIA	"quick-tempered." Pop.: Ignatia
ISSA	"iron-like; strong." Name given to a Maltese at the time of Apostle Paul, Publius Roman governor of Malta.
KELT	"grey cloth of black and white yarn."
KIRLEAS THE LARK	K. name for an Italian Greyhound.
LADY ANN	K. name for a Ch. Maltese.
LAILA	"dark as night." Name for a European Ch. Maltese.
LAMBIRE	"to lap; to lick."
LEGGIARDRIA	"beauty; grace; elegance."
LETIZIA	"happy; glad." Pop.: Letitia
LINDA	"gentle." Name of the Greyhound owned by Percy B. Shelley.
LIVONIA	K. name for a Maltese.
LUCREZIA	"lucky one." Pop.: Lucrese
LOUISA	"famous battle maid." Also: ELOISA Pop.: Louise
LUNGO	"long."
MAID OF SILK	K. name for a Ch. Italian Greyhound.

MAFFEA	"gift." Pop.: <u>Mattea</u>
MARTA	"mistress." Pop.: <u>Martha</u>
MARRONE PIED	"brown feet."
MAURA	"the dark one." Also: MAURIZIA Pop.: <u>Maura</u>
MELISSA	"honey; sweet." Pop.: <u>Melissa</u>
MELINA	"quince yellow."
MERCEDE	"pity or mercy."
MINERVA	"wisdom; purpose, force." Pop.: <u>Minerva</u>
MODESTA	"modest; a virtue name." Pop.: <u>Modesty</u>
MISS NINETTE	An Italian Greyhound name.
NEROLIA	"black." A princess of Ancient Italy. F. of Nero.
NICOLA	"A Christmas name." Pop.: <u>Nicola</u>
NEVER SAD	K. name for an Italian Greyhound.
NORD NUVALA	"North cloud."
ODES	"noble; rich." Pop.: <u>Odelia</u>
OLIVIA	"peace." Pop.: <u>Olga</u>
OLIMPIA	"heavenly." Pop.: <u>Olympia</u>
ORAZIA	"punctual." Pop.: <u>Horatia</u>
PALTO	"overcoat.
POCO	"little."
POCO SORELLA	"little sister."
PASQUINA	"born in the spring." Also: PASQUA, PASCHINA Pop.: <u>Pascha</u>
PAOLA	"little." Also: PAOLETTA, PAOLINA Pop.: <u>Paula</u>

PACIFICA	"peace." Pop.: Peace
PEPE	"pepper."
PEPERONI	"pepper."
PERPETUA	"ever-lasting." An Italian favorite; honors St. Vivia Perpetua.
PETRONELLE	"adamant." Pop.: Petra
PIPPA	"lover of horses." Also: FILIPPA, FILIPPINA Pop.: Philippa
PRASSEDE	"active." Pop.: Plaxy
QUEEN'S BEAUTY	K. name for an Italian Greyhound.
REFRESHING	K. name for an Italian Greyhound.
REINA	"queen." Italian favorite. Pop.: Regina
RACHELE	"a lamb; soft; mild." Pop.: Rachel
ROSETTA	"the rose." Also; ROSA, ROSALIA, ROSINA Pop.: Rhoda
ROSALBA	"white." Pop.: Rosalbe
ROSAMONDA	"rose of the world." Pop.: Rosamond
ROSSO	"red."
ROSSICCIO	"ruddy, tawny."
SABINA	"one of an ancient Italian people, little holy one."
SABRINA	"to rest." Pop.: Sabra
SARA	"princess." Pop.: Sarah
SERAFINA	"the ardent." Pop.: Seraphine
SIBILA	"a sibyl; prophetess." Pop.: Sybil
SIDONIA	"enchantress." Pop.: Sidonia
SALE	"salt."
SHIFTY SUE	K. name of an Italian Greyhound.

SILVER FALCON	K. name of an Italian Greyhound.
SILVER FLUTE	K. name for an Italian Greyhound.
SNOWBALL	Name of the greyhound in Sir. Walter Scott's poem, which was jet black.
SOFIA	"the sensible." Pop.: <u>Sophronia</u>
SUSANNA	"white." An Italian greyhound is named Oh, Susanna. Pop.: <u>Susan</u>
TERESINA	"reaps the harvest." Also: TERSA, TERESA
TOMASINA	"twin." Pop.: <u>Thomasa</u>
TRAVIATA	"she who goes away, or strays."
VALENTINA	"strong; valorous." Also: VALERIE Pop.: <u>Valentina</u>
VANNA	"butterfly." Pop.: <u>Vanessa</u>
VENETIA	"to dare to give." Pop.: <u>Venda</u>
VAIR	"tones of silver and blue."
VITTORIA	"victorious." Also: VINCENTIA, VINCENZINA Pop.: <u>Vincenta</u>
VIOLET	"shy, violet." Also: VIOLANTE, VIOLA Pop.: <u>Violet</u>
VIRGILIA	"a twig; unmarried." Also: VIRGINIA Pop.: <u>Virginia</u>
VIVIANA	"animated; vital." Pop.: <u>Vita</u>
VOLANTE	"flying."
VEGA	"brightest star in the Lyra constellation." K. name given to an Italian Greyhound."
VIVA	"long live!"
WHITE FLASH	K. name given to a white Maltese.
ZEPPA	"lame."
ZUCCHERO	"sugar."

MEXICAN DOGS

Chihuahua (long coat)
Chihuahua (smooth coat)

Spanish Names

Male

ADAN — "of the red dust; man of red earth." Pop.: Adam

ADOLPHO — "hero." Pop.: Adolphus

ADRIAN — "black." Also: ADRIANO Pop.: Adrian

ALANO — "fair; speedy; harmonious." Pop.: Alan

ALARICO — "ruler of all." Pop.: Alaric

ALBERTO — "brilliant; attaining fame." Pop.: Albert

ALEJANDRO — "helper of mankind; ward off, or protect man." Pop.: Alexander

ALFONSO — "eager for battle." Also: ALONSO, IDLEFONSO Pop.: Alphonso

ALFREDO — "wise." Pop.: Alfred

ALUINO — "beloved by all." Pop.: Alvin

ANDRES — "strong; manly." Pop.: Andrew

ANIMODO — "spirited."

ANTONIO — "beyond praise." Pop.: Anthony

AQUILES — "a fighter with compressed lips when tense." Pop.: Achilles

ARCHIBALDO — "bold." Pop.: Archibald

ARNALDO — "strong as an eagle." Pop.: Arnold

171

ARTURO   "rock, or firm; valorous; brave."
                        Pop.: Arthur

AZABACHE   "blue black hair."

BASILIO   "kingly; royal; lit. the basilisk."
                        Pop.: Basil

BELTRAN   "bright raven; or glorious raven."
                        Pop.: Bertram

BENITO   "blessed." Also: BENEDICTO
                        Pop.: Benedict

BERNADO   "bold; brave; strong."
                        Also: BERNAL   Pop.: Bernard

BLANCO   "white."

BONDADOSO   "soft hearted."

CADENADE ORO   "gold chain." K. name for a Chi-
                        huahua.

CABALCLO   "hairless." K. name given to a
                        Mexican Hairless.

CENTON   "patchwork quilt."

CIRO   "king; sun." A name made famous
                        by Cyrus, the Great. Pop.: Cyrus

CHIQUITO   "tiny."

CRISTIANO   "follower." Pop.: Christian

CLARO   "light-colored."

CLODOVEO   "of holy fame." Pop.: Clovis

COLOR DE ROSA   "pink."

CONRADO   "wise." Pop.: Conrad

CONSTANTINO   "firm; constant; steadfast."
                        Pop.: Constantine

CORNELIO   "crowned." Pop.: Cornelius

DE OJOS NEGROS   "dark-eyed."

DE PALO BLANCO   "white-haired."

DE PALO RUBIO   "light haired."

DE PELO LISO	"short haired."
DE PELO ROJA	"red haired."
DE PIES LIGEROS	"swift footed."
DIONISIO	"fun-loving." Also: DIONIS Pop.: Dennis
DOCIL	"obedient."
DON JUAN	K. name for a Ch. Chihuahua, meaning, "Master, or Lord John; gracious master."
DUKE	K. name for a Chihuahua, meaning, to draw, or lead."
EDMUNDO	"defender of property; blessed peace." Pop.: Edmund
EDUARDO	"guard of goods; fortunate; blessed." Pop.: Edward
EL PELO LARGO	"long haired."
ENRIQUE	"home lord; ruler of property." Pop.: Henry
ESTEBAN	"fitly crowned." Also: ESTEVAN Pop.: Stephen
EUGENIO	"well-born." Pop.: Eugene
EUSTAQUIO	"fruitful; well put together." Pop.: Eustace
FELIPE	"lover of horses." Pop.: Philip
FERNANDO	"faithful to trust; beauty." Also: HERNANDO Pop.: Ferdinand
FLASH	K. name of a Chihuahua.
FRANCISCO	"free." Also: FRANCISQUITO, PANCHO Pop.: Francis
GALOPIN	"ragamuffin."
GASPAR	"treasure holder." Pop.: Jasper
GERARDO	"brave with the spear; bold." Pop.: Gerard

GIL	"a shield-bearer." Pop.: <u>Giles</u>
GILBERTO	"bright of will; illustrious pledge or hostage; bright servant." Pop.: <u>Gilbert</u>
GUALTERIO	"mighty warrior; ruling the host; leader of the army." Also: GUITTERE Pop.: <u>Walter</u>
GUIDO	"to steady; guide." Pop.: <u>Guy</u>
HARAPOS	"rags."
HEBERTO	"lit. bright warrior." Pop.: <u>Herbert</u>
HILARIO	"cheerful; merry; hilarious." Pop.: <u>Hilary</u>
HORACIO	"keeper of the hours; timekeeper; keen-eyed." Pop.: <u>Horace</u>
HUBERTO	"bright of mind." Pop.: <u>Hubert</u>
HUGO	"intelligent; home lord." Pop.: <u>Hugh</u>
JEREMIAS	"uplifted; appointed." Pop.: <u>Jeremiah</u>
JERONIMO	"holy; sacred; prophet." Pop.: <u>Jerome</u>
JONATAN	"God has given." Also: JONATAS Pop.: <u>Jonathan</u>
JORGE	"tiller of the soil." Pop.: <u>George</u>
JOSE	"the Lord shall add unto me another son." Pop.: <u>Joseph</u>
JUAN	"gracious." Pop.: <u>John</u>
JUANILLO	K. name for a Ch. Chihuahua, meaning, "little gracious one."
JULIUS	"divine; downy-haired; soft-haired." Pop.: <u>Julius</u>
LEAL	"faithful."
LAZARO	"God hath helped." Pop.: <u>Lazarus</u>

LEANDO	"tawny."
LEANDRO	"lion man; courageous; renowned." Pop.: Leander
LEON	"the lion; name assumed by 13 popes." Pop.: Leo
LEOPOLDO	"patriotic; bold and beloved." Pop.: Leopold
LORENZO	"benefactor; victor." Pop.: Laurence
LUCAS	"light." Pop.: Luke
LUCIO	"born at daybreak." Pop.: Lucius
LUIS	"famous warrior; famous in battle." Pop.: Lewis
MALO	"wicked."
MARCELO	"hammer; war-like." Pop.: Mark
(de) NARIZ NEGRO	"black-nosed."
NEGRO	"black."
NICOLAS	"victory." Pop.: Nicholas
OJINEGRO	"black eyed."
OJOS VIVOS	"bright eyed."
OLIVERIO	"keeps peace." Pop.: Oliver
PABLOCITO	"very little one." Also: PAULINO, PABLO Pop.: Paul
PASCUAL	"born during the Passover." Pop.: Pascal
PEDRO	"firm foundation." Pop.: Peter
PELIRROJO	"red-haired."
PEQUENITO	"little one."
PIMIENTO	"red pepper."

| QUERIDO | "darling (favorite)." |
| QUIXOTE | "romantic." |

RAIMUNDO	"wise protector."
REYES	"king." Pop.: Roy
REYNALDOS	"strong ruler." Pop.: Reginald
RICARDO	"strong." Pop.: Richard
ROBERTO	"bright in fame." Pop.: Robert
ROGERIO	"famous spearman." Pop.: Roger
ROLDEN	"fame of the land." Pop.: Roland
RUBIO	"blond hair, yellow hair."
RUY	"champion; famous." Pop.: Roderick

SANSON	"strong man." Pop.: Sampson
SANCHO	"sanctified." The amusing esquire of Don Quixote.
SERVETUS	"one who protects." Pop.: Service
SIMON	"obedient." Also: XIMON Pop.: Simon
SUAVE	"soft."

Female

ADONICA	"sweet."
AGUEDA	"good and kind." Pop.: Agatha
AGUEDEZA	"quickness of mind."
ALEGRE	"gay or happy."
ALEJANDRA	"helper of mankind." Pop.: Alexandria
ALERTO	"alert."
ALICIA	"cheerful." Pop.: Alice
AMATA	"the beloved." Pop.: Amy
AMOR MIA	"my darling."

ANA	"grace; merry; prayer." Also; ANITA, NITA Pop.: Ann
ANIMADA	"spirited."
AZUL	"blue."
BARBARITA	"little stranger." Pop.: Barbara
BEATRIZ	"she who blesses; makes happy." Pop.: Beatrice
BENIGNA	"kindly; gracious." Pop.: Elizabeth
BENITA	"the blessed." Also: BENICIA Pop.: Benedicta
BERTA	"bright; glorious; illustrious." Pop.: Bertha
BLANCA	"dazzling; white."
BRIGIDA	"the mighty; high; or strong." Pop.: Bridget
(de) CARA PALIDA	"white faced."
CAROLINA	"strong and womanly." Also: CARLOTTA, LOLA Pop.: Caroline
CASANDRA	"helper of men; inspiring." Pop.: Cassandra
CATALINA	"pure." Pop.: Catherine
CECILIA	"blind; dim-sighted." Pop.: Cicely
CHE CHE	A K. name for a Chihuahua, meaning, "che is the letter ch."
CHOCOLATE DROP	K. name for a Chihuahua.
CLOTILDE	"famous; illustrious war-maid." Pop.: Clotilda
COLOR DE NARANJA	"orange colored."
CONSTANZA	"firm; constant." Also: COSTENZA Pop.: Constance
CRIADA	"servant."
CRISTINA	"follower." Pop.: Christine

DE NADA	"it is nothing."
DIANA	"the divine." Pop.: <u>Diana</u>
DOROTEA	"gift." Pop.: <u>Dorothy</u>
DULCE	"soft of disposition."
ELENA	"light; sweet and good." Also: HELENA, ELLENIS, LEONOR. Pop.: <u>Helen</u>
EL ORA	"gold."
EL PALA LARGA	"long-haired."
ELOISA	"white."
EMA	"ancestress, or grandmother." Also: MANUELA Pop.: <u>Emma</u>
EMILIA	"industrious." Pop.: <u>Emily</u>
ESMERALDA	"bright hope."
ESTER	"a star." Also: ESTELA, ESTREL-LITA, ESTRELLA Pop.: <u>Esther</u>
ENGRACIA	"graceful; beloved; favored." Pop.: <u>Grace</u>
ENRIQUETA	"ruler of private property; mistress of the house." Also: NETTY, ETTA Pop.: <u>Henrietta</u>
EUFREMIA	"of good report; fair fame." Also: EUFEMIA Pop.: <u>Euphemia</u>
EVA	"life; with vitality." Also: EVITA Pop.: <u>Eve</u>
FE	"faith."
FEDERICA	"peaceful ruler; rich peace." Pop.: <u>Frederica</u>
FELIPA	"lover of horses." Pop.: <u>Philippa</u>
FELISA	"the fortunate; happy." Pop.: <u>Felicia</u>
FLORENCIA	"to flourish." Also: FLORENCITA, FLORINDA Pop.: <u>Florence</u>
FRANCISCA	"free." Pop.: <u>Frances</u>

FURIA   "spitfire."

GERTRUDIS   "spear loved maiden."
                       Pop.: Gertrude

GITANA   "gypsy." F. of Gitano.

GUILLERMINA   "chosen protection; resolute protectoress." Pop.: Wilhelmina

INES   "pure; chaste; gentle; meek."
                       Also: MESILA Pop.: Agnes

JUANA   "gift." Also: JUANITA, NITA
                       Pop.: Jane

JUDIT   "the praised." Pop.: Judith

JULIA   "soft-haired." A favorite name.
                       Also: JULIETTA, JULIANA
                       Pop.: Julia

LAURA   "receiving recognition."
                       Pop.: Laura

LETICIA   "joyful; glad." Pop.: Letitia

LIPRE   "free."

LISO   "glossy hair."

LITTLE CARMINCITA   K. name for a Chihuahua, meaning, "little rose."

LUCIA   "bright." Also: LUISA, LUISITA, LULU Pop.: Lucy

LUCRECIA   "bringer of riches." Pop.: Lucretia

LUISA   "famous warrior." Also: ELOISA
                       Pop.: Louise

MAGDALENA   "guardian." Also: MADELENA
                       Pop.: Magdalen

MARTA   "lady; or mistress." Pop.: Martha

MERCEDES   "rewarding." Pop.: Mercy

MUNECA DE TRAPO	"rag doll."
MUNECA	"doll."
NATALIA	"A Christmas child; born on Christmas day." Also: NATALITA Pop.: Natalie
(de) NARIZ NEGRA	"black-nosed."
NEGRA	"black."
PAMELA	"beloved elf." lit. "the loved." Pop.: Pamela
PAOLA	"little." Also: PAULINA, PAULA, PAOLINA Pop.: Paula
PALOMILLA	K. name for Ch. Chihuahua, meaning, "little dove."
(un) PEDAZODE plus (color)	"a patch of (color)."
PENELOPE	"faithful." Pop.: Penelope
PEPA	"she shall add." Also: PEPITA, PEPILLA, JOSEFA Pop.: Josephine
PRUDENCIA	"discretion; prudent; a virtue name." Pop.: Prudence
PEQUENUELA	"little one."
RAQUEL	"gentle innocence." Pop.: Rachel
REBECA	"to bind; snare; firm." Pop.: Rebecca
RINA	K. name for a Ch. Chihuahua, meaning, "a ringing cry."
ROJO ORO	"red-gold."
ROSALINDA	"fair; pretty rose." Pop.: Rosalinda
ROSITA	"rose." Pop.: Rhoda
ROSAMUNDA	"rose of the world." Pop.: Rosamond

SANCHA	"sanctioned; holy." Pop.: <u>Sancia</u>
SARA	"high-born; princess." Pop.: <u>Sarah</u>
SENALDA	"sign; destiny." Pop.: <u>Signa</u>
SEVILLA	"a sibyl; prophetess." Pop.: <u>Sibyl</u>
SOFIA	"wisdom." Pop.: <u>Sophia</u>
STARLITE	K. name of Ch. Chihuahua.
SUSANA	"white; lily." Pop.: <u>Susan</u>
TERESA	"reaper." Also: TERESITA Pop.: <u>Theresa</u>
TERASINA	K. name for a Ch. Chihuahua, meaning, "little harvester."
TOMASA	"a twin." Pop.: <u>Thomasa</u>
URSOLA	"strong as a bear." Pop.: <u>Ursula</u>
VALIENTE	"dashing (spirit)."
VELOZ	"swift."
VENTURA	"adventurous." Pop.: <u>Ventura</u>
VIOLANTE	"violet; shy."
VIGILANTE	"alert."
XAVERIE	"the bright." Honors St. Francis Xavier.
XENA	"the hospitable." Xena was the wife of the Cid, in Spanish legend.
ZEREKA	K. name for a Ch. Chihuahua.

ORIENTAL DOGS

Chow Chow
Japanese Spaniel, or Chin
Lhasa Apso
Pekingese
Pug

Oriental Dog Names

Male

ABSO SEN KYE   "a Tibetan name, meaning 'bark sentinel lion dog,' given to the Lhasa terrier."

ACE   K. name given to a Pekingese, meaning, "the ultimate."

AMA-GASA   "rain."

AMI (f. or m.)   "sweet."

BANNIN (m. or f.)   "a watchman."

BARA   "rose."

BEAU   "handsome." K. name given to a Pekingese.

BEAU BRUMMEL   K. name for a Pug, meaning, "a fop."

BIRŌDO (f. or m.)   "velvet."

BUZZ   K. name given to a Pekingese, suggesting "constant activity."

CHA IRO NO   "brown."

CHANG TANG   "sweet in the palm of my hand?" K. name for a Lhasa Apso.

CHAO-PU-CHO   "cannot find; seek but cannot get."

CHAWAN	"a tea bowl."
CH'I	"strange, wonderful, rare."
CHIA PAO	"pride of the house."
CHIEN	"sturdy, strong."
CHIISAI MONO	"little thing."
CHIJIRIGE NO	"curly."
CHING	"light on the feet."
CHINKY CHOG	K. name given to a Pekingese.
CH'Ū	"interesting; amusing."
CHŪJITSU NA	"faithful."
CHOCHŌ	"butterfly."
CLICK	K. name for a Pug.
CONFUCIOUS	A Chinese philosopher whose teachings were on loyalty, intelligence. K. name for a Pekingese.
DAITAN NA SENSHI	"bold warrior."
DŌ KA	"copper coin."
DOKONI MO	"everywhere."
DOMINO	A name given to a Pekingese with a face like a mask.
FEI YING	K. name for a Ch. Pekingese, meaning "brave rebel, or flying shadow."
FOX	K. name for a Pekingese.
GEININ	"entertainer."
GENKI NO YOI	"lively."
GIN NO (f. or m.)	"silver."
GORO	"fifth boy."
GUNJIN	"soldier."
HACHI	"bee."

HACHIRO	"eighth boy."
HAIIRO NO	"grey."
HASHI	"chopsticks."
HEN K'UAI TE P'AO	"run very quickly."
HETA NA	"clumsy."
HI LO JACK	K. name for a Pug.
HING CHEN	"star dust."
HIROSHI	"generous."
HO	"the good."
HO HUA	"faithfulness."
HOTARU	"firefly."
HOTEI	"Cheerful Japanese god of happiness, beloved by the children."
HUANG CHUNG	"lit. yellow bell."
HUNG HU TZE	"red beard."
HSAIO HENG	"mighty mite."
ICHIRO	"first boy."
IMP	K. name for a Chow Chow.
INKA	"ink."
ITSMO UGOITE IRU	"always on the go."
KAI	"royal dignity."
KAI LUNG	"King Dragon." K. name for a Ch. Pekingese.
KABUKI	"lit. eccentric, impudent."
KAMINŌ NO ARU	"crested."
KASŌ	"house fortune."
KAWA	"river."
KHAN-DU	K. name for a Pekingese.
KHI KI	K. name for a Ch. Pekingese.
KI IRO NO	"yellow."

KI IRO NO MAMORU	"yellow guard."
KIKU	"Chrysanthemum; noble flower; on the emperor's crest."
KINSHOUKU KAMI	"golden hair."
KISHU	"surprise."
KITSUNE	"fox."
KO	"elder brother."
KOKO KASHI KO	"here and there."
KOW TENG	"the highest rank."
KU CHI	"many trousers?" K. name for a Pekingese.
KUAN YIN	Protector of children.
LANDEBU	"rendezvous."
LANG	"prince."
MANCHU	"pure."
MIDORI NO	"green."
MIGHTY MO	K. name for a Pekingese.
MIGHTY RED	K. name for a Chow Chow.
MING	"bright."
MING YUIN	"bright cloud."
NAGAI KE	"long hair."
NANI NO	"nothing."
NIHON	"sunrise."
OCHITSUITA	"calm."
ŌJI	"prince."
Ō-SAMA	"king."
OTHELLO	K. name for a Pug.
PAI	"white."

P'AO	"to run, walk."
PAO	"to guard, protect."
P'IEN	"cheap."
PEPPER POT	K. name for a CHOW CHOW.
PO	"waves of the sea."
POO CHU TU	K. name for a Chow Chow.
PRINCE GENJI	in the Tale of the Genji, this prince is exiled, to rise to high office in the kingdom.
RIJŌKEN	"a hunter-dog."
RIKONA	"intelligent."
ROBIN HOOD	K. name for a Ch. Pekingese.
SABURO	"third boy."
SAKE	"rice wine."
SANDUR	K. name for a Lhasa Apso.
SENSHI	"warrior."
SHO GUNJIN	"little soldier."
SHO HOTEI	"little god of happiness."
SHO SUBON	"little trousers."
SILVER WINGS	K. name for a Ch. Chow Chow.
SNO BOI	K. name for a white Pekingese.
SOCRATES	K. name for a Ch. Pekingese.
SORA IRO	"sky blue."
STORMY NIGHT	K. name for a Chow Chow.
SUMI	"black ink stick."
SUN	K. name for a Pekingese.
SUN STAR	K. name for a Pekingese.
SWAPS	K. name for a Pug.
TAIKOO	black and white Lhasa Apso, the first to be brought to this country.

TAKASHI	"noble."
TAKE	"bamboo."
TANOSHII	"happy."
TENGU	"the goblins, gnomes that haunt the mountains and forests."
TOPPER	K. name for a Pug.
WONG TONE	"brown sugar."
WRINKLES	K. name for a Ch. Pug.
YAMI	K. Japanese Spaniel.
YAV-SHIH NI LAI, WO CHIU LAI	"I shall come, if you do."
YAWARAKAI	"soft."
YOI	"good."
YOKI NA	"gay."
YOROKOBI NO MOTO	"source of delight."
YOSHI	"well, good."
YUKI	"snow."
YUN YUN	"dizzy revolving."
ZUTTO	"straight, direct, directly."

Female

AH CUM	K. name given to a Pekingese.
AKAI (f. or m.)	"red."
AKAGANE	"copper."
ANGEL FACE	K. name for a Pug.
AOI (f. or m.)	"blue."
ASAHI (f. or m.)	"morning sun."
ASHI NO KARUI (f. or m.)	"light."

ATSUKAI NIKUK	"hard to get along with."
BEE	"she who blesses; makes happy." From: _Beatrice_
BEETLE	K. name for a Pekingese, having the connotation of smallness.
BLACK ANGEL	K. name for Ch. Chow Chow.
BLACK DUST	K. name for a Pekingese.
BLUE DAWN	K. name for a Ch. Chow Chow.
BUNG TONG	"sugar."
BUTTERFLY	K. name for a Pekingese, suggesting "lightness," "agility," "beauty."
CHA IRO NO MAMORA	"brown guard."
CHARM-A-PLENTY	K. name for a Pekingese.
CHERUB	K. name for a Pug.
CHIISAI	"little."
CHIISAI HOERU MONO	"little barker."
CHIN LONG	"close relationship with a clever active one," possibly. K. name for a Pekingese.
CHŌDO YOI	"just right."
CHU CHI	"marvel."
CHUN	K. name for a Pekingese, meaning "standard.'
CHUNG	"a bell."
CINDERELLA	K. name for a Pug.
CINNAMON SUE	"Cinnamon color with the character of a lily, pure?" K. name for a Pug.
COQUETTE	"a flirt." K. name given to a Pekingese.
CRICKET	K. name given to a Pekingese, suggesting activeness, smallness.

DERRIE	K. name given to a Ch. Pekingese.
DINKIE	Name for the first Lhasa Apso female brought to the U.S., the color of raw silk.
DUSKIE PRINCESS	K. name for a Pekingese.
EIKIN	"a pound." (weight)
FIREFLY	K. name for a Ch. Pekingese.
FUBUKI	"lit. blowing snow." K. name for a Japanese Spaniel.
GAITŌ	"overcoat."
GAY FEATHERS	K. name for a Pekingese.
GAZELLE	K. name for a Pug.
GEISHA	"entertainer."
GINA	"silvery."
HANA	"flower."
HANTEN NO ARU	"spotted."
HATA	"flag."
HATSUBOKA	"ink splashing forth; a technique to give a quick, wet, splashing effect."
HAYAI	"swift."
HIGASA	"sun."
HOGOSHA	"defender."
HOSHI	"star."
HOSHI NO YŌ NI	"star bright."
HSI	"fine, delicate."
HU	"pepper."
HU LU	"guardian of travellers."
HUA	"lotus lady." (Japanese)

HUA	"flower." (Chinese)
HUMMINGBEE	K. name for a Ch. Pekingese.
IGENOARU	"dignified."
INU	"dog."
JASMIN	K. name for a Pekingese.
JOCHŪ	"maid servant."
JOŌ	"queen."
JOYŪ	"actress."
JUJIGŪN NO SENSHI	"crusader."
KAGE	"shadow."
KAGEDE	"in the shadow."
KAI TAI KAI	K. name for a Chow Chow. "lit.- KAI-times, story (floor); TAI- large, great. Many times from floor to floor?"
KAIKATSU NA	"pleasant."
KAMI	"a wonderful thing."
KAMINARI	"lightning fast."
KAWAII	"dear."
KE	"hair."
KE NO MUKU SHITA	"wooly hair."
KEI	"orchid." Suggests a dainty one.
KINIRO NO	"golden."
KINU	"silk."
KIREI NA	"pretty."
KIREINA	"pretty princess."
KIREGIRE NO	"scrappy."
KO UN	"good luck."
KOKKEIBON	"comic book."
KOMAKAI	"small, minute."

KOROGI	"cricket."
KUMO	"cloud."
KUAI	"extraordinary, unusual."
KUNG CHU	"princess."
KURO TO SHIRO	"black and white."
KUROI	"black."

LADY JENIFER	K. name for a Pug, meaning, Lady White.
LI LI	"lively Plum; or polite Plum." One of the first English Pekingese to be imported to America.
LING	"clever, active, or honorable." K. name given to a Chow Chow.

ME	"eyes."
MIJIKAI KE	"short hair."
MING	"famous; fame."
MIZU	"water."
MOSS	K. name for a Pug.

| NAMERAKA NA | "sleek." |
| NOEL | K. name for a Pekingese that might have been born on Christmas Day. |

O DOKE NO	"clownish."
ŌJIJO	"princess."
OKURI MONO	"a gift."

| PRINCESS MING HSING | "Princess Bright Star." |
| PSYCHE | K. name for a Chow Chow, meaning in Greek Mythology, the soul, sometimes represented in art as a butterfly, or a tiny winged thing. |

PUFF BALL	A fungi which has a ball-like fruit body, which emits a cloud of spores when broken. K. name given to a Pekingese.
QUEEN OF SPADES	K. name given to a Pug.
RAN	orchid, meaning "noble, graceful, perfection."
RAZZLE	K. name for a Pekingese.
SAKURA	"flowering cherry."
SHAO-HSING	K. name for a Chow Chow, meaning, "little star."
SHIRAKABA	"white birch."
SHIROI	"white."
SHIROSA	"whiteness."
SHITAGAU MONO	"follower."
SHO	"small."
SHO AMAI	"little sweet."
SHO HANA	"little flower."
SHO KAGE	"little shadow."
SHO KEIBO	"little escort."
SHO KISHU	"little surprise."
SHO MAMORU	"little guard."
SHŌ YŌSEI	"fairy."
SUKOSHI	"little, not much."
SUMI	"charcoal."
TALLIS	"the learned, the wise."
TANG LA	K. name for a Ch. Lhasa Apso, meaning, "finished, then lies down?" or, "sugar sweet to the very end?"
TAPO'	"smashed."

TOMONI	"friendly."
TORMA	K. name for a Lhasa Apso Ch. Might mean, "pulls, drags sugar."
TSAO	"early."
TSUYOSHI	"strong."
TZU	"elder sister."
YARI	"lance; fast as a lance."
YŌJINBAKAI	"watchful."
YOKITA	K. name for Japanese Spaniel. "much spirit?"

RUSSIAN, HUNGARIAN & BALKAN DOGS

Borzoi (Russian Wolfhound)
Komondor
Puli
Kuvasz
Vizala

Names

Male

ADRIAN	"black."
AFANASSIJ	"undying."
AGAFON	"good."
AGOSTON	"venerable."
AHABB	"dear; dearest."
AKIN	"judge." Pop.: <u>Acim</u>
AKTEP	"actor."
ALBAN	"white."
ALEXEI	"help; defence." Also: SASCHA, ALESCHA Pop.: <u>Alexander</u>
AMOROSIZ	"one who accumulates." Pop.: <u>Ambrose</u>
ANDREJ	"strong; manly." Also: ANDREIAN Pop.: <u>Andrew</u>
ANIKITA	"unconquered."
ARPAD	K. name given to a Ch. Puli.
ALYWIN	"good friend."
AYOUB	"persecuted."
BACYA	"kingly." Pop.: <u>Basil</u>
BARBAR	"barbarian."
BELI-TZAR	"white prince."

BAKKIIR	"early."
BIRKAS	"shepherd."
BETYAR	Ch. Pulik name.
BOJA	K. name for a Borzoi.
BOLESLAV	"great glory."
BONIFACIJ	"a good fate." Pop.: <u>Boniface</u>
BORIS	"warrior; great fighter." A Boris was Czar of Bulgaria.
BRONZE	K. name for a Ch. Borzoi.
BUNDAZ	K. name for a Ch. Puli.
CHER	"snow."
CHRISTOF	"protected traveller." St. Christopher is patron saint of travellers. Also: CHRISTOPFER Pop.: <u>Christopher</u>
CITATION	K. name given to a Puli.
CZAR	first Borzoi dog of prominence in the movies.
DANIELA	"God is my judge." A Biblical prophet. Pop.: <u>Daniel</u>
DAVEED	"beloved." Pop.: <u>David</u>
DEREKAS	"valiant."
DIMITRE	"spring from the earth." Pop.: <u>Demetrius</u>
DON PACO	K. name for Ch. Borzoi.
DUKE BORI	K. name for a Borzoi, coming from the first part of the word 'Borzoi,' which means Russian Wolfhound.
ENCHANTED SHADOW	K. name for a Puli.
EISAAK	"laughter, fun."
EMILIJ	"industrious." Pop.: <u>Emil</u>
EPHREM	"fruitful."

ERICH	"ever king."
EVGENE	"of noble race." Pop.: <u>Eugene</u>
FANFARE	"a flourish; blow a fanfare." K. name given to a Puli.
FEELEEP	"lover of horses." Philip, the Great inherited the title 'horse-lover.'
FEODOR	"gift." Also: FEDYA, FEDOR Pop.: <u>Theodore</u>
FEYLAM	"wolf." Pop.: <u>Phelan</u>
FOMA	"twin." Pop.: <u>Thomas</u>
FRIDRICH	"peaceful ruler." Pop.: <u>Frederic</u>
GOTCHINA	K. name for a Ch. Borzoi.
GOUSTOFF	"staff." K. name for a Borzoi.
GREAT RUBINOF	"great son." K. name for a Ch. Borzoi.
GRISCHA	"watchful guard." Also: GRIGORIJ Pop.: <u>Gregory</u>
GUHLOOBOY	"light blue color." (guh-loo-BOYO)
GYPSY	K. name given to a black Puli.
HABIIB	"loved one."
HASSAN	"the goodly." K. name given to a Ch. Kuvasz.
HILARIAON	"merry." Also: GILARIJ Pop.: <u>Hilary</u>
JAKOV	"take the place of." Also: <u>JASCHA</u> Pop.: <u>James</u>
JEREMIJA	"uplifted." Pop.: <u>Jeremy</u>
JERONIM	"sacred." Pop.: <u>Jerome</u>
JOSEF	"to add." Also: JOSEEF, OSEEP Pop.: <u>Joseph</u>

JOV	"patient." Pop.: <u>Job</u>
JURGI	"farmer." Also: JURIJ, YURI Pop.: <u>George</u>
KAZIMIR	"command for peace." Pop.: <u>Casimir</u>
KEEREEL	"splendor." Also: CIRIL, CIRO Pop.: <u>Cyril</u>
KLAVDIJ	"lame." Pop.: <u>Claude</u>
KLEMENT	"mild." Pop.: <u>Clement</u>
KOHMEHTAH	"comet."
KOPEK	"small coin." Humorous name for a mutt. Not worth a Kopek.
KONRAD	"wise; bold." Also: KUNRAT Pop.: <u>Conrad</u>
KONSTANTINE	"firm." Pop.: <u>Constantine</u>
KUSTBAAN	"thimble."
LASAR	"helper." Pop.: <u>Eleazar</u>
LEON	"courageous." Pop.: <u>Leon</u>
LUKA	"light." Also: LUKEZ, LUZIAN Pop.: <u>Lucius</u>
LEV	"a lion." Pop.: <u>Leo</u>
MALCHICK	K. name for a Ch. Borzoi, mean- ing, "little boy."
MAZEPPA	"a page to the king of Poland, and as such acquired various useful accomplishments." K. name for a Borzoi.
MEHTEHOHR	"meteor."
MELANCTHON	"black flower."
MERLIN	"a magician and seer in the Ar- thurian Romances. K. name for a Borzoi.

MIKHAIL	"great power." Also: MISHA, MISHENKA Pop.: <u>Michael</u>
MILAN	"lovely."
MOHLMEEYAH	"lightning."
MORIZ	"dark." Pop.: <u>Maurice</u>
MIRKO	"work ruler."
NAJME	"star."
NIKOLAI	"victory." Also: NIKON, NIKOLAJ Pop.: <u>Nicholas</u>
PAVEL	"little." Also: PAVLIN Pop.: <u>Paul</u>
PEEDZHAHK	"coat." (peed-ZHAHK)
PHADDEI	"devoted." Pop.: <u>Thaddeus</u>
PETR	"adament." Also: PETRUSCHA Pop.: <u>Peter</u>
PRINCE IVAN	"gracious." K. name for a Borzoi.
RIKE	"guardian." K. name for a Borzoi.
RURICH	"rich in fame." Pop.: <u>Roderick</u>
SACHAR	"all power given." Pop.: <u>Zachary</u>
SERGIJ	"to serve." Popular name in Russia. From St. Sergius. Also: SSERGIE, SERGE Pop.: <u>Serge</u>
SNOWMAN	K. name for a Puli.
TIMOFEI	"shining example." Also: TEEMOFE Pop.: <u>Timothy</u>
TOBIJA	"good." Pop.: <u>Tobias</u>
VIKENTIJ	"conquering." Pop.: <u>Vincent</u>
VLASSIJ	"a blaze." Pop.: <u>Blaze</u>

VLADIMIR	"world prince." First Christian ruler of Russia. Deeply loved by the Russians for the great Russian saint, Prince Wladimir.
VELIKA	"great."
ZAMNOJ	"after me."
ZIGANKA	"gypsy."
ZHEYK	"beetle." Name given to a Ch. Borzoi.
ZIRR	"button."
ZIVAN	"lively."
ZHOLTII	"yellow."
ZOLETE	"gold."
ZONAZO	K. name given to a Ch. Borzoi.
ZWETLANA	"star."
XARUFF	"lamb."
YAKOF	"supplanter." Pop.: <u>Jacob</u>

Female

ADRIANA	"black."
AGAFIA	"kind & good." Nurse in story of Anna Karenina, by Leo Tolstoy.
ALBINA	"white."
ALMA	"learned."
ALVA	"white."
ANASTASIA	"one who shall rise again." Also: NASTENKA Pop.: <u>Annstasis</u>
ANNUSIA	"grace." Also: ANNIKA, ANNUSCHKA, ANNJUSCHA Pop.: <u>Ann</u>
ANTONETTA	"inestimable." Pop.: <u>Antonia</u>

AQUILINE	"eagle power." Saint Aquila made the name a favorite in Russia.
ARDRA	"ardent." Pop.: Ardeha; Ardith
AVGUSTA	"high; august." Pop.: Augusta
AZANDE	K. name.
BANDOR	"curly."
BARIKA	"little lamb."
BEATRICA	"she who makes happy." Pop.: Beatrice
BISTRI	"rapid; fast."
BOODEELNEEK	"alarm clock." Mah YAH boo DEEL neek - My alarm clock.
BRONISLAVA	"weapon of glory."
BELLONA	K. name for a Ch. Borzoi.
CHARADEI	"magician."
CHYAWRNIHY	"black." (CHYAWY nih y)
CHEHRNEELAH	"ink." (Chehr-NEE-lah)
CLEOPATRA	K. name for a Puli. She was Queen of Egypt.
DASCHA	"given by God." Also: FEODOSIA, FEDORA Pop.: Theodosia
DARK MOON	K. name for a Borzoi.
DANICA	"morning star."
DITTA	"rich, happy." Also: DITINKA Pop.: Edith
DRAGA	"dear."
DUSCHA	"happy one." Also: DUSCHINKA (dim) Pop.: Edith
EEPEEHEN	"peace." Pop.: Irene

ELISIF   "consecrated to God."
Also: LISENKA   Pop.: <u>Elizabeth</u>

EUDOKHIA   "esteemed."   Pop.: <u>Eudocia</u>

EVVA   "life."   Pop.: <u>Eva</u>

FEODORA   "gift of God."   Also: DASHA
Pop.: <u>Theodora</u>

FOMAIDA   "twin."   Pop.: <u>Thomasa</u>

FOTIE   "bright; brilliant."   Pop.: <u>Phoebe</u>

FRANZISKA   "the free."   Pop.: <u>Frances</u>

GAVRILA   "heroine."   Pop.: <u>Gabrielle</u>

GERTRUDA   "true spear."   Pop.: <u>Gertrude</u>

GLOUKERA   "honey sweet."   Pop.: <u>Melissa</u>

GOLDEN GLOW   K. name given to a Ch. Puli.

HEBECTA   "bride."

HABAAYIB   "loved one."

ILARIA   "cheerful." Also: MILARIA
Pop.: <u>Hiliary</u>

INDIGO BLUE   K. name for a Puli.

JACOVINA   "to take the place of."
Also: ZAKELINA Pop.: <u>Jacqueline</u>

JEVLALIJA   "well spoken."   Pop.: <u>Eulalee</u>

JULIJA   "soft haired."   Pop.: <u>Julia</u>

KOSTANCIA   "firm."   Also: STANCA
Pop.: <u>Constance</u>

KRISTINA   "anointed."   Also: KINA
Pop.: <u>Constance</u>

KRYEHMUHVIHY   "cream colored." (KRYEE - muh -
vih - y)

KSEENIA	"hospitable." Pop.: <u>Xena</u>
LALA	"tulip."
LENKA	"light."
LIBUSA	"darling." Name of a 7th century queen."
LUDMILLA	"love of the people." A favorite Russian name. St. Ludmilla was a favorite saint.
LUISE	"lady warrior." K. name for a Kuvasz.
LUZIJA	"lustrous." Pop.: <u>Lucy</u>
MADELINA	"watchful." Pop.: <u>Madeline</u>
MAHLY ENKEEY	"small." (MAH-lyen-kee-y)
MARFA	"mistress." Pop.: <u>Martha</u>
MARISKA	K. name for a Ch. Borzoi.
MARUSHKA	K. name for a Ch. Borzoi.
MARJARITA	"pearl." Also: MARJETA Pop.: <u>Margaret</u>
MAVRA	"dark." Pop.: <u>Maura</u>
MILA	"lovely."
MILCA	"industrious." Also: MILICA Pop.: <u>Emily</u>
MICHELINE	"God-like." Also: MIKELINA Pop.: Michaela
MITRA	Greek Goddess, huntress of all the fruits of the earth. Also: DIMITRA Pop.: <u>Demetria</u>
MILICA	"love." Pop.: <u>Mila</u>
MUSHKA	"little fly." Dog sent up in space by the Russians.
MYAKHKE	"soft."
NADEZNA	"Christmas." The supreme Christ-

	mas name. Also: NATASHA, NATALIJA, NATASCHA Pop.: <u>Natalie</u>
NAWOIHY GAWT	"New Years."
NJUUM	"star."
NEDA	"Sunday's daughter."
NESSA	"meek; pure; chaste." Also: NESSIA, AGNESSA, AGNESIJA Pop.: <u>Agnes</u>
OLGA	"peace." Lit. olive emblem of peace. Name of the daughter of Nicholas II, Czar of Russia. Masculine is OLEG Also: OLINKA Pop.: <u>Olga</u>
PAHS-KHAH	"Easter."
PAVLA	"little." Pop.: <u>Paula</u>
PAWST	"Lent."
PCHELKA	"little bee." Dog sent up into space by the Russians.
PUSHINKA	"dog." Owned by Caroline Kennedy, given to her by Premier Khrushchev.
PYEHRYEETS	"pepper." (PY EH-ryets)
RACHIT	"lamblike; innocent." Pop.: <u>Rachel</u>
RADMILLA	"of joyous affection."
SAKHHAHR	"sugar." (SAH - khahr)
SAVA	"to rest." Pop.: <u>Sabra</u>
SEENEEY	"blue" (SEE-nee-y)
SEVASTJANA	"reverenced." Pop.: <u>Sebastinana</u>
SHAPKA	"cap."
SHYAWLK	"silk."
SIVILLA	"wise one." Pop.: <u>Sibyl</u>

SONIA	"sensible." Also: SONYA Pop.: Sophronia
STANCA	"steadfast." Also: KOSTANCIA Pop.: Constance
STAR	"bright." K. name for Borzoi.
STEFANIDA	"crowned fitly." Pop.: Stephana
TANIA	K. name given to a Borzoi.
TARAZAH	K. name given to a Borzoi.
TERESA	"bearer of the harvest." K. name given to a Kuvasz.
TIRAN	"tyrant."
ULRIKA	"powerful." Pop.: Alarice
URRSULA	"unknown strength." Pop.: Ursula
VALESKA	"ruling glory."
VARVAR	"little stranger." Also: VARINKA Pop.: Barbara
VELIKA	"great." Pop.: Guinevere
XIRFAAN	"lamb."
ZELDA SHAWN	K. name for a Borzoi.
ZENEVIEVA	"white one." Pop.: Genevieve
ZENOVIA	"of noble birth."
ZOIA	"full of life." Pop.: Zoe
ZORA	"dawn." Also: ZORANA Pop.: Aurora
ZORE	"princess."
ZKINYI	K. name for Ch. Puli.
ZIZI	"ornament."
ZADACHA	"problem."

ZHENA   "wife."
ZRAAR   "button."

SCOTTISH DOGS

Cairn Terrier
Collie
Dandie Dinmont Terrier
Golden Retriever
Scottish Deerhound
Scottish Terrier
Shetland Sheep Dog
Skye Terrier
West Highland White Terrier

Scotch Names

Male

AENGUS	"the choice; excellent strength; virtue." Pop.: Angus
AIZLE	"cinder."
ALICK	"to ward off; protect man." Pop.: Andrew
ARISTOCRAT	K. name for a Scotch Terrier.
AULD	"old."
AMAZEMENT	K. name for a West Highland White Terrier.
AWNIE	"bearded."
BAIRN	"child."
BALDIE	"sacred prince, probably a cognate with Baldur, the beautiful."
BALIFF	"a guard."
BAIRD	"a minstrel, or bard; poet." Pop.: Bard
BARTY	K. name for a Ch. Scotch Terrier.
BICKERIN	"noisy contention."

BIRKEE	"fellow."
BARNEY	K. name for a Cairn Terrier.
BIZZ	"flurry."
BIZZIE	"busy."
BLACK LANCE	K. name for a Collie.
BLATE	"modest; bashful."
BOGLE	"hobgobblin."
BONNIE	prefix for any name, as Bonnie Laddie, meaning, boy sweetheart, a term of endearment.
BOTTOMS UP	K. name for a Scotch Terrier.
BOYD	"white; fair-haired." A Scottish favorite.
BRAW	"handsome; gaily dressed."
BRIGADOON	K. name for a West Highland Terrier.
BRIGHT FUTURE	K. name given to a Collie.
BROCADE	K. name given to a Ch. Scottish Terrier.
CAMERON	"crooked nose." A clan name.
CANCE	"gentle;quiet; prudent; careful." Also: CANNIE
CAUK	"chalk."
CHARLEMAGNE	K. name for a Collie. King of the Franks; Charles the great.
CLATTER	"noisy; talkative; babble."
CLINKER	K. name given to a Collie. Small pieces left after burning coal.
CLISH-MA-CLEAVER	"nonsense."
CONQUEROR	K. name for a Collie.
CORBIE	"raven."
COUTHIE	"loving, affable."

DAFFIN	"larking, fun."
DANDIE	"strong." Pop.: <u>Andrew</u>
DARK KNIGHT	K. name for a Shetland Sheep dog.
DAVIE	"beloved." Pop.: <u>David</u>
DEIL-MA-CARE	"devil may care."
DRED	"to endure."
DUFF	"the dark, black-faced." A clan name.
DUNCAN	"brown chief." Duncan was a King of Scotland, slain by Macbeth.
ECLIPSE	K. name for a Collie, meaning, "to obscure, to darken."
ENCHANTER	K. name for a Collie.
EXPLORER	Sunnyside K. name for a Collie, meaning, "adventurous; seeking."
FIER	"companion." Also: FIERE
FIRST EDITION	K. name for a Scottish Terrier.
FLANE	"arrow."
FRANCIE	"free." Pop.: <u>Francis</u>
FRIGATE	K. name for a Shetland Sheep Dog.
FROST	K. name for a Dandie Dinmont Terrier.
GASH	"wise."
GAMIN	K. name for a Shetland Sheep Dog.
GAVIN	"hawk of battle. Pop.: <u>Gawain</u>
GILLIES	"servant."
GLAUD	"the lame." Pop.: <u>Claude</u>
GOLD CHIPS	K. name for a Shetland Sheep Dog.
GOLDEN RULER	K. name for a Collie.
GOLDEN SULTAN	K. name for a Collie.

GRAY DAWN	Sunnybank K. name for a Collie.
GREYFRIARS BOBBY	Name of a Skye Terrier in the book by the same name by Eleanor Atkinson, meaning, "grey, bright in fame."
GOLD SIXPENCE	K. name for a Shetland Sheep Dog, a Ch.
HATHOR	K. name for a Ch. West Highland White Terrier.
HILTIE - SKILTIE	"helter-skelter."
HOURL	"to trail."
HUTHER-MY-DUDS	"ragged one; tatter-demalion."
INK-SPOT	K. name for a Collie.
JOCK	"beloved." Also: JOHNY, IAN, IAIN Pop.: John
KAIRD	"Gypsy."
KENNET	"old Scotch dialetic word for 'hunting dog.'"
KERNE	"foot soldier." Pop.: Kearney
KILTIE	K. name for a West Highland White Terrier..
KING COAL	Sunnybank K. name for a Collie.
KNURL	"dwarf."
LACHLAN	"warlike."
LADDIE	"boy." Pop.: Ladd
LAIRD	"landowner."
LAYLO	K. name for a White Collie.
LERO	K. name for a Collie.
LIBERATION	K. name for a Collie.

LOAFER	K. name for a Collie.
MAGISTRATE	K. name for a Collie.
MERIT	K. name for a West Highland White Terrier.
MERRY DANCER	"northern lights."
MESSIN	"our; mongrel."
MIRK	"dark."
MISLEAR'D	"mischievous."
MORRICE	"dark." Pop.: <u>Maurice</u>
NICHOL	"victory."
NIETS	"chief; champion."
NIGEL	"black."
NOBELMAN	K. name for a Collie.
NORN	"from the North."
OLD TWIG	K. name for a Collie.
PARADER	K. name for a Collie.
PARAGON	K. name for a Collie, meaning, "a match; an equal."
PATIE	"noble." Also: PATE, PAYTON, PEYTON. Pop.: <u>Patrick</u>
PICADOR	K. name for a Collie, meaning, "to prick; irritate."
PRIDE	K. name for a Golden Retriever.
RABBIE	Old Highland pet name, meaning, "bright fame." Also: ROBBIE Pop.: <u>Robert</u>
RANDY	"tough; rascal."
RASCAL	K. name for a Ch. Scotch Terrier.

RITCHIE	"stern." Pop.: <u>Richard</u>
RIGH	"king."
RIGHTAWAY	K. name for a Collie.
ROMMIE	K. name for a Carn Terrier.
ROYAL	a Collie in Rip and Royal by Sir Walter Scott whose full name is Prince Royal Robert Mackenzie III.
ROYAL RIBBONS	K. name for a Shetland Sheepdog.
SANDPIPER	K. name for a Dandie Dinmont Terrier. So named because of the color of a sandpiper.
SAUNT	"saint."
SAWNEY	"sandy."
SCEPTER	K. name of a Collie.
SCOTTISH CHIEF	K. name for a Skye Terrier.
SEA BREAZE	K. name for a Collie.
SHAVER	"funny fellow."
SINBAD	K. name for a Cairn Terrier, meaning, a character in the Arabian Nights Entertainment who relates the stories of his seven voyages.
SIN	"son."
SINNY	"sunny; sonny."
SKEAN DHU	"black blade; knife."
SODA	K. name for Scotch Terrier.
STEENIE	"crown."
STRONGHEART	Triple Ch. Collie, of the movies.
TAM GLEN	K. name for a Scotch Terrier.
TAMMIE	"a twin." Pop.: <u>Thomas</u>
TELEK	Dwight Eisenhower's Scotch Terrier when in the army.
THANE	Sunnybanks K. name for a Collie.

TOWN TOPIC	K. name for Collie.
THUNDER	K. name for Scottish Deerhound.
TRIAD	the collie resulting from the crossing of rough and smooth collies.
WARLOCK	"a wizard."
WILLOUGHBY	K. name for a Shetland Sheepdog, meaning, "from the place of the willows."

Female

AILIE	"famous fighter." Also: ALISON, LEOT Pop.: Louise
ANNIE LAURIE	K. name for a Scotch Terrier.
ASE	"ashes."
AWA	"away."
AWANK	"awake."
BABBIE	"little stranger." Also: BABIE Pop.: Barbara
BANG	"to thump."
BAULD	"bold."
BAWS'NT	"white streaked."
BELLE	K. name for a West Highland Terrier.
BERTA	"bright." Also: BERTINA Pop.: Bertha
BEWITCHING	K. name for a Scotch Terrier.
BIRR	"force; vigor."
BIRSES	"bristles."
BIT	"small; nick of time."
BLACK BRIDESMAID	K. name for a Collie.
BLACK NEBBIT	"black nosed."
BLAE	"blue."

BLASTIE	"a little witch."
BLEEZE	"blaze."
BODIE	Scotch coin worth only 2 cents.
BONNIE	"pretty, beautiful, good." Scottish love this name.
BONNIE BELLE	A K. name for a Scottish Terrier, meaning, "good, beautiful."
BONNIE GRETA	"the beautiful and good pearl."
BOOT	"payment to the bargain."
BRATTLE	"to scamper."
BRIDGET	K. name for a Scotch Terrier, meaning, "the mighty, or high." An Irish name.
BRIDE	"the mighty or high." Pop.: Bridget
BUFF	"to bang, thump."
CANTIE	"cheerful; lively; jolly."
CANTS	"merry doings."
CATRIN	"pure." A K. name given to a Collie.
CHEARY	"cheery."
CLEG	"gadfly."
CLUNNY	K. name for a Collie.
CRONIE	"intimate friend."
DAFT	"mad; foolish."
DAKE	"First Scotch terrier registered in America." In Scottish law Daker meant ten or twelve. Then Dake might have been the 10th in the litter? Or the 10th owned by her master?
DAWTIE	"darling; or dearly beloved."
DIDDLE	"move quickly."
DONALDINA	"world princess." Pop.: Donalda

DOOFLU	"woeful."
EDIE	"happy."
EFFIE	"pleasant; of good report." Also: PHEMIE Pop.: <u>Euphemia</u>
ELECTORA	K. name for a Ch. Collie, meaning, "bright."
ENCHANTING	K. name for a Ch. Collie.
ENCHANTRESS	K. name for a Ch. Scotch Terrier.
FAIR ELLEN	Sunnybanks K. name for a Collie.
FALA	F. D. Roosevelt's Scotch terrier.
FANCY	K. name for a Collie.
FLORY	"to flower; flourish." Pop.: <u>Florence</u>
FRIZETTA	"rich peace." K. name for a Collie.
FUTURE	K. name for a Collie.
GLINT	"sparkle."
GORM	"blue."
GOWD	"gold."
GRACIE	"the loved." Pop.: <u>Grace</u>
GRIZE	"gray battle-maid; grey-eyed one." Pop.: <u>Griselda</u>
HAND-WAL'D	"hand picked; choicest."
HANSEL	"a first gift."
HEATHER	K. name for a Scottish Deerhound.
HEIDI	"modest; beautiful." K. name for a Collie.
HELP AND HAND	A Scottish Deerhound that belonged to King Robert Bruce.

ILKA	"each and every one."
ISBEL	"royal name." Also: TIBBIE Pop.: Isobel
JEANIE	"gracious." Also: JOANNA, JANET, JEAN, JOAN, JENNY. Pop.: Jane
KATIE	"pure." Pop.: Catherine
KELDA	"spring, or fountain."
KELL	"red chalk."
KINTLIN	"cuddling."
KIRSTY	"a patrician; little follower." Also: KIRSTIE, CHRISTEL, CHRISTIE Pop.: Christina
LAMMIE	"lamb."
LASSIE	"little maid; term of endearment."
LEDDY	"lady."
LEESE-ME-ON	"dear to me."
LINT-WHITE	"flax color."
LITTLE STARLIGHT	K. name for a Shetland Sheepdog.
LOGIC	K. name for a Collie.
LOOSOME	"loveable."
LORINDA	"little learned one." K. name given to a Scottish Deerhound.
LOYALTY	K. name for a Ch. Collie.
MAIDA	"maiden." Name of Scottish Deerhound owned by Sir Walter Scott.
MAK'O	"pet."
MELL	"meddle."
MIM	"prim; meek."

MOTTIE	"dusty."
MEGGIE	Name of Scottie belonging to F.D. Roosevelt, which is a more endearing and familiar a term than Meg.
MISCHIEF	K. name for a Shetland Sheepdog.
MYSIE	"a pearl." Also: MEG, MARJORIE MAISIE. Pop.: Margaret
NANTY	"gracious." Pop.: Ann
NUTMEG	A mustard colored Dandie Dinmont Terrier.
PACK AN'THICK	"confidential."
PATTERN	K. name for a West Highland White Terrier.
PENNY FEE	"wage in money."
PERFECTION	K. name for a Collie.
PLISKIE	"tricky."
PRIMSIE	"precise."
PRUDENCE PRIM	Name of White Collie belonging to Calvin Coolidge.
PURITY	K. name for a Collie.
QUEAN	"a lass."
RAG-A-BASH	"idle; ragged one."
RAG DOLL	K. name for a Ch. Scotch Terrier.
RAGGIL	"rascal."
RANTS	"merry meetings."
REAM	"cream."
RED-WAT-SHOD	"red, wet, shod."
REEKIE	"smoky."
RIBBON-RAIDER	K. name of a Ch. Scotch Terrier.
RIN	"to run."

RIVE	"tug; tear."
ROOSTY	"rusty."
SATISFACTION	K. name of a Collie.
SAVEY SUE	K. name of a Ch. Cairn Terrier.
SAXON MAID	"from Robin Hood stories."
SELMA	"fair; courageous; constancy."
SHADOW	K. name of a Scotch Terrier.
SIBBIE	"wise." Pop.: Sibyl
SILLER	"silver."
SILVER LASS	K. name for a Skye Terrier.
SNAW	"snow."
SNOW WHITE	K. name for a West Highland White Terrier.
SWEEP	Name of a working Border Collie.
TEVIS	"quick temper."
TWIG	K. name for a Collie.
VAUNTIE	"proud."
WANRESTFU'	"restless."
WARL'Y	"worldly."
WHINSTONE	K. name of a Scotch Terrier.
WHITE HOPE	K. name of a West Highland White Terrier.
WIGHT	"stout; strong."
WINDFLOWER	K. name for a Ch. Dandie Dinmont Terrier. Showy, multi-colored sepals; anemone.
WISHFUL	K. name for a Cairn Terrier.
WORDY	"worthy."
YULE	"Christmas."

WELSH DOGS

Sealyham Terrier
Welsh Corgi (Cardigan)
Welsh Corgi (Pembroke)
Welsh Springer Spaniel
Welsh Terrier

Names

Male

AED	"witness." Pop.: Ed
ALDEBARAN	"red star."
AMBASSADOR	K. name given to a Welsh Springer Spaniel.
ARROW STRAIGHT	"fast as an arrow; straight as an arrow."
ARVEL	"wanderer."
AWST	"implies awe; respect; admiration." Also, "belonging to August." Pop.: August
BOOTLEGGER	Name given to a Ch. Sealyham Terrier.
BRIGADE	Name given to a Sealyham Terrier.
CADELL	"strength in war."
CI SAWDL	"welsh heeler."
CLYDE	"heard from afar." A river in Scotland.
CONCERTO	Name given to a Pembroke Welsh Corgi.
CORGI	"cattle dog; dwarf dog." Comes from Curgi, cur meaning, "to

watch over."

DEINOIL	"judge." Pop.: Daniel
DICK TURPIN	Name given a Welsh Terrier show dog of 1893.
DUFAN	"the tamed; taming." Pop.: Damon
DYLAN	"the sea." Honors the Brythonic god of the waves.
FOX	Name given to a Pembroke Welsh Corgi.
GIROEL	"lordly." Pop.: Cyril
GOLD CHARM	Name given to a Ch. Welsh Terrier.
GRIFFYN	"red-haired." Also: GRIFFETH, GRUFFYDD, GRIFFYDD. Pop.: Rufus
GUILLIM	"protector." Also: GUILLYN Pop.: William
GYDION	"of the hill; destroyer of trees." The god of magic and sky.
GWYN	"white or fair." A god and mighty hunter.
HAPPY TALK	K. name for a Welsh Corgi.
HARRIBOY	K. name for a Welsh Terrier.
HOWELL	"the spirit."
HU	"lofty." Pop.: Hugh
IOLA	"divine." Pop.: Julius
ILAR	"cheerful; merry; hilarious." Pop.: Hilary
JON	"God is gracious." Also: JONE Pop.: John

JORWARTH	lit. "a guardian or defender of property." Pop.: Edward
JULION	"belonging to Julius." Pop.: Julian
KYNAN	"chief; king." Pop.: Conan
LLEW	"famous warrior." Pop.: Lewis
LLEWELLYN	"fast as lightning." Also: LUGH Pop.: Lllewellyn
LLOYD	"the gray." Also: LLWYD Pop.: Lloyd
LUCIFER	Name given to a Welsh Terrier.
LUD OF THE SILVER HAND	"god of the flocks."
MACSEN	"the greatest." Pop.: Maxmilian
MEGAN	"the great." K. name for a Welsh Corgi. Also: MEGHAN
MEURIZ	"dark in color." Pop.: Maurice
MISCHIEF	Name given to a Sealyham Terrier.
MR. SNOWMAN	Name given to a Sealyham Terrier.
MORVYRN	"sea friend." Also: MORVRAN Pop.: Morven
MUSICMAKER	Name given to a Pembroke Welsh Corgi.
MYRRDIN	"a falcon." Pop.: Merlin
OWAIN	"youth; young warrior." Also: JEVAN Pop.: Evan
PEMBROKE	"from the headland."
RAINDROP	Name given to a Sealyham Terrier.
RARE-BIT	Name given to a Ch. Welsh Terrier.

ROCKET

Name given to a Cardigan Welsh Corgi.

STARSMAN

K. name given to a Welsh Terrier.

Female

ARIANA

"silver."

AVELINE

"pleasant."

BEATA

"she who makes happy."
Also: BETTRYS   Pop.: Beatrice

BELINDA

"shining; bright."

BRIDE

"mighty or high; strong."
Pop.: Bridget

BRONWEN

"the white bosomed." Old Welsh name honoring the goddess queen of pagan Ireland.

CAINTIGERN

"fair lady."

CATHWG

"pure."

CORDULA

"the sea jewel." Also: ULA
Pop.: Cordelia

DAVIDA

"the beloved." Also: TAFFY, TAFLINE   Pop.: Vida

ELLIN

"light."   Pop.: Helen

ENAID

"the soul; spotless purity."
Pop.: Enid

ELIDAN

"belonging to Julius; downy-face; soft-haired."

GANORE

"the white one."   Also: GAIVRE
Pop.: Genevieve

GRISAILLE	"various tones and shades of gray."
GWENDOLEN	"white or fair." Pop.: Gwyn
GWETHALYN	"life; vitality; animated." Pop.: Vita
JODOTHA	"happiness; playful." Pop.: Jocosa
JOSKET	K. name for a Pembroke Welsh Corgi.
KYNA	"wise lady." F. of Kynan, or Conan, meaning, "the wise or chief."
LLEULU	"light." Pop.: Lucy
LYNETTE	"flaxon-haired." Also: LYNET Pop.: Linnet
MADONNA	K. name for a Welsh terrier.
MAIDOC	"goodly; have benefit." F. of the Welsh Madoc. Welsh favorite name, as Madoc was the hero who was supposed to have discovered Amer- ica.
MAIR	"star of the sea; lady of the sea." Pop.: Mary
MISS	Name given to a Sealham Terrier.
MORGAN	"shore of the sea; sea woman."
PRIMROSE	K. name given to a Welsh Corgi, meaning, "the first rose."
RAPUNZEL	"golden-haired." K. name for a Welsh Corgi.
RED WING	K. name for a Ch. Welsh Corgi.
ROCKET	K. name for a Ch. Welsh Corgi.
RUTHIN	Name given to a Ch. Welsh Corgi.

SEREN	K. name given to a Welsh Corgi, meaning, "calm."
STARMIST	Name given to a K. Sealyham Terrier.
SUNBOW	K. name given to a K. Sealyham Terrier.
SUNDEW	Name given to a Ch. Welsh Terrier.
TANGO	Name given to a Welsh Terrier.
TEWDIVER	"gift." Pop.: <u>Theodore</u> and <u>Theodosius</u>
TOP-BID	K. name given to a Welsh Terrier.
T'OTHER AND WHICH	First pair of Welsh Terriers brought to America.
TREFOR	"prudent." Pop.: <u>Trevor</u>
TUDOR	"God's gift." Pop.: <u>Theodore</u>
VENTURE	K. name for a Welsh Terrier.
VORTIGERN	"king with the soul of a sacred dragon."
WALLIS	lit. "a Welsh girl."
WOOD	"from the forest."
YNYR	"honorable." Pop.: <u>Honour</u>

FISH & AMPHIBIANS
SALAMANDERS & NEWTS

FISH & AMPHIBIANS
SALAMANDERS & NEWTS

ALLIGATOR

  "ALLY OP, JR."

ANGEL FISH

  BEAU GREGORY   "Beautiful."

  CRACK SHOT   Sends jets of water straight at a blue bottle fly; the fly falls and is caught by the fish. It has been called "Shooting Fish," "Archer Fish."

  FINGER PRINT   Marks like thumb prints are seen on its sides, near the back.

  HALF MOON   Another name for this fish.

  SILVER DOLLAR   It looks like a silver dollar.

  LADDER   There are bars on its fins, and is called Ladder, or Scalare fish.

BEACON FISH

  SPOT LIGHT   Head and tail lights are bright red glowing spots above the eye pupil and at the tail.

BLACK WIDOW FISH

  ELECTRA   From the play, "Mourning Becomes Electra," by Eugene O'Neill. The fish is black as though in mourning.

  RAINCOAT   Or Black Raincoat. Any fish has scales and slime to protect it from water; though it is not completely water proof.

BLOODFIN

  FLAME   The fins are fire-like in color.

BLOODFIN (continued)

IRISH	An Irishman usually has red hair, and the fins are red.
RED FLAG	All the fins are bright red.

BLUE DEVIL

POMACE	From the Scientific name which is, "Pomacentrus."

BULLHEAD

CONVOY	Parents keep their young together like a convoy, guarding them by swimming around them.

CATFISH

CAMOFLAGE	Dark spots on the body change according to the surroundings.
SCAVENGER	Eats things other fish will not eat.
SHOW OFF	It swims in an inverted position.
WATER KITTEN	It has whiskers like a kitten.
WHISKERS	For the whiskers.
X-RAY	The glass catfish looks more like an X-Ray picture than a fish.

CHAMELEON

ACROBAT	Leaps from leaf to leaf in the trees.
LIGHTNING	It thrusts out its tongue very fast.
NIGHT LOVER	Strictly dirunal.
SLIM	It is very slender.
TURRET	He has turret mounted eyes that swivel independently.
VERMILION	The dewlap under the chin is this color.

COOLIE

PINK LEMONADE	Half-banded coolie is orange-pink colored, looks like pink lemonade.

CRAB

MASQUERADE	Spider crab looks like a spider in

CRAB (continued)

	disguise.
PAGOO	A crab in "Pagoo," by Holling C. Holling.
SEAWEED	The spider crab carries seaweed about for a disguise.
SPIDER	Spider crab looks like a spider in disguise.
CHRISTOPHER	After Christopher Columbus who discovered the Sargasso Sea where he found a crab swimming in the thickly tangled weed.
BLACK FINGERS	The mud crabs have black-fingered claws.
BULLY	The green crab is a pugnacious fighter.

DANSEL FISH

NIGHT & DAY	It has black and white markings.
SHARPS AND FLATS	Piano keys are black and white.

EEL

GRACE	The eel is graceful.
OSTRICH	It buries all but its head in the sand or mud; while ostrich buries only its head.
HELENA	The Romans esteemed the eel the Helena of their feast for it is a dainty fish.
QUEEN	It is also considered by some to be the queen of palate pleasure.

FROG

BANJO	Bull frog's call is like a plucked banjo string.
"BETTER GO ROUND"	Bull frog's deep bass voice seems to say this.
BLINKER	The frog blinks.
BUBBLES	The tree frog inflates bubbles that act as a sounding board.

FROG (continued)

'CELLO	Some say green frog has a deep voice like a cello.
CHUG-A-RUM	Some think that the frog says this.
CROAKER	Name of a frog in "Wild Folk at the Pond," by Carroll Lane Fenton.
FLIP TONGUE	Frog's quick tongue.
"GARUMPH"	Or "Humph," says frog.
GOGGLES	Frog looks as though he wore goggles.
JUG A RUM?	Asks frog in "Here Come the Beavers."
LEAPER	Frog jumps high.
MR. SPITTLETOES	In "Two Little Mice," by Katharine Pyle.
PIGMY	Young tree frog is as small as the tip of a finger.
PROPHET	Tree frog has an undeserved name as a weather prophet, of predicting a storm, for they are stirred to life by unusual moisture in the air.
"MY PLEASURE."	Grins bullfrog, smirking at you.
OLD CLOCK	"Swamp tree frog sounds as though he was winding up a slow, noisy old clock."
SPLASH	Frog splashes into the pond.
TIM TADPOLE	In "Tim Tadpole and the great bullfrog," by Marjorie Flack.
THEODORE	In the Freddy Stories by Walter Brooks.
TUNG!	Sound that green frog makes.
WAGTAIL	In "Wagtail," by Alice Gall & Fleming Crew.

GLASSFISH

UNITED NATIONS	A peace loving fish; can see what

GLASS FISH (continued)

is going on inside it. So is the United Nations a peace loving organization and everyone knows just about what it is trying to do.

GOLDFISH

BRIDE — The Veiltail has beautiful fins that look lacy and soft, like the clothes of a bride.

CHECKS — Red and white colors make one think of a red and white checked tablecloth.

PLUMES — The Veiltail has plumy, wavy fins.

STUBBY — The Chinese has a short tail.

GUPPY

AURORA — From Aurora Borealais, for the male guppy is all colors.

BLACK STAR — The European Veil type guppy is all black best produced in Europe, therefore a star.

BLUE FLAG — Trinidad's tail is blue.

BROOM — Also, SWEEPER, and BRUSH. Broad tail's tail looks like a sweeping broom.

CANNIBAL — Guppy parents eat their young sometimes.

CIRCUS — A guppy is many colored like a circus.

FLORABELLE — A veiled tailed guppy has a fancy tail and the name Florabelle is a fancy name.

"HAPPY-GO-LUCKY" — Always happy.

JEWEL — The male guppy is jewel-like in coloring.

MIDGET — The guppy is tiny.

MIDNIGHT — A black guppy.

MOSQUITO — It eats mosquito larvae and is a tiny fish.

GUPPY (continued)

OLIVE	For this colored guppy.
PEACOCK	So called because of his many colors.
POP EYE	The young guppies develop all-seeing pop-eyes to escape being eaten by parents.
PRISM	All colors of a guppy are like many colors in a prism.
RAINBOW	Its many colors, like a rainbow.
SLIM	Scartail has very slim waist.

HOG CHOKER

RIBBONS	It looks like ribbon, thin, wavy as it swims.
STARS & STRIPES	Spots look like stars; it has stripes.

GOURAMI

EVENING GOWN	It looks like pearls and lace.
POLKA DOT	The pearl gourami has a speckled look.
PUDGY	The dwarf gourami is round, short, plumpish.

LIONHEAD

BUTTERBALL	It is short and plump.
KING	The "lion" is king of the beasts.
GLUTTONHEAD	It is only interested in what it is going to have for dinner.
LITTLE WIGGLER	It wiggles when it swims.

LIZARD

DESERT DRESS	Horny toad, or lizard is like the brown earth.
FAKIR	Horned toad puffs up, hisses, which is all show, for it is harmless.
FLECK	The sand lizard, or horned toad, is flecked with brown, yellow,

LIZARD (continued)

	black.
"GECKO"	Western Gecko lizard squeaks "gecko."
HOT ROD	The fence lizard runs very fast.
LIGHTNING	The fence lizards are as quick as lightning.
PRICKLES	Sand lizard or horny toad has horns and spikes.
RACER	Fence lizards are fast runners.
ROCKY	Ground Uta lives in rocky nooks.
SHIMMY	Horned toad, when frightened, shimmies from side to side, pushing into the sand.
SPECK	Horned toad, or sand lizard are flecked with colors.
SPEEDY	Fence lizard for his speed.
VIGILANTE	The night lizards are vigilant.

LYREFISH

CHIFFON	His tail is airy and light.
FILLY	The tail is made of fine fillaments.

MOLLIES

BLACK MOLLY	The color is black.
SOOT	For a black moll.
BLACK VELVET	The black mollie.
MIDNIGHT	The black mollie.
QUAKER	The grey speckled with black.
DON JUAN	Enthusiastic, follow the female ceaselessly.

MOUSEFISH

FISHER, the	The mousefish fishes.
MARBLE	They are spotted, like marble.

MUD PUPPY

RED FEATHERS	The gills are fringed with red at

MUD PUPPY (continued)

	the neck.
RED RUFFLES	The fancy gills are red.
WET SOAP	It is very slippery and slip and slips away like wet soap.

NEWT

CARMEN	The red color of its underparts.
GORGEOUS GEORGE	The red color is beautiful.
PITCH	The color of its back is black.
TARI	From the Scientific name Taricha, the western newt.

OBLIQUE FISH

SNOOTY	It swims with its head turned up.

PARADISE FISH

DAWN	It has many colors like the dawn.
JACOB	Jacob, in the Bible, had a coat of many colors.
RAINBOW	It has many colors that make one think of a rainbow.

PLATYS

MOONFACE	It has a crescent moon marking at the base of its tail.
HARVEST MOON	The red moon platy is a deep rich red, like the harvest moon.
WITCHES MOON	The black moon have a greenish sheen. The Gold Wagtail has gold body with black fins and black caudal.
SPARKLES	The blue platy has an iridescent blue-green over olive.
BLUE VEIL	For the blue-green over the olive.
WASH OUT	Sometimes the gold is pale, and looks washed out.

PUFFER

BIG SWELL	The puffer puffs up, inflates, to three times their original size.

PUFFER (continued)

TICKLER — The smooth puffer has prickles confined to area on belly.

TICKER — It makes a clicking sound when air escapes from its throat.

I'LL HUFF & I'LL PUFF — It puffs up.

OPAL — Its eyes look like opals.

LITTLE SQUIRT — It squirts water out at the mouth, and is small.

TETRO — The scientific name for it is "Tetrodon."

RED WINGED SEA ROBIN

FINGERS — Long white fingers grow out of the breast fins.

FLYER — It seems to fly when it swims; a flying fish.

ROBIN GREEN — It's green color.

WHITE FINGERS — See above.

WHITE LACE — Fins look lacy.

HELMET — Has an armored head.

SALMANDER

DOTTY — It is spotted.

GAUDY — The yellow spotted is profuse with spots.

HIDEAWAY — It hides in caves.

MORSE CODE — There is a series of dots and dashes on the tiger salamander.

NICKAJACK — The green salamander was first found in the Nickajack Cave, Tennessee.

PEPPER — The red salamander has pepper spots.

ROCK — The hellbender masquerades as a rock for safety.

SALAMANDER (continued)

LORELEI	The eel-like salamanders are called sirens and Lorelei was a siren.
SLIM JIM	Salamander is long and slender.
TWILIGHT ZONE	Salamander has developed eyes adapted to the dimly lit caves, the 'twilight zone.'

SALMON

HIGH JUMPER	Leaps upward farther than the length of their bodies when young; when older they leap up small water falls.
COOL WATERS	They like the cool water.

SCAVENGER FISH

CAPTAIN HOOK	For his hook nose.

SALLY GROWLER

OLD GROUCH	It looks as though it grumbled and grouched. Makes a growl sound.
SALLY	For the first part of its name.

SEA HORSE

ANCHOR	It holds onto the grasses with its prehensile tail.
DOBBIN	It looks like a horse.
DRAGON	The Australian sea horse is sometimes called 'sea dragon.'
FAIRY	It looks like a sea fairy, or a fairy horse.
FANCY BALL	The Australian sea horse has fancier costume than its plain cousin.
GADGET	Its tail is a handy gadget for winding around anything when not swimming.
GREEN SCARF	The Australian sea horse looks as if it had a scarf flowing around it, for it has many ragged appendages.

SEA HORSE (continued)

INSIDE OUT	It looks as though it had its skeleton on the outside.
CREST	There are shields that ride on the back of it and produce a crest on head, neck and back.
LET GEORGE DO IT	The father hatches the eggs in its pouch.
SAFE POCKETS	Its pouch is used to hide the young when they become frightened.
SEA PONY	It looks like a pony or horse.
SMACKER	It has no teeth, so snaps its jaws when it eats making a faint smacking sound.
TAIL CLUTCH	It anchors its tail to weeds or grasses.
VEST POCKET	Sea horse has a pouch.
YELLOW TRIM	Males have the dorsal fin trimmed in yellow.
YELLOW EYES	The color of its eyes.
CREEPER	It can creep on the bottom by little movements of tail and body.
BLACK KNIGHT	It is usually a black or dark grey, flecked with brilliant spots.
BLACK CHARGER	A black sea horse.
JEAN PAINLEVÉ	After the man whose skillful studies with the motion picture camera made it possible for the layman to observe and understand sea horses.
STAR	Its pigmentation look like stars that cover the whole body in adulthood.

SEA URCHIN

SHOCK ABSORBER	The sea urchin has long, sharp pointed spines covering it, which act as shock absorbers against

| | the violent contact with rocks. |
| NEEDLES | It has needle pointed spines. |

SIAMESE FIGHTING FISH

BETTA	The first part of the Scientific name, "Betta splenders."
BUBBLES	It is a bubble nest builder.
SPLENDOUR	Long flowing colored finnage trail through the water on the male.
SUB	It looks like a little submarine.
VEILTAIL	It has a tail that is veil like.
BANNERS	The flowing finnage larger than the fish itself.
GAY BANNERS	As above.
BULLY	Pugnacious fish.
CORNFLOWER	Color of the blue fighting fish.

SNAIL

FLAT FOOT	Its one foot that moves when it walks.
POKE ALONG	It doesn't move very fast.
SLOW POKE	As above.
PLODDER	It takes snail a long time to get where he is going.
TRAILER	It leaves a transparent ribbon in its wake.

SNAKES

BUZZTAIL	In "Buzztail," by Robert M. Mc Clung.
CHECKERS	The belly of the milk snake is checkered.
GREEN CHECKS	The garter snake's skin is checked.
HIGH WIRE	The chicken snake climbs to 25 feet above the ground.
JOE	An Anaconda in the Bronx Zoo.

SNAKES (continued)

KAA	In the Jungle Books, by Rudyard Kipling.
KALA NAG	"Black snake," in the Jungle Books.
KARAIT	A snakeling in the Jungle Book.
KEE - NA - BEEK	American Indian name for 'snake.'
KING	King snakes rule the serpent family. They attack and kill other snakes including the poisonous, though they are gentle themselves.
LITTLE BURROWER	The Worm snake resembles earthworm and burrows into the earth.
MÁ NA TÓ	American Indian name for 'snake.'
NAG	"Black cobra," in Jungle Book. Shortened form of Kala Nag.
NAGAINA	Nag, the black cobra's wife, in Jungle Books.
PLAID BLANKET	The Corn snake's skin is plaid.
PLAIN JANE	Water snake is plain bellied.
RED BAND	The Mountain King snake has red bands.
RING NECK	King Snake has rings around it.
SHOVELER	Common hog nosed snake digs up toads; is harmless.
SLIM GREEN	In "Slim Green" by Louise Dyer Harris & Norman Dyer Harris.
SOUND OFF!	Sounds that snake makes.
LOTTA SPOTS	The Garter snake has a lot of spots.
TRIO	The Garter snake has 3 stripes the length of its body.
WA RUH	American Indian for 'snake.'
WAKA	American Indian for 'snake.'
FERDINAND	A King Cobra in the Staten Island Zoo.

STICKLEBACK FISH

BULLY, the Guard	The Stickleback male guards the nest even from the other parent, butting the female out of the way.
PERT	A characteristic of the stickleback.
SCARLET TIE	It has a red splash on its neck.
WORRY WART	The male worries over the nest of eggs and guards it.

SUNFISH

HEAD HUNTER	It hunts for snails to eat.
PUMPKIN	Looks like a pumpkin seed.
RUBY	Its eyes are like rubies.
SATIN	Its skin glistens.

SWORDTAIL

SILVER	The lower part of the body is silver.
SPIKE	It has spikes on its tail.
QUAKER	The female wears subdued colors.

TOAD

BUFO	In "Bufo" by Robert McClung.
CHOIR BOY	Toad's voice, singing.
LUMPY	A toad's skin feels lumpy.
MIMIC	Tree toad takes an hour to change his clothes to look like his surroundings.
MISTER TOAD	From "Wind in the Willows," by Kenneth Grahame.
PUFFIN	The toad puffs.
TOUGHY	The skin is tough; warty.
TRILLER	The voice of toad.
WARTS	Toad has warts on him.

TORTOISE

ARMORED TANK	The first armored tank was a tortoise.

TORTOISE (continued)

TOP SPEED	360 yards an hour.

TURTLE

BUKH KE NOK	"Great turtle." American Indian name.
CAROLINA	The box turtle Scientific name is "Terrapin carolina."
HUMPHREY	Because it humped along in such a funny way, in "Humphrey," by Marjorie Flack.
ME SHE GA	"Little turtle," in American Indian language.
MIS KE NAKE	"Turtle" in American Indian language.
MISTAKE	A child thought her turtle was masculine, found it to be female.
MISTER TURTLE	In "The Cunning Turtle," by Kurt Wiese.
NO MA THA	"Turtle," in American Indian language.
OSMOND	The turtle in "Judy and her turtle Osmond," by Jane Quigg.
PROWLER	The turtle prowls around.
RED EYE	The male box turtle has red eyes.
SLOW WIT	It took 39 trials for the turtle to master a simple elevated maze test given by Dr. Riess at the American Museum of Natural History.
SERPENTINA	The snap turtle.
SLOW FREIGHT	Takes turtle a long time to get anywhere.
SNAPPER	The turtle snaps.
SNORKEL	The Soft shelled turtle has a 'snorkel,' a snout in its head.
THEODORE	In "Theodore Turtle," by Ellen MacGregor.

TURTLE (continued)

TILLY THE TURTLE	Name given it by small boy.
WE LOON SEE	American Indian name for "small turtle."
WEB FOOT	The snapping turtle has a web foot.
YELLOW EYE	The female box turtle has yellow eyes.
YERTLE	In "Yertle the turtle" by Dr. Seuss.
MIN	In "Min of the Mississippi" by Holling C. Holling. Min travelled down the Mississippi river from its source to the mouth.

WEATHERFISH

SAND STORM	It works in sand, sending clouds of sand above its head.
WHISKERS	It has whiskers.

ZEBRA FISH

ARROW	It moves very quickly.
PRISON STRIPES	Both male and female are horizontally striped.
OLD LADY	The female is silvery white.

HORSES

HORSES

ABBE, THE	A leading pacer, male.
ABBOTT, THE	In 1900 best mile, performed by world champion.
ABDALLAH	The most amazing trotting horse ever lived. It is also the name of a Barb. It means, 'servant of God.'
ABOYEUR	His sire was Desmond. He is winner of English Derby, 1913.
ABU BAHA	An Arabian, a champion stallion and sire.
ABU ZEYOD	Arabian, male. Hero in the Arabian Nights Entertainment.
ACE OF DIAMONDS	Race horse.
ACT NOW	Race horse.
ADELINE	Won Castleton Farm Stake in 1947.
ADIO ABE	A pacer, leading money maker in 1952.
ADIOS	"Goodbye." A pacer and leading money maker.
ADMIRAL	Grand Champion Stallion in 1942, at Maryland Show.
ADORABLE SUE	Race horse.
ADOUNAD	An Arabian stallion.
AGGIE DOWN	A pacer.
AGILE	Won the Kentucky Derby in 1905.
AHMUR	A red Arabian horse.
AIDA DE BIERBEEK	A Grand Champion Belgian mare.
AIMIE	A Percheron.
AIMWELL	Winner of Epsom Derby in 1785.

242

AIRDALE	Sired by Tregantle.
AL AZHAR	Arabian horse, meaning, 'after the oldest university in the world,' which is now in Cairo.
AL HADR AL BASHIR	Hadr means, <u>descent</u>; Bashir, <u>Messenger of victory.</u>
AL MARAH TAI	"Fun; good time." Name given to an Arabian horse.
ALACRAN	Means, "scorpion." Name given to a mustang. The raised tail resembles the tail of a scorpion.
ALAN A DALE	Kentucky Derby Winner in 1902.
ALCADE	A thorough bred stallion first in team tying in 1946.
ALCAZAR	An Arabian chestnut stallion.
ALEMITE	A pacer in 1949.
ALDEBARAN	The Arabian horse in "Ben Hur" by Lew Wallace.
ALHAAMED	"Famous; thankful." Arabian horse name.
ALIBI BLUE	A race horse.
ALIBASTRO	A race horse.
ALL OUR LOVE	Name given a race horse.
ALLEN WINTER	A leading trotter.
ALLERTON	A leading sire of thoroughbred horses, up to 1918.
ALLIFAH	An Arabian mare, meaning, 'tamed very well.'
ALSAB	Name given an Arabian, meaning, "phenomenal."
AMAGANSETT	A steeple chaser.
'AMAYIR	"Flourishing." Name given an Arabian horse.
AMBEGINNING	Name given a race horse.
AMBUSH	Name given a race horse.
AMELIA	Name given an American Saddle

	Horse.
AMERICAN ECLIPSE	One of the most famous horses ever raced in the U. S. Began to be hailed as fastest horse in America when he was challenged by Sir Henry of the South.
AMERICAN FLAG	Sired by Man O'War.
AMERICAN GIRL	A race horse.
AMERICAN WAY	Steeple chaser.
ANCHORS AWEIGH	Sired by Man O'War.
ANDIAMO	In "The Turn of the Wheel," by Dorothea Donn Byrne.
ANDREW JACKSON	Considered the fastest trotter of his day.
ANDY'S BEACON	Race horse.
ANGEL FLIGHT	Race horse.
ANGEL'S ORPHAN	Race horse.
ANGELS PEAK	Race horse.
ANGIOLA	A leading trotter.
ANITA	A Mustang mare.
ANKERWYCHE CRIBAN SNOWDON	A Welsh pony.
ANNIBAL	A steeple chaser.
ANNA BRADFORD'S GIRL	A leading pacer.
ANTARES	Arabian horse in "Ben Hur," by Lew Wallace. Antares was a hero in Arabian History.
APOLLO	Kentucky Derby winner, 1882.
APRIL	A race horse.
APRIL STAR	A leading pacer, and a money maker.
APUKWA	A Clydesdale that won 37 prizes, on the honor roll of Clydesdale sires given by the Clydesdale Horse Society of Great Britain.

APOGEE	A race horse.
APRIL FLIRT	A race horse.
APRIL FOOL	1891 Quarter Horse racer.
ARABIAN LAD	A race horse.
ARC LIGHT	Steeple chaser.
ARCTIC QUEEN	A race horse.
ARD PATRICK	English Derby winner in 1902.
ARDELIE	A leading pacer and money maker.
ARIDE	A Percheron.
ARIEL	A sprinter and sire of precocious sprinters, a speed horse.
ARION	Was purchased for 125,000. A race horse.
ARISE	A race horse.
ARISTIDES	Kentucky Derby Winner in 1875. Meaning, an Athenian statesman and general.
ARKABI	"One with the large knee." Name given to a Arabian.
ARMED	Named horse of the year in 1947.
ARMED SOUTH	A race horse.
ARNABI	"Hare-like." Name given an Arabian horse.
ARRETE	Gold medal winner in the Grand Prix des Nations.
ARSLAN	"lion-like." Name given an Arabian.
ARTFUL	Race horse that was a money maker.
ASKMENOW	Race horse.
ASSAULT	Horse of the year in 1946. Won the Triple Crown.
ASSASSIN	Epsom Derby winner in 1782.
ASTRAL KING	American Saddle Horse, 1906.

ATAIR	An Arabian horse in "Ben Hur," by Lew Wallace, which means, 'the flyer, speedy.'
ATROCIOUS	Race horse.
ÄTTILA	Leading money maker, a pacer. Attila was King of the Huns, who invaded Europe.
ATTORNEY	A pacer, leading money maker.
ANGEAS	The top payoff in Tijuana, Mexico in 1933.
AUGUST SUN	A race horse.
AUNT JINNY	A race horse.
AUREOLE	Queen Elizabeth's horse.
AUTUMN DOUBLE	In 1935, this horse made 11,650 on a 60 cent wager. (18,892 to 1)
AVALANCHE	A race horse.
AVENGER BOY	A race horse.
A'WAJ	Lit. "horse of the crippled one." Name given to an Arabian horse.
AXWORTHY	Foaled in 1892, leading sire of thorough bred horses up to 1918.
AZAM	"The great." Name given to an Arabian.
AZBARI	"Of Great shoulder width." Name given an Arabian.
AZIZA	"Dear." Name given an Arabian female.
AZOFF	Son of Peter the Great, and sired Peter Manning. Held the trotting record 15 years.
AZOR	"To visit." Winner of Epsom Derby, 1817.
AZRA	Kentucky Derby Winner 1892.
AZTEC KID	A race horse.

B' HAVEN	A race horse.
BAAL	1932, record pay off.
BABETTE	A Belgian mare.
BABRAM	A Quarter Horse, 1770.
BABY BE READY	A race horse.
BABY DAN	A Percheron.
BACCARAT	Name for a race horse.
BACCHUS	Name given to a Quarter horse in 1778. In Roman Mythology, he was the god of wine.
BACK PAY	Won 289 races.
BADEN	A trotter and a leading money maker.
BADEN BADEN	Kentucky Derby Winner in 1877.
BAGATELLE	A famous steeple chaser.
BAKER STREET	A race horse.
BALA	A horse in "King Solomon's Horses," by Nora Benjamin Kubie. "White swallow."
BALD EAGLE	A pinto in "Cowboy Reader."
BALLOT	In 1908 won $19,750.
BANGAWAY	Earned $124,637.66 through 1952.
BANKRUPT	Foaled 1883, won 348 races.
BAR NONE	A Shire, foaled 1877, won Shire Society Championship in 1882.
BAR PEST	A race horse.
BARAKAT	An Arabian, ridden by Tyrone Power in the motion picture, "Suez."
BARBADECHE	Took the Bickerstaffe Plate in 1948.
BARD, the	1883 race horse.
BARNUM	Won 290 races.
BARON	A Clydesdale. On honor role of Clydesdale sires, given by Clydes-

dale Horse Society of Great Britain.

BARON WORTHY   A Pacer, leading money maker.

BARON'S PRIDE   A Clydesdale. Son of Topgallant, mother was Forest Queen. He won 13 prizes in 1915. One of the greatest Clydesdale sires in Scotland.

BASTARD, the   Won World record in England 1929.

BATEAU   A Mare sired by Man O'War, a race horse.

BATTLE PRINCE   A Pacer.

BATTLESHIP   Won Grand National in England in 1948. A small, splendid jumper. Sired by Man O'War.

BAY BOLTON   English racing mare, bred to Bully Rock 1740, and foal was first thoroughbred born on American soil.

BAY STATE WARDISSA   A Morgan mare.

BAYARD   Sired by Mouton de Gony. A Belgian chestnut roan.

BE GOOD BUSTER   A race horse.

BEAT THE DRUM   A race horse.

BE SURE NOW   His father was Real Sure.

BEAU LYS   A Belgian.

BEAU BUTLER   Considered a real threat in 1926 Kentucky Derby.

BEAU WHITE   A race horse.

BEAU ZAC   A race horse.

BEAUTIFUL BELLS   In 1872 was sired by The Moor, his mother was Minnehaha.

BEAUTY PRINCESS   A race horse.

BED O' ROSES   A race horse.

BEE BEE TEE   A race horse.

BEEFEATER   A race horse.

BEHAVE YOURSELF	1921 Kentucky Derby winner.
BELDAME	1905, Saddle Horse.
BELGIAN FARCEUR	A Clydesdale, in 1917 purchased for $47,500.
BELL BOY	A race horse.
BELLFOUNDER	Hackney horse important in the development and history of the hackney. Foaled in 1815, imported in 1822 from England.
BELLINGSBOROUGH BELLE	A Shire, mare, sold for highest price of a shire mare - $6,200.
BELSIZE	An Arabian race horse.
BEN ALI	Kentucky Derby winner 1886, a pacer, leading money winner.
BEN BRUSH	Descendent of Eclipse. Kentucky Derby winner in 1896.
BEN EAR	A Pacer, leading money maker.
BENEDICT	A race horse.
BERK	'Lightning,' an Arabian stallion.
BERLO	A bay filly. Rang up fifth consecutive victory in the $86,250 dollar Coaching Club American Oaks at Belmont Park, 1960.
BERTS REWARD	Won at Belmont Park, 1949.
BET 'N FRET	A race horse.
BESIGUE	A Percheron.
BETSY GRAY	A pacing filly. Abbedall Stake winner.
BEUZETTA	A trotter, leading money maker.
BEWITCH	A race horse.
BEYOND TIME	A race horse.
BIANCA	"White." A white mare.
BIENFAISANT	A Percheron. Meaning, 'charitable; beneficial.'
BIG BRITCHES	A race horse.

BIG PEBBLE	A race horse.
BIG RACKET	World record in 1945 at Mexico City.
BIG STRANGER	A race horse.
BIG WHITE, the	Sired by Dan, a Percheron, stallion. Old canal horse in Pennsylvania who broke all records in pulling loads. Jan Kip's half-brother.
BILL CODY	A Quarter Horse stallion.
BILL GALLON	A Trotter, leading money maker.
BILL OF RIGHTS	A race horse.
BILLY BARTON	A famous steeple chaser.
BILLY DIRECT	A pacer, bettered Dan Patch performance in 1938. Fastest harness horse the world has ever known.
BIMILECH	Black Toney's last son. Called 'the Boy.'
BINGEN	Leading sire of thoroughbred horses up to 1918.
BITEN	A Thoroughbred gelding.
BITTER FEUD	A race horse.
BLACK ANGEL	Foaled 1927, sire Merry Boy, mother Nell Bramlett. A Tennessee walking horse.
BLACK BESS	Cross the plains pulling a covered wagon. A Percheron.
BLACK COMMENT	A race horse.
BLACK FOG	A race horse.
BLACK GOLD	Kentucky Derby winner in 1924.
BLACK HAWK	A black stallion captured with Black Kettle. A Mustang. Sometimes called Black Pot. Later drew a milk wagon.
BLACK HELEN	A race horse.
BLACK JIN	Mare, descendent of Charles Kent.

BLACK KETTLE	A Kentucky thoroughbred in a Mormon wagon train, a year old black stud that escaped from the Cheyenne Indians that swooped down on the train camped on the trail, only a day from Fort Wallace. Later he was sold to a milkman.
BLACK RAFTERS	An American Quarter horse.
BLACK SQUIRREL	In 1876 foaled. American Saddle Horse.
BLACKHAWK	A Pacer, and leading money maker.
BLACKSTOCK	Winner of the Excelsior Handicap. A four year bay colt by Hanover.
BLACKSTONE	A Pacer, leading money maker.
BLAKE'S FARMER	A Shire.
BLANK CHECK	A race horse.
BLAZE	An Arabian.
BLITZ	A notable Arabian horse, stallion. Had a remarkable record in India as a race horse.
BLOCKADE	Won the Maryland Hunt cup.
BLUE MURDER	In the short story, "Blue Murder," by Wilbur Daniel Steele.
BLUE SKIES	Abbedale Stake Winner, a Pacing filly.
BLUESKIN	Owned by George Washington.
BOATSWAIN	Sired by Man O'War.
BOBCAT	A horse that learned to shake hands.
BOLD VENTURE	Kentucky Derby winner, 1936.
BOLIVAR	A Pacer, leading money maker.
BOMBS AWAY	In 1945, a 2 year old trotter, winner of the Arthur S. Tompkins Memorial.

BONNIE BUCHLYIRE	A Clydesdale that won 16 prizes in 1915. At 9 years brought $26,250 in 1915 at a dispersal sale.
BONNIE SCOTLAND	Imported in 1853 by IAGO.
BOOJUM	Sire of Snark, world's record sprinter.
BORO BLUSTERER	A Shire. Grand Champion Shire Stallion at Panama Pacific and International Live Stock Exposition, 1915.
BOSTON	A great race horse, greater as a sire, son Lexington one of greatest of all sires, and a great race horse.
BOSTON BLUE	In 1818, the first time a horse ever trotted in public, a match against time for $1000.
BOURBON CHIEF	Especially distinctive.
BOURBON KING	In whom great Chief family of Saddle Horses culminated.
BRACADALE	Brilliant performer.
BRANHAM BAUGHMAN	A Pacer, leading money maker.
BRIARD	A Percheron.
BRIDGET	12th Earl of Derby horse winner. Winner of the first Oaks (Epsom Oaks) in 1779.
BRIGHAM PEARL	A Hackney mare.
BOER	A Percheron.
BONAPARTE	A Percheron, imported from France.
BROKERS TIP	Kentucky Derby Winner 1933.
BROOK, the	Famous Steeple Chaser.
BROOMFIELD CHAMPION	Notable sire and great grandson Glancer sired Clyde.
BROOMSTICK	Had great staying power.
BROOMTAIL	A pony, brother to Lightning in "Lightning," by Miriam Mason.

BROWN HAL	Leading sire of Pacers in 1918. He also had a trotting record.
BROWN JACK	Rugged individualist. For 6 consecutive years won Alexandria Stakes at Ascot. Loved crowds, excitement. Seldom lay down to rest, in low iron manger.
BUBBLING OVER	Kentucky Derby Winner 1926.
BUCEPHALUS	"Ox head." A favorite war horse of Alexander, son of King Philip of Macedonia in the story "Wonder Tales."
BUCHANAN	Kentucky Derby Winner 1884.
BUCKSHOT	A Trotter.
BULLDOG	Had speed rather than stamina, most of his offsprings were sprinters.
BULLE ROCK	Imported to Virginia in 1730, first thoroughbred to come to America. A race horse, also called Bully Rock.
BULRUSH	Son of Justin Morgan.
BUNN'S TRINKET	A Shetland pony, and notable sire.
BURGOO KING	Kentucky Derby winner 1932.
BUSHER	Horse of the year, 1945.
BUSHRANGER	A famous steeple chaser.
BUT WHY NOT	A race horse.
BUTTERCUP	A Hackney stallion.
BUTTERMILK	A race horse.
BUZZARD	Imported in 1787.
BYERLY TURK	Introduced into England, famous as a sire and his descendents called the Byerly Turk horse. It is uncertain whether he is of Barb or Arabian origin. Imported in 1690 to England. This line produced the famous Herod.

CADEAU	Highest pay off to players, U. S., in 1913.
CADET	In "Riding," by Benjamin Lewis.
CADET BOOTS	A race horse.
CADMUS	A Percheron.
CAESAR	In "Ben, Story of a Cart Horse."
CAESAR BEY	An Arabian horse.
CALL ME TONY	A race horse.
CALL UP	A Trotter in 1950.
CALLIOPE	In "Caravan," by John Galsworthy.
CALYPSO	Name given a Percheron.
CAMEL	Name given race horse in 1909. Largest pay off on $5.00 win ticket, which was $956.30.
CANNON BALL	Winner in Harness Horse racing, 1940.
CAPOT	Horse of the year in 1949.
CAPTAIN	A Cow pony sorrel in "Cowboy Reader."
CARBINE	He had an artistic temperament. Musket sired him, and Carbine became a better racer than his sire. He performed giant feats. His nickname was "Old Jack."
CAREFREE	Won 67 races. He had wild, eccentric habits, and when you bet, you would bet on whether he would jump the rail, or duck through a gap or stop and look at the landscape.
CARLOS	Don Hernando de Soto's horse, which he brought to Cuba and took to Florida with him.
CARNOT	Name given a Percheron.
CASTLE BOMB	A trotter, champion in 1952.
CAT CALL	A race horse.
CATOMAR	Winner at Fairgrounds in New Orleans, in 1938.

CAVALCADE	The sensation of 1934. He was strictly a router. Up to a mile he was never conspicuous in a race. After the mile mark he gained speed and came on with a terrific burst. Kentucky Derby winner in 1934.
CEDRIC	Name given a Clydesdale.
CENTURION	A race horse.
CHALK EYE	A race horse.
CHARMANTE	Name given to a Percheron.
CHARMING SCOTT	A Pacer.
CHASE ME	Son of Purchase, a brown thoroughbred, a family pet that became famous overnight.
CHALLEDON	Horse of the years, 1939-1940. A favorite son, a plain bay. Thrilling stretch runner.
CHANCE PLAY	A race horse.
CHANT	Kentucky Derby Winner in 1894.
CHASAR	By Crusader-La Belle Helene. Slow to start, great rush in the stretch.
CHELAK	In "Wonder Tales..."
CHENANGO	A famous Steeple Chaser.
CHERI	Name given a Percheron.
CHERRY MALOTTE	A famous Steeple Chaser.
CHESTER DARE	In 1882, an American Saddle Horse.
CHESTNUT	A Shetland pony, and a notable sire.
CHESTNUT BAR	A Trotter.
CHESTNUT PEPTER	He had an illustrious career.
CHICKO	A burro, in "Little Don Pedro," by Helen Holland Graham.
CHIEF COUNSUL	A Pacer, and leading money maker.

"CHIEF OF FOUR MILE" An Appaloosa stallion.

CHAMPION   In 1913, a 2 year old stallion
                     that sold for $20,664.

CHILHOWEE   Means "speedy."

CHOCOLATE SOLDIER   Nickname for Equipoise, because
                     of his color and his courage.

CHINA RED   A race horse.

CHOU CHOU   A French donkey, in "Chou Chou,"
                     by Françoise it means, "dear,
                     darling."

CHÚCARO   In "Chúcaro, wild pony of the
                     Pampa;" by Francis Kalnay.

CICERO   A Cyllene sire, in 1905 winner of
                     English Derby.

CIRCLE IT   A race horse.

CIRCUMNAVIGATOR   A race horse.

CITATION   Became the first horse in history
                     to pass $1,000,000 in earnings.
                     He was triple crown winner in
                     1948 and Horse of the Year in
                     1948. He made $1,085,000 for
                     his owner.

CITOGEN   Name given a Belgian.

CLAN DONA   Name given a Welsh Mountain pony.

CLANDESTINE   A race horse.

CLANG   Had Domino blood.

CLEAR COAST   A race horse.

CLEVELAND FARNLEY   A Cleveland Bay Stallion.

CLOUDY WEATHER   His sire was Mud.

CLOWN PRINCE   A race horse.

CLYDE   Alias Glancer, a Clydesdale and
                     leading in honors at Scotch Exhi-
                     bition.

COALTOWN   A 1948 Sprinter.

COCKATOO   In "Philippa's Fox Hunt," by
                     Somerville and Ross.

COLD DECK	An 1876 American Quarter horse.
COLIN	In 1907 made $24,830 for his owner.
COLLECTOR	In 1831, a Trotter.
COLUMBUS	In 1831, a Trotter.
COMMANDER III	Won the Cambridgeshire.
COMANDO	Almost as fine a race horse as Domino, his sire.
COME ON POP	A race horse.
COMET	A Tennessee Walking horse, chocolate colored.
COMPRE ME ORO	A race horse.
CONFIDENCE	A Hackney mare; sire of many horses of this type of gait (hackney); high stepper with extravagant action.
CONNIVER	A race horse.
CONNOR	A Pacer, leading money maker.
CONQUEROR	A Grand Champion Shire stallion.
CONQUISTADOR	Sired by Spanish Gold.
CONSTANCE	Name given to a Percheron.
COOLE	World's longshot record 3,400-1.
COPPERBOTTOM	1832, an American Quarter horse.
CORIANDER	A son of Messenger.
CORONATION	Winner of the Epsom Derby 1841.
COPPER BOTTOM	Through female line, traces to Janus. Sire was Sir Archy.
COSSACK	In 1847 winner of Epsom Downs Derby.
COTTESMORE	A famous Steeple Chaser.
COUNT FLEET	Horse of the year in 1943. Won triple crown that year.
COUNT HER IN	A race horse.
COUNT TURF	Kentucky Derby winner, 1951.
COUNTERMARCH	A race horse.

COUNTERSPRINT	Horse of the year in 1951. A Pacer.
COUNTESS VIVIAN	A Pacer, champion in 1952.
COUNTRY CAT	A race horse.
COURT JESTER	A Pacer, leading money maker.
COWBOY BOOK	A racer.
COYOTE	A chestnut, in "Cowboy Reader."
CRAFTY SKIPPER	A race horse.
CREATION'S KING	A Hackney stallion.
CREOLE MAID	A race horse.
CRICKET	A Palimino. Also name of a Pacer and leading money maker.
CRISP HORSE	Mare, a Suffolk, in 1768 belonged to Mr. Crisp of Ufford, Sussex. To this horse are traced all pedigrees of the breed that may be registered in the stud book of either England or America. A remarkable breeder.
CRISP'S CUPBEARER	A Suffolk.
CRISTIANO	A mustang.
CROCKETT	A cow pony sorrel in "Cowboy Reader."
CRUSADER	Sired by Man O'War. Also an Arabian gelding.
CRYSTAL BELL	A race horse.
CUCO BRITCHES	In "Gunsmoke," on T. V.
CUMBERLAND	A Clydesdale.
CUNNINGHAM	A notable Arabian Stallion.
CYLLENE	A race horse that sold for $150,000.
CZAR WORTHY	A Trotter and leading money maker.
DAIRING JET	A race horse.
DAIR'ING RED	A race horse.

DAJJANI	"Tame, domesticated one." Name given an Arabian.
DAN	A famous black Percheron.
DAN O'ROURKE	Won Epsom Derby, 1852.
DAN PATCH	A Shire stallion. Champion of International Stock Exposition in 1910 and sold to an Illinois importer for $10,000. A Pacer, whose forebears were trotters.
DANCE OF SPAIN	A race horse.
DANCING DOE	A race horse.
DANDELION	A race horse.
DANDY DAY	An American Quarter horse.
DANDY JIM	In 1900 was an American Saddle Horse.
DANGEGELT	Is important in the history and development of the Hackney horse.
DANGEROUS	Wom Epsom Derby in 1833.
DANIEL LAMBERT	Son of Ethan Allen. Greatest distinction achieved of all his 36 producing sons and daughters.
DAPHNE THE GREAT	A sensation in her time.
DARK PRINCE	A race horse.
DARK SECRET	A gray, or roan that was almost black at first; became lighter and ended up as white as Golden Meadow.
DARK SHADOWS	A race horse.
DARK STAR	A race horse. Winner Kentucky Derby 1953.
DARKER SHADOW	A race horse.
DARLEY ARABIAN	A bay, supposed to be a pure Maneghi Arabian. To the Darley Arabian can be traced the choicest of thorough bred blood. From his line came Eclipse, generally known as the greatest stallion that ever lived.

DARN FLASHY	A champion trotter in 1952.
DARN SAFE	A race horse.
DARNLEY	A Clydesdale. Sire was Conqueror, Dam Keir Peggy, her sons were Darnley, Pollock, Newstead, the latter, all prize winners.
DART SO	A race horse.
DARGAN	An Arabian stallion, meaning 'to proceed, to walk.'
DAVID HARUM	A Shetland and a notable sire.
DAWN HORSE, the	Called Eohippus. Not a true horse; had 3 toes on each hind foot, 4 toes on each fore foot. Teeth were like those of a pig.
DAY STAR	In 1878 was Kentucky Derby Winner.
DEANNA	A Trotting filly, winner of the Acorn.
DEBORAH HANOVET	A Pacing filly, winner of Abbedale Stake.
DECORATED LADY	A 5 gaited Champion American Saddle Horse.
DEERSTALKER	In "Caravan," by John Galsworthy.
DELIA	Name for a Percheron.
DELEGATE	A Sprinter.
DENMARK	A Thoroughbred, foundation stock. American Saddle Horse.
DEPTH CHARGE	A race horse.
DESTINADO	A race horse.
DESTROY	A race horse.
DESTRUCTOR	A race horse.
DETERMINE	In 1954 Kentucky Derby Winner.
DEVALUATION	A race horse.
DEVIL DARE	A race horse.
DEVIL DIVER	A race horse.

DIAMOND DENMARK	Sire of Montrose. A notable sire of the breed.
DIAMOND JUBILEE	Won English Derby in 1900. Sire was St. Simon. He sold for $150,000.
DIAMOND POINT	A race horse.
DIFFERENT THINGS	A race horse.
DILHAM PRIME MINISTER	At one time the most famous Hackney pony in America; noted prize winner and sire.
DILIGANCE	Imported from France. A Percheron.
DIAMOND MOON	A race horse.
DIG DOWN	A race horse.
DIMITY	A race horse.
DIOMED	Winner of Epsom Derby, the first ever run. Imported for breeding purposes. Sired Pacemaker.
DIRECT HAL	One of leading pacers to 1918.
DIRECT RHYTHM	A Pacer.
DISCOVERY	In a class by himself. He took all weights, all comers. Son of the Iron Horse. He had a blaze face, intelligent; dignified; perfect manners. Broke track records. Sired by Display.
DISPLAY	One of toughest handicap horses of recent times. Leading money maker; called the Iron Horse; a born fighter; son of Fair Play and sired Discovery.
DISTANT SHORE	A race horse.
DITTO	Won Epsom Derby 1803.
DIVINE COMEDY	A race horse.
DJERANDA	"The locust." An Arabian horse.
DOBBIN	A Hackney.
DOES	A Morgan gelding.

DOLLY   A Percheron, descendent of Big
                         White, old canal horse in Pennsyl-
                         vania who broke all records in
                         pulling loads.

DOMINO   A descendent of Eclipse. His
                         nickname was 'Black Whirlwind.'
                         Sired by Himyar. Domino line is
                         looked to for pure speed. On
                         his grave is "the fleetest runner
                         the turf has ever known." He
                         competed in one of the most sen-
                         sational match races in American
                         turf history.

                         Also the name of an Appaloosa
                         Stallion.

DONALD   A Morgan stallion. Noted as a
                         show horse and sire. Fine ex-
                         ample of true Morgan type.

DON'T FOOL   A race horse.

DOTTED SWISS   A race horse that won the Holly-
                         wood Gold Cup, $162,100.

DOTTIES PICK   A race horse.

DOUBLE DAILY   A race horse.

DOUBLE EAGLE   A race horse.

DRAGON   A champion Percheron stallion
                         seen at the 1906-7 International
                         Live Stock Exposition.

DREAD   A Trotter in 1831.

DRIFTWOOD   An American Quarter Horse, sire
                         of Red Button (Old Roany).

DRINKER OF THE WIND   In "Drinkers of the Wind," by
                         Carl R. Raswan.

DUDIE ARCHDALE   A trotter, and leading money mak-
                         er.

DUCKS AND DRAKES   A horse in "Destiny Bay," by
                         Donn Byrne, which was by Drake's
                         Drum out of Little Duck.

DUENNA   A Shetland mare.

DUETTISTE   A famous Steeple Chaser.

DUKE OF LULLWATER   A Trotter, champion in 1952, won Castleton Farm Stake 1951, sired by Volomite.

DUMPTY HUMPTY   A race horse.

DUKHI   "The sod-like one." Arabian horse.

DURBAR II   In 1914 won English Derby. Sired by Rabelain.

DUTCH BOY   A champion Trotter in 1952.

EAGER   Winner of Epsom Derby in 1791.

EARL THE PEARL   A race horse.

EARLOCKER   A famous Steeple Chaser.

EARLS MOODY GUY   A Trotter.

EARLS SONG   A Trotter, Champion in 1952.

EARLY DELIVERY   A race horse.

EARLY DREAMS   A Trotter and leading money maker.

EARLY MIST   A race horse.

EASTER BELLE   Champion roadster at National Horse Show in 1904.

EASY ECHO   A race horse.

EASY STREET   A race horse.

EBENEZER   Horse in "Justin Morgan..." by Marguerite Henry.

ECHO DRUMS   A race horse.

EDNA MAY   Some horsemen say she was the greatest saddle type ever seen in America.

EDUCATION   A race horse.

EDWARD'S OLD BRITON   A Suffolk.

EIGHT THIRTY   A race horse known to be a perfect gentleman. He had substance and quality; speed and endurance; fine disposition; exceptional intel-

ligence. He had absolute game-
ness; seldom late; never completely sound.

EL AROUSSA	"The bride." An Arabian horse.
EL BULAD	"Steel; strong." An Arabian horse.
EL EMIR	"The prince." Notable Arabian stallion.
EL GRECO	A race horse.
EL SABOK	"The racer." An Arabian horse.
ELECTIONEER	Leading sire thoroughbred horses to 1918. A great Trotting sire.
ELEPHANT	A Shire.
ENCHANTER	Grand Champion Percheron stallion.
ENDFIELD NIPPER	Well known prize-winning Hackney Stallion.
ENGLISH KEEL	A race horse.
EQUIPOISE	Domino blood; nicknamed by the crowds, "Come on Ekky." Balanced and proportioned; held record for fastest mile in history of American racing for many years...1:34 2/5 at Arlington Park, Chicago. Won Keene Memorial Stakes.
ERNE II	Familiar Steeple Chaser.
ESQUIRE	Sired by William Conqueror, a shire.
ETAWAH	A Trotter, leading money maker.
ETERNAL BEAU	A race horse.
ETHAN ALLEN	Greatest son of Sherman Morgan. Very popular as a successful Trotter, and a great sire.
ESTUDIANT	A Champion Percheron stallion in France, 1908. Imported to America in 1909.
EUGENIA	An American Saddle Horse, mare.

EXILE	A Cleveland Bay Stallion, imported in 1820.
EXPECTATION	A familiar Steeple Chaser.
EXTERMINATOR	Kentucky Derby Winner, 1918. Best loved thoroughbred; most intelligent. Nicknamed "Slim" and "Bones."
FABULIST	Race horse.
FADING SKY	Race horse.
FAIR ELLEN	An Arabian mare.
FAIR PLAY	A stayer and sire of horses of stamina. His sire dangerous in his most vicious mood and Fair Play at worst showed unfriendliness, stubborn willfulness. Fair Play line looked to for stayers.
FAIRMOUNT	A Steeple chaser.
FAIRY CHANT	A race horse.
FAIRY VISION	A race horse.
FALL WIND	A race horse.
FALSE COLORS	A race horse.
FALSETTO	A race horse.
FAMOUS SONG	A Trotter in 1951.
FANCY LADY	A Thoroughbred.
FARANA	A bay, Arabian stallion, meaning, 'to be arrogant, or overbearing.'
FARCEUR	A Belgian, champion at Brussels and the International Livestock Exposition; great show horse and sold for $6,500.
FASHION	One of the really great American racers of last century, won on Union Race Course 1842. First heat was a world record.
FASHION PLATE	A race horse.
FATALIST	A race horse.

FATHERS RISK	A race horse.
FAY'S NIGHT OUT	A race horse.
FEARNAUGHT	Son of Regulus-Silvertail. Imported in 1764. Represented best blood in England.
FENELON	A Percheron.
FIBBER	A Trotter, won Will Gahagan Memorial.
FIESTA	A Trotter, leading money maker.
FIGHTING FOX	World record 1939. Brother of Gallant Fox.
FIGHTING STEP	A race horse.
FINANCE	Sired by Bulldog; an unusually handsome horse; speed was his forte.
FIND	A race horse.
FIREAWAY	A race horse in 1782.
FIRENZI	One of the greatest American thoroughbreds, began racing 1886.
FIRETHORN	A race horse.
FIREWORKS	A race horse.
FIRST BALCONY	A race horse.
FIRST EDITION	A race horse.
FIRST FIDDLE	A Stallion race horse.
FIRST LANDING	A race horse.
FIVE DOLLARS	A Cow pony in "Cowboy Reader."
FIXIT	A race horse.
FLAME QUEEN	A race horse.
FLAMING ARROW	A race horse.
FLARES	Son of Gallant Fox, a dark solid bay.
FLASH COMMAND	A race horse.
FLASHING COLORS	A race horse.
FLASHWOOD	A Clydesdale.

FLASHY PRINCESS	A Trotter, champion in 1952.
FLASHY TOKEN	A race horse.
FLASHY WINNER	A race horse.
FLEET BIRD	World Record, Golden Gate Fields.
FLEET TOWER	A race horse.
FLIRTEUR	A 3 year old French Coach Stallion, Champion at Paris Horse Show in 1908.
FLOATING DREAM	A race horse. Pacing filly, won Abbedale Stake.
FLORIAN	In "Florian," by Felix Salten.
FLORICAN	In 1949 won Castleton Farm Stake. Trotter, Sired by Spud Hanover.
FLOWER BOOK	A race horse.
FLUTTERBY	A race horse.
FLUTTERBY GHOST	A race horse.
FLY UP	A race horse.
FLYING ATLAS	A race horse.
FLYING EBONY	Kentucky Derby winner in 1925.
FLYING FOX	In 1904 sold for $187,500.
FLYING JIB	A Pacer, 1894.
FLYING KITTY	In "The Turn of the Wheel," by Dorothea Donn Byrne.
FO FO	In "Black Horses," by Luigi Pirandello.
FOLLOW ME	In 1942 won Coaching Club Trotting Oaks.
FONSO	In 1880 won Kentucky Derby.
FOREIGN MONKEY	A race horse.
FOREST QUEEN, the	A Shire, son Forest King.
FOREST SQUIRREL	In 1890 an American Saddle Horse.
FORWARD GUNNER	A race horse.
FOUR CENT STAMP	A race horse.
FOUR FREEDOMS	A race horse.

FOUR TRICKS	A race horse.
FOX	A sorrel, so called as was foxy. In "Cowboy Reader."
FOX ALONG	Sired by Gallant Fox, rode by Billy Pearson.
FOXBOROUGH	A race horse.
FOXHALL	Important to America. A Suffolk.
FOXHUNTER	A race horse.
FRANCES JEWELL	A Pacer and champion in 1952.
FREE COPY	A race horse.
FREE FOR ALL	A race horse.
FREEMAN	A race horse.
FRENCH FILLY	A race horse.
FRESH AS FRESH	A race horse.
FRESH DOC	A race horse.
FRESH PAINT	A race horse.
FRILLS	A race horse.
FROZEN MARCH	A race horse.
FULL STEAM	A race horse.
FUN'S FUN	A race horse.
FUSCHIA	A Shire, the heaviest mare ever seen by Mr. M. G. Truman, a noted importer and authority on this breed. Junior Champion at Shire Horse Society Show in London, weighing in her 4 year form 2475 pounds.
GABILAN	The pony in "The Red Pony," by John Steinbeck, meaning, 'hawk.'
GALLAHADION	In 1940 Kentucky Derby winner.
GALLANT FOX	Triple Crown winner, 1930 - the Preakness, Kentucky Derby, Belmont Stakes. Called 'the fox;' clever, opionated, exceptional class; curiosity his strongest

trait; too much of a gentleman; a real individualist. When he got ahead of a horse, he slowed up and waited for him. He was defeated in his first race as a 2 year old because he stood and looked at an airplane overhead.

GALLANT MAN — Won Belmont Stakes in 1957. Won $77,300.

GALLEY SLAVE — A race horse.

GANDER — A Pacer, won American National.

GARAVEEN — A notable Arabian stallion.

GAVILÁN — 'Hawk.' A Mustang. A snow white mane, so heavy it bent his neck when grazing; white stripe down face.

GAY GHOST — A race horse.

GAY MAC — A dark bay, dam was Dewdrop.

GAY WARRIOR — A race horse.

GET RICH — A race horse.

GHAZALAH — Lit. 'gazelle.' An Arabian horse.

GHEZALA — "The gazelle." An Arabian horse.

GERTIE — Horse in "Gertie the Horse," by Margarite Glendinning.

GHOST OF LLANO ESTACADO — A Mustang stallion with a band of mares.

GINGBOW — A race horse.

GINGER — A dark chestnut Cayuse, in "Cowboy Reader."

GIROUST — A Pacer, Futurity winner.

GITANA — 'Gipsy,' a horse in "Chúcaro, wild pony of the Pampa," by Francis Kalnay.

GLADIATOR — 1833 race horse.

GLANCER — Alias Thompson's Black Horse, a Clydesdale, sired by Blaze.

GLENCOE — A Clydesdale of merit in America

	before 1915.
GLOAMING	A race horse.
GLORIFY	A race horse.
GO BETWEEN	In 1906 a Saddle Horse, worth $16,800.
GO BOY'S SHADOW	A Tennessee Walking Horse Stallion.
GO MAN GO	A race horse.
GODOLPHIN ARABIAN	Of uncertain origin, produced Matchem.
GOLD BAR	A race horse.
GOLD COPY	A race horse.
GOLD COVER	A race horse.
GOLD FOAM	A race horse.
GOLD KING	A golden Palomino.
GOLD MINER	A race horse.
GOLD VENUS	A race horse.
GOLDEN BOY	A Shetland stallion.
GOLDEN CHIEF	Copperbottom Quarter Horse.
GOLDEN MEADOW	A white horse, the people choice, crowd roared, "Hi ho Silver."
GOLDEN MELODY	A racer.
GOLDSMITH MAID	Most amazing Trotting horse ever lived. 1874. Earned $364,200. Originally called The Maid.
GOOD START	A race horse.
GOOD TIME	A Pacer in 1949.
GOOD AND PLENTY	A Famous Steeple Chaser.
GOODNESS GRACIOUS	A race horse.
GRACE DIRECT	A Pacer, leading money maker.
GRAND BASHAW	A Barb stallion, foaled 1816, imported from Tripoli Africa.
GRANDEE	A Shetland, notable sire.
GRANDPA	Famous Steeple Chaser.

GRANDVILLE   In 1936 Horse of the Year. Sired
                              by Twenty Grand.

GRATTAN BARS   A Pacer, leading money maker.

GRAY VAN   Father Vandy, mother Lady Gray.

GREAT BRITAIN   A Shire; important stallion, weigh-
                              ed 2830 pounds.

GREAT CROSSING   A race horse.

"THE GREAT HORSE"   Painted by Albert Dürer, is horse
                              of the 16th century from which the
                              Shire is supposed to have derived
                              its ancestry.

GREEN CHEESE   Famous Steeple Chaser.

GREEN FINGERS   A race horse.

GREEN MOUNTAIN MAID   Most famous brood mare of the
                              American Trotting Horses. Sire-
                              Henry Clay; dam, Shanghai Mary.

GREY PHANTOM   Arabian filly.

GREYHOUND   A Trotter. Greatest of trotters,
                              and extraordinary intelligence,
                              called the 'gray ghost.' Fastest
                              trotter ever lived. The Man O'
                              War of trotters.

GRO-UP   Won 1949 in Atlantic City.

GUIDE BOOK   A race horse.

GUEMERA   "The moon." Arabian horse.

GUINEA GOLD   A Pacer, leading money maker.

GULL FLIGHT   In "The Turn of the Wheel," by
                              Dorothea Donn Byrne.

GUN BOX   A race horse.

GYPSY QUEEN   A Saddle Horse, mare, prize
                              winner.

GYPSY'S ALIBI   A race horse.

HADBAN   An Arabian stallion, meaning,
                              'shaggy hair; dense long eyelashes.'

HAGAR	A notable Arabian horse, meaning, 'abandon; to desert.'
HAIDEE	Meaning, "quiet," notable Arabian mare.
HAIL TO REASON	Victor at Atlantic City in Sept. '60, winning $135,065, World's Playground Stakes.
HALEB	"Brown." Arabian horse.
HALF ACRE	A race horse.
HALMA	Kentucky Derby winner 1895. Meaning, "patient; long suffering."
HALF BAR	A chestnut sorrel American Quarter horse. Mother was Half Chick and father was Three Bars.
HULUJ	"The cotton like one." An Arabian horse.
HALWAJI	"Lit. of the sweet one." An Arabian horse.
HAMAMA	"The dove." An Arabian horse.
HAMBLETONIAN	Son of Messenger.
HAMRAH	"Red." Bay, Arabian stallion, sired by a Hamdani, dam a Seglawi Jedran.
HAND AND FOOT	A race horse.
HAND IN HAND	A race horse.
HANGMAN	Horse in "Caravan," by John Galsworthy.
HANNIBAL	A Coach stallion, important prize winner of highest rank at many shows.
HANOVER	Thoroughbred Stallion, foaled in 1884. In 1886 made racing appearance. One of the greatest American thoroughbreds, sired by Hindo.
HANOVER'S BERTHA	A Trotter; leading money maker.
HAPPY MEDIUM	Sired by Hambletonian. Sire of Pilot Medium.

HAPPY NEWS	A race horse.
HARB	An Arabian horse, meaning, lit. "war."
HARDTACK	A race horse.
HAROLD	A Shire. Foaled 1881. Won numerous important prizes in show ring. Sired by Lincolnshire Lad II.
HARRY'S DREAM	A race horse.
HARUM SPARKE	A Shetland show mare.
HARVARD	At Brighton Beach, New York in 1887 largest pay off on $5.00 win ticket - $760.00.
HARVESTER, the	One of the fastest Trotter stallions as well as great sire.
HASH	Race horse.
HASTINGS	Sire of Fair Play.
HASTY BIT	Race horse.
HASTY HIKE	Race horse.
HASTY LANE	Race horse.
HASTY ROAD	Race horse.
HATS	Race horse.
HAVE TUX	Race horse.
HAWB	"An exclamation of displeasure or impertinence to animate the horse." Name given to an Arabian horse.
HAY FI	"Coming from the South." Name given an Arabian horse.
HAY FIDDLE	Race horse.
HAZEL DAWN	American Saddle Horse, mare.
HE DID	Race horse.
HEART CALL	Race horse.
HEART OF OAK	Famous sire; sired 19 prize winners.
HE'SADOLL	Race horse.

HEATHER HAWK	Race horse.
HEATHERBLOOM	Jumped 8 feet 3 inches. Barnum and Bailey Circus offered $25,000 for Heatherbloom.
HEEL FLAME	Race horse.
HEGIRA	Arabian stallion belonging to General Ulysses Grant.
HEIR IN LAW	Race horse.
HELIX	A Percheron, champion stallion in 1911.
HELLENIC HERO	Race horse.
HELL'S ANGEL	In "Cowboy Reader."
HER LADYSHIP	A Pacer in 1938.
HEROD (KING HEROD)	Foaled in 1758. On the race course, then retired to the stud. A direct descendent of the Byerly Turk. To Herod, Eclipse and Matchem every living thoroughbred traces in direct male line.
HI-LO'S FORBES	A Pacer.
HIAWATHA	A Clydesdale. Won 7 prizes to 1915.
HIBLER	A famous Steeple Chaser.
HICKORY SMOKE	A race horse.
HIGH BUTTONS	A race horse.
HIGH CLOUD	Had Domino blood.
HIGH COMET	A race horse.
HIGH FLEET	A race horse.
HIGH GUN	Won Belmont Stakes 1954, made $89,000.
HIGH JINKS	A race horse.
HIGH SPY	A race horse.
HIGHFLYER	By Herod, out of Rachael. In 1774.
HIGHLAND CHIEF	A Percheron.
HIGHLAND ELLEN	Sire was Highland Scott.

HIGHLAND MAID	American Saddle Horse.
HILDRED	One of most perfect mares in history of the American show ring. A Hackney.
HILL GAIL	Kentucky Derby winner 1952.
HILL PRINCE	Horse of the Year 1950.
HILLSOTA	A Pacer, champion in 1952.
HIMYAR	In 1875, sire was Alarm, out of Hira. Was the Sire of Domino. (A country in So. Arabia.)
HIMYARITE	Meaning, "from Himyar." An Arabian stallion.
HINDOO	In 1881 a Kentucky Derby Winner. He had courage and speed of highest order.
HIS EMINENCE	Kentucky Derby winner in 1901.
HIT SONG	In 1951, won Arthur S. Tompkins Memorial. A 2 year old Trotter. One of the leading money winners.
HIT THE TRAIL	A race horse.
HITCHIN CONQUEROR	A Shire, foaled in 1883. Sired by William Conqueror, his dam Flower (by Honest Prince).
HOE DOWN	A race horse.
HOLYSTONE	Hunter champion with quality and finish; scope and power.
HOME FLEET	Race horse.
HOME JOURNAL	Race horse.
HOME TO ROOST	Race horse.
HONEST	Race horse.
HONEST PRINCE	Sire of Flower. A Shire.
HONEST TOM	A Shire, foaled in Lincolnshire, in 1806. Prominent sire of the day; descendents proved his merit. Also called, OLD TOM, LITTLE DAVID, OLD DAVID.
HONE	Race horse.

HONEST TRUTH	Race horse.
HONEY GOLD	Tennessee Walking horse, registered as Rosy O'Grady. A sorrel mare.
HONEY PATCH	Race horse.
HONEY PIE	Race horse.
HONEY'S GEM	Race horse.
HONK	Race horse.
HONOR BRIGHT	A Trotter, won the Acorn.
HOOT MON	A Trotter, leading money maker.
HORSE SHOES	Race horse.
HOST PETER	Race horse that had an illustrious career.
HOT SLIPPERS	Race horse.
HOT ROBBER	Race horse.
HOTSPUR	Race horse.
HOUSE OF LORDS	Sire was Volomite.
HOW ARE THINGS	Race horse.
HOWDY RICH	Race horse.
HUMAH	"Protectors." Arabian race horse.
HUMORIST	A horse with only one lung.
HURMAH	"Lit. of woman." Arabian race horse.
HURRY BACK	Race horse.
I FIGURE	Race horse.
IDEOLOGY	Race horse.
IDLE STAR	Race horse.
IDOLITA	A Trotter, leading money maker.
IKE'S DELIGHT	Race horse.
IMAM	A bay, Arabian horse; stallion; meaning, "Imam is the priest in the Islamic Religion."
IMAMZADA	Arabian horse.

IMPATIENT	In "The Turn of the Wheel," by Dorothea Donn Byrne.
IMPOSTER	Race horse.
IMPRECATION	A Percheron.
IN THEE	A race horse.
INAUGURAL DAY	A race horse.
INDIAN AGENT	A race horse.
INDIAN CHIEF	Harness stallion.
INDIAN VILLAGE	A race horse.
INIMITABLE	A race horse.
INKY	A horse in "Horse in Danger," by Glenn Balch.
INTERFERENCE	A race horse.
IRON MASK	He had Domino blood.
IRON SHOT	A famous Steeple Chaser.
IRONSIDES	Race horse.
IRISH DUMPLING	Race horse.
IRISH HAL	A Pacer in 1952.
IRISH LANCER	Won the 23,900 Lamplighter Handicap by two and three quarters lengths at Monmouth Park.
IRON LIEGE	Kentucky Derby Winner, 1957.
ISHTAR	Arabian horse, mother of Imam. Means, 'smart.'
ISMAEL	Arabian stallion belonging to General Ulysses S. Grant.
ITSA GREAT DAY	Took second place at Atlantic City September 1960 by a nose over Ross Sea.
IT'S MUTINY	Race horse.
IVONDALE FARCEUR	A Grand Champion Belgian Stallion.
JAM	A Steple Chaser.

JAN KIP   In Erie Canal service from Bel-
                           gian stock. Out of Nita who had
                           raced Peter Cooper's Tom Thumb.

JANECIA   A Percheron.

JAWHARAH   "Pearl." An Arabian stallion.

JANUS   Foundation sire of the American
                           Quarter Horse. Imported. Lived
                           from 1746 to 1780. 9 lines car-
                           ried a strong infusion of imported
                           Janus blood.

JAY EYE SEE   Best mile performance by world
                           champion.

JEAN GRATTAN   A Pacer and leading money maker.

JEANNETTE RANKIN   A Trotter and leading money mak-
                           er.

JEDRA   Meaning, "competence, or effi-
                           ciency." An Arabian.

JENKO HANOVER   A Trotter.

JENNY CAMERON   A Mare important to American
                           Race History.

JET HOSTESS   A race horse.

JET PILOT   Kentucky Derby Winner in 1947.

JET WHIZ   Race horse.

JEWEL JADE   Race horse.

JEWELLED CAP   Race horse.

JIMMINY WICKED   A race horse.

JOCASSE   A 2 year old Percheron.

JOE BLAIR   A Quarter horse.

JOE COTTON   Kentucky Derby Winner 1885.

JOE PATCHEN   A Pacer, leading money maker.

JOE QUEEN   A Quarter Stallion that will appear
                           with Audie Murphy in "Whisper-
                           ing Smith" series on NBC. Ap-
                           peared in Roy Rogers Chevy Show,
                           "You Asked For It." Track win-
                           nings, $13,305.

JOE'S DOLL   Race horse.

JOHNNY ONE EYE	Race horse.
JOHN BULL	A Shire. 1853 imported to Illinois from England.
JOHN DILLARD	By Indian Chief (Canadian). Foundation Stock. American Saddle Horse.
JOHN NOLAN	A Trotter, leading money maker.
JOHNNY COPE	A Clydesdale of merit in America before 1915.
JOHNSTOWN	Who almost had everything; he was lop-eared, seemed lazy, sleepy, one of best behaved horses, made a runaway race of Kentucky Derby.
JOLLY ROGER	A famous Steeple Chaser. Big, powerful, imported in 1762.
JOSEDALE ALATE	A Pacer.
JOY BET	A race horse.
JOY BRINGER	A race horse.
JUDGE MOORE	In 1947, won Arthur S. Tompking Memorial. A 2 year old Trotter. Won The American National Stake.
JULES	A Percheron.
JULIAN'S BOXER	A Suffolk. Sired superior sons and daughters.
JUMPIN' SPEED	A race horse.
JUNE THE FOURTH	A Trotter 1940.
JUPITER	His sons in great demand. Some regard Jupiter as the greatest Belgian sire in the history of the breed.
JUST REGARDS	A race horse.
JUSTA DRIZZLE	A race horse.
JUSTIN MORGAN	American Trotter, sired by True Briton whose ancestry traced to Godolphin, also to Barb. Dam, Diamond. Called little giant. A

small stocky bay, founded a line
without parallel in breeding history. Helped win the Civil War.
The true Morgan is small, seldom
more than 14 hands in height,
short legged, powerful shoulders
and quarters. Has a willingness
and intelligence.

KAABA	Means, "a sacred place for Mos-lems in Mecca, Saudi Arabia." A Grey Arabian Stallion.
KABAR	An Arabian Stallion, meaning, "to regard as great, magnify."
KADAAN	An Arabian horse, meaning, "brave, strong."
KHADEJA	"Mohammad's wife." An Arabian stallion.
KAHAR	Arabian stallion, meaning, "to conquer, overcome."
KAHTAN	"Name of a Bedouin tribe." An Arabian horse name.
KALIF	"Caliph." An Arabian mare.
KAMIL	"The perfect." An Arabian horse.
KATAR	An Arabian bay Stallion. Means, "stingy."
KAUKAB	Lit. 'star.' Grandaughter of El Sabok. Arabian mare.
KAYAK II	Brilliant stablemate of Seabiscuit.
KEEP QUIET	A race horse.
KEMAH	"Worthy." Arabian horse.
KENTUCKY CHOICE	American Saddle Horse, in 1905.
KESIA	"Severe." A notable Arabian mare.
KETTLEDRUM	Won Epsom Derby in 1861.
KEYSTONER	A Pacer.
KHALED	An Arabian sire. Khaled was an Arabian hero who invaded Palestine.

KHAHL — An Arabian Stallion, meaning, 'friend.'

KHARISH — "Scratched one, from pasturing on prickly desert plants."

KHARTUM — Name of an Arabian horse, meaning, "elephant trunk."

KHEILAN — The generic name of the true Arabian horse. It means 'friend.'

KHASHINIYAH — "Rough; tough." Arabian horse name. For mare.

KIMBERLY KID — A Trotter.

KING CRABB — Foaled in 1885 won 310 paces.

KING JACK — In 1933 top pay off to players at Tijuana, Mexico.

KING JET — A race horse.

KING LARIGO — A Shetland. Notable sire. Champion Stallion, at leading shows. Highest priced animal of the breed selling for $10,000.

KING NIBBLE — Champion 1952 Trotter.

KING SAXON — Peerless as a sprinter. Carried speed to a mile and sixteenth.

KING VULTURE — Was exceedingly clever.

KING'S CURRENCY — A race horse.

KING'S PASS — A race horse.

KINGLY TOKEN — A race horse.

KINGMAN — Kentucky Derby winner 1891.

KINGSTON — One of the greatest American Thoroughbreds.

KINSCEN — Means, "my treasure" in Hungarian. This horse was never defeated, but in parade was a pathetic sight, dragging wearily along. Then the pounding hoofs awakened her.

KIOWA — A Mustang.

KISMET — A notable Arabian stallion with a

	remarkable record in India as a race horse. Won $150,000.
KISS ME KATE	A race horse.
KITTIWYNK	A horse in "The Maltese Cat," by Rudyard Kipling.
KNIGHT DREAM	A Pacer, 1948. A bay colt.
KNIGHT GALLANT	Race horse.
KNOTTY PROBLEM	Race horse.
KOOL KARAT	Race horse.
KUBAYSHAN	"The little ram." Arabian stallion. KUBAYSHAH for mare.
KUHAYLAN	"A black eyed horse." A Mare is KUHAYLAH.
KUTCH	A Quarter horse.
KYRAT	An Arabian horse in Longfellow's poem, "The Leap of Roushan Beg." "The strong and fleet." A chestnut horse with four white feet.
LA BELLE	A Percheron mare. Champion American bred, in 1911.
LABRADOR	A Pacer, leading money maker.
LADY BEE	A race horse.
LADY JACKSON	In 1831 a Trotter.
LADY OF THE MANOR	A Pacer, leading money maker.
LADY PATCH	A Yearling, Pacer, in 1924.
LADY THORN	Daughter of Mambrino Chief.
LADYSMAN	American Turf star.
LAGOS	A Percheron.
LAMINATED STEED	By Cedric.
LANCINANTE	Grand Champion Percheron mare.
LAND OF HOPE	Race horse.
LAP DOG	Won Epsom Derby 1826.
LARK	A Quarter horse racer.

LAWRIN	Kentucky Derby Winner, 1938.
LEAPING LENA	A horse in "Cowboy Reader."
LEASURE	A race horse.
LEONATUS	In 1883 Kentucky Derby Winner.
LEOPARD	An Arabian stallion belonging to General Ulysses S. Grant.
LEVEL BEST	A race horse.
LEXINGTON	A great race horse.
LIBERAL LADY	Sequois Handicap winner 1960. $16, 850.
LIBRETTO	A Percheron Stallion.
LIGHT TALK	A race horse.
LIGHT AND GAY	A race horse.
LIGHTNING	A pony in "A Pony called Lightning," by Miriam E. Mason. Another horse, a racer, was notoriously sluggish, lazy.
LIGHTNING JACK	Race horse.
LIGHTS UP	Race horse.
LIKELY MISS	Race horse.
LILIANA	"Flower, name of a girl." An Arabian horse.
LIMIRICK PRIDE	In "Destiny Bay," by Donn Byrne.
LINCONSHIRE LAD II	Foaled in 1872. Best known of show ring winners of the period. Ranked first in list of common progenitors. A Shire.
LINDA	A Percheron.
LINDEN TREE	An Arabian horse belonging to General Ulysses S. Grant.
LION HEART	Famous Steeple Chaser.
LITTLE ALBERT	A Trotter, leading money maker.
LITTLE BEAR	A Stallion. Mustang.
LITTLE BROWN JUG	A Pacer.
LITTLE BUB	In "Justin Morgan Had a Horse,"

	by Marguerite Henry.
LITTLE CHARGE	A race horse.
LITTLE DAVID	A race horse, alias Honest Tom.
LITTLE JOE, the Wrangler.	Horse.
LITTLE JUDY	A Pacer.
LITTLE KATE	An American Saddle Horse.
LITTLE OLD ME	A race horse.
LITTLE PAT	A Pacer.
LITTLE SIZZLER	An American Quarter Horse Stallion.
LITTLE SPINET	A race horse.
LITTLE SQUIRE	Jumper extraordinary, white; a real showman; sleek; a pleasure for him to perform.
LITTLE TIPPER	Race horse.
LITTLE WHITE STAR	A Pony in "The Old Pony," by Dorothy Clewes.
LITTLE WONDER	A Hackney Stallion.
LITTLE WONDER	Winner of Epsom Derby in 1840.
LITTLE ZIDA	Race horse.
LIVE COAL	Race horse.
LIVELY LADY	Winner The Acorn, a Trotter mare. 2 year old Trotter of the year in 1952.
LIVERPILL	Horse in "Cowboy Reader."
LOAFER	A black thoroughbred gelding.
LOCK OUT	Race horse.
LOGAN	Called "the Iron Horse." Won 388 races to 1952, foaled in 1888.
LONG EARS	Race horse.
LONG ISLAND BELLE	A Pacing filly, winner of Abbedale Stake.
LONGFELLOW	Race horse in 1860's.
LONWAY	A Pacing filly, winner of Abbedale

	Stake.
LOOKOUT	Kentucky Derby winner, 1893.
LORD JIM	A Trotter, leading money maker.
LORD MURPHY	Kentucky Derby winner 1879.
LORENZO	Famous Steeple Chaser.
LOST WAR	Race horse.
LOTSOLOOT	Race horse.
LOU DILLON	A Trotting mare, sensational trotter in American turf history.
LOUIS NAPOLEON	A great sire.
LOVE IN VIEW	Race horse.
LOVELY HOSTESS	Race horse.
LOVELY READING	Race horse.
LOYAL WOMAN	Race horse.
LOVER'S AID	Race horse.
LU PECK	A Trotter, champion 1952.
LUCKY BARS	By Three Bars, a thoroughbred.
LUCKY NIXON	Race horse.
LULU LULLWATER	Race horse.
LUSTY SONG	Race horse, Trotter. Winner of Arthur S. Tompkins Memorial, a 2 year old in 1949. Sire was Volomite.
LUXURIANT	In 1949 at Narragansett Park, R. I., highest payoff to players in U. S.
LUXURY LADY	Race horse.
MAÂROUF	"The known." An Arabian horse.
MACARONI	Epsom Derby winner 1863.
MACBETH II	Kentucky Derby winner 1888.
MACGREGOR	A Clydesdale.
MCGREGOR, the Great	A Trotter, leading money maker.

MAD HATTER	A great cup horse.
MAD PLAY	Race horse.
MAGNA	An American Saddle horse, mare.
MAHUBAH	Dam of Man O'War. By Rock Sand and Fair Play. Means, 'smart.'
MAIDAN	Means 'battlefield.' Notable Arabian stallion. Had a remarkable career as cavalry and racing horse in India. Taken to France, then England. Lived to be 23 years old. Fem. MAIDANEH.
MAJOR	A Shire that won 45 prizes.
MALICIOUS	"The beloved." Power and drive were amazing.
MAMBRINA	Sired in England by Mambrino. A Thoroughbred filly, appeared in U. S. in 1787.
MAMBRINO	Was the Sire of Messenger, famous in harness horse lore. A Sire of Trotters.
MAMBRINO CHIEF	Race horse.
MAMBRINO CHIEF II	Trotter foaled in 1844. Fountainhead of Chief family. American Saddle Horse. Produced speed; never sired colts of quality; coarse in appearance, bay in color, 16 hands.
MABRINO KING	Was regarded as the most beautiful horse in America in his day.
MAMBRINO PATCHEN	Sired scores of trotters. His daughter Dolly was dam of ONWARD, DIRECTOR, THRONDALE, all a remarkable trio.
MAN O' WAR	Champion of Champions; a celebrity in Ky., lived on Faraway Farm; defeated every horse sent against him. Called "big Red." None of his family, or himself have been admitted or accepted for registry in the English "Stud Book." This

was because records dealing with the ancestors of Man O' War were lost or destroyed during the Civil War and never did get to England.

MANIFESTO   A race horse.

MANSOUR   "The victorious," an Arabian Stallion.

MANUEL   Kentucky Derby Winner, 1899.

MANY STINGS   Race horse.

MARCH IDOL   Race horse.

MARCHIONESS, the   A Trotter, leading money man.

MARENGO   Was owned by Napoleon.

MARFA   A Palomino.

MARGIN   A Trotter, leading money maker.

MARK ANTHONY   Racer, in 1767.

MARKET WISE   A great stretch runner.

MARS   A horse in "Ben Hur," by Lew Wallace. Also a horse sired by Man O' War.

MARY REYNOLDS   A Trotter, leading money maker.

MASHER   A race horse.

MATCHEM   An important son of Godolphin Barb named Cade. A great sire. Imported in 1773.

MATCHLESS   A Shire, ranked 2nd in list of common progenitors, 1883-1899.

MATINEE IDOL   In 1915 foaled. Won 334 races.

MAY MARSHAL   A Pacer, leading money maker.

MAYSAN   "A particular Arabian gait." An Arabian horse.

MEADOW MONEY   Highest payoff to players, U. S., Lincoln Fields, Ill. 1941.

MEADOW RICE   Race horse. Sire was The Widower.

MERELY EVER SO   Race horse.

MERCURY	A Belgian, foaled 1882. Unusual action. Champion at National Show, 1887 and 1888. Sired 40 prize winners at Brussels between 1894 and 1901.
MERLIN	A Welsh pony; a small race horse crossed with a Welsh pony.
MERRY-GO-ROUND	Foaled 1943, Sire was Merry Boy, Dam Wise's Dimples. A Tennessee Walking Horse.
MERRY MONARCY	Winner Epsom Derby 1845.
MESSAOUD	"The happy." Arabian horse name.
MESSENGER	Commonly known as Imported Messenger. Was imported in 1788, as a Thoroughbred to improve the running horse; became distinguished progenitor of Trotters. Traces back to Flying Childers and the Darley Arabian. He was a grey stallion. Never trotted a mile, nor did any of his get. His four sons were the actual founders through their offspring, MESSENGER, HAMBLE-TONIAN, MAMBRINO, CORIANDER.
MERSHED	"Name of a mule, which means guide." Name for an Arabian horse.
MIDAFTERNOON	In 1956 made World Record at Jamaica, N. Y.
MIDDLEGROUND	Kentucky Derby winner, 1950.
MIDNIGHT DATE	Race horse.
MIDNIGHT STAR	Champion 5 gaited gelding.
MIDNIGHT SUN	Grand Champion Stake at the Tennessee Walking Horse National Celebration, in the '40's.
MIGHTY FAIR	Race horse.
MIGHTY GONE	Race horse.
MIGHTY KINGDOM	Race horse.

MIGHTY LUCKY	A Pacer, champion in 1952.
MIKES FIRST TRY	Race horse.
MILESTONE	A Trotter.
MILKMAN	Sire of Pasteurized, Buttermilk and Early Delivery.
MIRABELLE	Never won a race, though sister of Man O' War.
MISS AQUILA	Race horse.
MISS COLVILLE	Imported mare, registered in English stud book as Wilkes Old Hautboy.
MISS CUTTY SARK	Race horse.
MISS EVERYTHING	Race horse.
MISS FIREFLY	Race horse.
MISS FLIRTATION	American Saddle Horse, mare.
MISS LA VISTA	Race horse.
MISS MANIE	A Pacer.
MISS ORB	Race horse.
MISS RUSSELL	One of the greatest American brook mares. Her fifth dam was Thoroughbred Diomed.
MISS SASSIE	Race horse.
MISS TILLY	In 1940 won Arthur S. Tompkins Memorial, Castleton Farm Stake. 2 year old Trotter. Won American National Stake.
MR. CHAN	Race horse.
MR. CONSISTENCY	Race horse.
MRS. MURPHY	Race horse.
MR. AMERICA	Race horse.
MR. SMACK	Race horse.
MR. SLIP UP	By Vandy, out of Hot Slippers.
MR. TURK	Race horse.
MITS	Race horse.
MOBOLIZE	Race horse.

MOIFFA	Champion Steeplechase horse in New Zealand, 1902 and 1903. Had an indomitable spirit. Won at Grand National at Aintree.
MOKO	Leading sire of thoroughbreds to 1918.
MONKEY	Stallion, imported in 1747 to America.
MONTROSE	Kentucky Derby Winner 1887.
MOONBAH	Race horse.
MOORE, THE	A Stallion, American Saddle Horse.
MORE GLORY	Race horse.
MORNING STAR	A Pacer, leading money maker.
MORON	Racer.
MUJAHID	"Patriot; struggler; to struggle." Name for an Arabian horse.
MUSICIAN	Leading money maker, Pacer.
MUSJID	"A church for the Moslems." Epsom Derby Winner 1859.
MUSKET	Sire of Carbine.
MUSTARD	Queen Anne's horse ran in race in 1713 without success.
MUZZETA	Top payoff to players in U. S. in 1910.
MY DARE	American Saddle Horse.
MY ETCHINGS	Race horse.
MY MAJOR DARE	American Saddle Horse.
MY OLD KENTUCKY	American Saddle Horse.
MY PLAY	Racer.
MY SLEEPY HEAD	Race horse.
MYSTIC COW	Race horse.
NANCY SONG	Champion Trotter, 1952.
NAOMI	Notable Arabian mare. Nazli, her daughter, sired by Maidan.

NARUSA	Race horse.
NASHUA	World's top money winning horse, $1,288,565. In 1955 won Belmont Stakes, $83,700.
NATAF	"To pluck feathers, or hair; to pull off." Name for Arabian horse.
NATIONAL ANTHEM	Famous Steeple Chaser.
NATIVE DANCER	Horse.
NATIONAL FLYER	Race horse.
NAWFALI	"Belonging to the generous one." Arabian horse.
NAWWAQ	"Of the one having or tending many camels." Arabian horse.
NAZEER	"Scant or small quantity." Arabian, out of Bint Samiha, by Mansour.
NAZLI	"Coming down a hill." Arabian horse, mare, a daughter of Naomi. Sired by Maidan.
NEALON	Saddle Horse, 1907.
NEARSIGHT	Horse.
NEAR RELATION	Won Cesar-witch Handicap.
NEEDLES	1956 winner Belmont Stakes $83,600. 1956 Kentucky Derby Winner.
NELLA DILLON	A Trotter, leading money maker.
NEVERMORE	A race horse.
NEW POLICY	In 1960 won Cinema Handicap at Hollywood Park.
NEW SHOOT	Race horse.
NEWPORT STAR	A Trotter, leading money maker.
NEWS BOY	Race horse.
NEWS SERVICE	Race horse.
NEXT MOVE	Horse.
NICKAJACK	Largest payoff on $5 win ticket.

NICKEL	Belgian.
NICKEL COIN	Race horse.
NIG	Drew flower wagon.
NIGHT HAWK	Race horse.
NIGHTINGALE	A Trotter, leading money maker.
NIMBLE FEET	Race horse.
NINO FORTH	Race horse.
NITA	Raced Tom Thumb, Peter Cooper's little engine. In 1830 the Baltimore and Ohio had a test of speed between a horse drawn car and their small experimental engine. Nita finally won the race.
NO CLOUDS	Race horse.
NO EXIT	Race horse.
NO QUARTER	Won 361 races to 1952.
NOBLE	Won Epsom Derby 1786.
NOBLE EFFORT	Race horse.
NOBLE MAESTRO	Race horse.
NORMANDY	Or Pleasant Valley Bill, a Percheron.
NORTHWIND	A Stallion in "The Way of the Wild," by Herbert Ravenel Sass.
NOW WHAT	Race horse.
NUGGET	A Palomino stallion.
NURI PASHA	A Prime Minister in Iraq who was killed in 1958.
NUT BOY	A Trotter, leading money maker.
NUTWOOD	Leading sire of thoroughbreds to 1918. Miss Russel's first foal. Her greatest son.
NYMPH	A Trotter, won The Acorn.
NOW I SIGH	A race horse.
OEDIPUS	Famous Stepple Chaser.

OH LEO	A race horse.
OLBERT	A Percheron.
OLD BECK	A Mare mule.
OLD BILL	A Percheron.
OLD BLUE HEN	A Champion Trotter in 1952.
OLD DAVID	Alias Honest Tom.
OLD MIN DE LA COZETTE	Sire of Blue Roan MESTIAUX DE RONQUIERES, a Belgian.
OLD PAINT	A race horse.
OLD ROSEBUD	Kentucky Derby winner in 1914.
OLD TENOR	N. Y. Subscription Plate, first run in 1725, won by him in Oct. 11, 1751.
OLDEN TIMES	Horse.
OLE FOLS	Race horse.
OLGA	Percheron.
OMAHA	A gold chestnut, a son of Gallant Fox, and stretch runner such as rarely seen. Triple Crown winner in 1935.
OMAR KHAYYAM	Kentucky Derby Winner in 1917.
ONE COUNT	Race horse. Horse of the Year, 1952.
ONE PUFF	Race horse.
ONWARD	Foaled 1875. Leading sire to thoroughbreds to 1918.
OPHIR	A mare, Arabian. Meaning, "horse with a good mane."
ORFA	"Mane."
ORBY	Winner of English Derby in 1907.
ORMONDE	Sold for $150,000. One of greatest, never beaten in sixteen starts.
ORO WILKES	Trotter and leading money maker.
OSOSO	Horse in "Chacaro, Wild Pony of the Pampa."

OURARDA	"The rose." Arabian horse.
OUR BOOTS	Race horse.
OUR COVER UP	Race horse.
OUR HOST	Race horse.
OUR LEGACY	Race horse.
OUR OSCAR	Race horse.
OUR RIGHTS	Race horse.
OUR TIME	Pacing filly, won Abbedale Stake.
OUSKOUB	"To pour out, spill." First horse possessed by the Prophet, by reason of his speed.
OUT AT LAST	Race horse.
OUTLAW	A Shire, painted by Zeitter in 1810.
OVER THE TOP	Son of Man O' War; resembled him so much; only moderate as a race horse.
PACESETTER	Race horse.
PACKINGTON BLIND	A Shire, foaled about 1760. Shire Stallion important in breeding fame in England.
PAINT BRUSH	A race horse.
PAINTED VEIL	A race horse.
PANTALOON	Imported in 1778.
PARIS PIKE	A race horse.
PARLOR BOY	Won 321 races. Foaled 1908.
PAROLE	Race horse.
PARROT	In "Caravan," by John Galsworthy.
PASTEURIZED	Race horse.
PATIENCE	Imported Hackney mare.
PATROLMAN PETE	Race horse.
PAT'S DANCER	Race horse.
PATSY MC CORD	By Black Squirrel, an American

	Saddle Horse.
PEACEMAKER	Son of Diomed and ran a 2 mile heat that remained a record for almost 3 decades.
PEACOCK	Race horse in 1764. Also name for a Tennessee Walking Horse Stallion.
PEGASUS	A creature of myth; the first recorded horse of ancient times. His wings were a symbol of man's early admiration for the speed and gracefulness of the horse.
PEARLY GATES	Horse in "Cowboy Reader."
"PEEWEE"	Horse in "Cowboy Reader."
PENNY FUND	Race horse.
PENNY LITTLE	Race horse.
PENSIVE	Kentucky Derby winner, 1944.
PEP APPEAL	Race horse.
PEPPER	Queen Anne's horse that ran in 1712 race.
PEPPY	American Quarter horse, sire.
PERFECT HOSTESS	Race horse.
PERHAPS	Won 350 races to 1952.
PERSIMMON	In 1893, a race horse.
PESKY'S PENNY	Race horse.
PET	A Pacer.
PETER ASTRA	Trotter, leading money maker.
PETER HENLEY	Had an illustrious career.
PETER HOPEFUL	Race horse.
PETER LINCOLN	Had an illustrious career.
PETER SCOTT	Most familiar son of Peter, the Great.
PETER THE BREWER	Had an illustrious career.
PETER THE GREAT	Leading sire of thoroughbred horses up to 1918. Has been called "the 250, 000, 000" horse,

because he founded a family. He
was harness horse sire, a son
of Pilot Medium, out of Santos.
In 1898 won Kentucky Futurity.
He sired Sadie Mac, mare that
won Kentucky Futurity in 1903.

PETER MANNING   A Trotter and leading money mak-
                       er. The mile record of this
                       great trotter stood for 15 years,
                       broken by Greyhound.

PETER VOLO   Sired 377 trotters and 156 pacers.

PETER WOOLLEN   Had an illustrious career.

PETONIA   Record bookmaking payoff - 500
                       to 1. (1894)

PETRIFY   Race horse.

PET'S DAY   Race horse.

PHANTOM   Won Epsom Derby in 1811.

PHANTOM AGE   Race horse.

PHAR LAP   A Thoroughbred, son of Night
                       Raider, foaled in New Zealand
                       in 1926. Sensational; won on any
                       kind of track; won at sprints;
                       over routes.

PHARI   A Pony in "Phari, adventures of
                       a Tibetan Pony."

PHENOMENA   In 1800 a Trotting mare. Impor-
                       tant in history and development of
                       the Hackney.

PHOSPHORUS   He won Epsom Derby 1837.

PICK UP   A Pacing filly, won Abbedale
                       Stake.

PILOT   A Pacer and Trotter, his greatest
                       son was Pilot, Jr.

PIMPERNEL, the   Race horse.

PINCHED   Race horse.

PINE THEME   Race horse.

PINK   A Percheron.

PINK STAR   Kentucky Derby winner, 1907.

PINK SWAN	A race horse.
PIRATE	A Shire painted by Zeitter in 1810.
PIRATE GOLD	A Palomino.
PIXIE	Race horse.
PLANET	Pacer, leading money maker.
PLATTER	Race horse.
PLAUDIT	Kentucky Derby winner, 1898. A Palomino Stallion.
PLAYFELLOW	Failed both on track and at stud.
PLAYMAY	In 1938 highest payoff to players-- U. S. at Santa Anita, Calif.
PLEASANT SURPRISE	A Pacer Champion in 1952.
PLENTY BABY	A race horse.
PLENIPOTENTIARY	Won Epsom Derby in 1834.
POCAHONTAS	By Iron's Cadmus, bred to Ethan Allen and became the dam of another Pocahontas.
POETS EVE	Race horse.
POLYNESIAN	A Sprinter.
POMCHICLE	Race horse.
POMPOON	Race horse.
PONCA	A Mustang, Stallion.
PONDER	Kentucky Derby winner 1949.
POPLAR DELL	A Pacer.
POSTMAN	Race horse.
POT-8-OS	By Eclipse, out of Sportsmistress.
POWER GLOW	Pacer, champion in 1952.
POWER SITE	Race horse.
PRECIOUS HAL	A Pacer, and leading money maker.
PREMIER	Foaled 1880. Sired by What's Wanted, a well known show and breeder. Successful sire of prize winning animals.

PRETENDER	A Hackney horse.
PRETTY BUCK	Father was Snipper.
PRIAM	Winner of 1830 Epsom Derby.
PRIM'S GIRL	Race horse.
PRINCE	"All-around" cow pony in "Cowboy Reader."
PRINCE ADIOS	A Pacer, leading money maker.
PRINCE ALBERT	A Pacer.
PRINCE OF ALBION	A Clydesdale, said to have sold for $15,000, highest price ever paid for 2 year old filly.
PRINCE OF WALES	A Clydesdale; also a notable Shetland sire.
PRINCE PALATINE	Cost $200,000. Winner of the St. Leger, the Ascot Gold cup, Eclipse Stakes, Doncaster Cup, Jockey Club Stakes.
PRINCE SCORPION	Race horse.
PRINCE WILLIAM	A Shire, head of the stud for 20 years; 52 sired by him.
PRINCE YAKIMA	A Pacer, 1943.
PRINCESS ANNE	A Welsh pony, mare.
PRINCESS FLARE	A race horse.
PRINCESS HANDSOME	American bred; first prize International Exposition in Chicago, 1901-2-3.
PROCEDURE	A race horse.
PROUD PATRIOT	A race horse.
PROXIMITY	Trotter, champion, American. Won 252,929.67 through 1952.
PRUDENCE	A Percheron.
PURE PITCH	A race horse.
PUTNAM	Army's hero; wheel horse in a crack battery; saw service in China, Mexico, World War; perfect artillery horse; decorated by

Pershing as best artillery horse in American Expeditionary Force.

QINYAN	"Date cluster." Arabian horse name.
QIYAD	"Easy to lead, guide." Arabian horse.
QUARE TIMES	Race horse.
QUEEN AMERICA	Race horse.
QUEEN ANN	A Belgian mare.
QUEEN'S CHOICE	Race horse.
QUESTIONNAIRE	Horse.
QUICK CHIEF	Race horse.
QUILL	Race horse.
QUIZ BRIAR	Race horse.
QUIZ WHIZ	Race horse.
RABBIT PUNCH	A race horse.
RADIUM RAYS	A race horse.
RAFID	Arabian horse, meaning, "to support or uphold." Mare is RAFIDEH.
RAGOUT	A Percheron.
RAGTIME	In "The Drifting Cowboy" by Will James, 'best bucking horse in the outfit.'
RAINS OVER	A race horse.
RAMLA	An Arabian mare.
RANGER	An Arabian horse owned by George Washington.
RASALEH	"Message, or letter." An Arabian horse.
RAS EL AYN	"Top of a spring." Horse imported from Spain.
RASH STATEMENT	Race horse.

RAVEN'S CLAW	Race horse.
RAWA	"Quick witted."
REAFFIRMED	A race horse.
REAL DELIGHT	A race horse.
REAL SURE	A race horse.
REALLY SUMTHIN	A race horse.
RED BUTTON	Quarter horse, also called 'Old Roany.'
RED DEER	Winner of Chester Cup in England in 1844.
RED FIGHTER	Race horse.
RED LANTADOS	A Palomino.
RED PEPPER	An Appaloosa Stallion.
RED PLUME	Race horse.
RED ROCKY	Race horse.
RED SAILS	A Pacer.
REDBIRD	A horse in "Cowboy Reader."
REGRET	Kentucky Derby winner, 1915.
REGULAR ONE	A race horse.
REIGH COUNT	Kentucky Derby winner, 1928.
RELIC	A race horse.
RENDITION	A race horse.
REPAY	A race horse.
RESEMBLANCE	A race horse.
REX PEAVINE	Supreme among Saddle Horse enthusiasts; not as outstanding in show ring as he was esteemed a sire.
RILEY	Kentucky Derby winner, 1890.
RISHAN	"Lit. the one with feather like wings." Arabian horse.
RELIABILITY	A male mule.
RENA GRATTAN	A Pacer, champion 1952.
REVELANTA	A Clydesdale, won 7 prizes to 1915.

REXECUTIVE	Race horse.
RHODABARB	Race horse.
RHUM JR	A Percheron.
RIBBON CANE	A Pacer, leading money maker.
RIBOT	A race horse.
RIGHT NOTE	Race horse.
RIENZI	Sheridan's horse.
RILMA	Trotter, leading money maker.
RIOTER	Famous Steeple Chaser.
RIPPER JACK	Race horse.
RISEN SUN	A Trotter, champion 1952.
RIVER CLIPPER	Race horse.
ROAN DICK	Race horse 1883.
ROBERT THE DEVIL	1877, race horse.
ROCK SAND	Had cost August Belmont $125,000 was sold by him, 13 years of age for $150,000. Sire of fine broodmares.
ROCKET FUEL	Race horse.
RODNEY	2 year old Trotter, won Arthur S. Tompkins Memorial.
ROMAN STORY	Race horse.
ROMAN SOLDIER	Only horse to win all four of big fall handicaps in Maryland.
RONDO	Race horse in 1884.
ROSE BOWER	Beat best 2 year old fillies in midwest in the $99,500 Princess Pat Stakes in August, 1960, at Arlington Park.
ROSE CROIX	A Trotter, leading money maker, means 'red cross.'
ROSE SONG	Champion Trotter 1952.
ROUGE DRAGON	"Red dragon." Famous Steeple Chaser.
ROUGH TIME	An orphan, mother died at birth.

	Had misfortunes, broke bone in foot. Noted for gameness. Race horse.
ROUND TABLE	Race horse.
ROUTE SIXTY SIX	Race horse.
ROWDY BOY	A Pacer.
ROXANNA	A Saddlebred mare.
ROYAL BLOOD	Trotting mare, won The Acorn.
ROYAL CLOVE	Race horse.
ROYAL FAVORITE	A Clydesdale, won 7 prizes in 1915.
ROYAL MAIL	Race horse.
RUN FOR NURSE	Race horse.
RUSTEM BEY	Half Arabian and half Standard bred.
RUSTIC VILLAGE	Race horse.
SAAD	"Happiness." Arabian stallion.
SAAIDA	"Happy," an Arabian mare.
SABER CHARGE	Race horse.
SABOK	"Rapid." An Arabian horse.
SABOT D' OR	Race horse. "Gold shoe."
SABRE	A Palomino. "Sword."
SABRINA	Race horse, mare.
SACRED GROVE	Race horse.
SA DA	"Son of the south wind." "Good luck," an off-spring of the 5 mares of the Prophet Mahomet. In "Wonder Tales," by Carpenter.
SA 'DAN	Named after a desert plant and monkey. A Stall on. The Arabian mare is SA ' DAH.
SADIE MAC	Sired by Peter the Great; won Kentucky Futurity 1903.
SAFY	"Pure." An Arabian horse.

SAGGY	Made world record in Maryland, 1947.
SAGE HEN	Mare, Quarter Horse. Mother was Driftwood.
ST. AMANT	In 1904 English Derby winner.
ST. PETER TEAZLE	Also known as ST. PETER, by Highflyer, out of Papillon.
SAILOR'S VISION	Race horse.
SALEM	"Saviour." An Arabian horse.
SALTRAM	Imported in 1780. Epsom Derby winner 1783.
SALTY DAY	Race horse.
SAN JU LEE	Race horse.
SANDY FORK	Race horse.
SARAZEN	Called "a grass cutter," for he ran close to the ground and had no tendency to 'climb.'
SARCASTIC	Race horse.
SARPEDON	Imported in 1828, by Emilus, out of Icaria.
SATIN PRINCESS	Race horse.
SAUCY JETTA	Race horse.
SAWR	"Aggressive." An Arabian horse.
SCAPA FLOW	Sired by Man O' War.
SCARLET SLIPPER	Race horse.
SCHALES, SHALES	The original Shales and Shields. Various names given to one horse, foaled in 1755, thought to be sired by Blaze, a son of Flying Childers. He is four generations from the Darley Arabian.
SCHNAPPS	A Trotter.
SCOTCH RHYTHM	Sire was Volomite. A Trotter, winner Castleton Farm Stake, 1950. Also Arthur S. Tompkins Memorial.
SCOTTIES IMAGE	Race horse.

SCREWTAIL	Horse in "Cowboy Reader."
SEA FALCON	Race horse.
SEA TOWER	Race horse.
SEA TREAD	Race horse.
SEA ORBIT	Race horse.
SEABISCUIT	Tough; honest; little bay; became world's greatest money winner. Beat War Admiral in the Pimlico Special match race. Horse of the Year in 1938.
SECA-PLACE	Race horse.
SEDUCTEUR	A Percheron.
SEE SEE TEE	Race horse.
SEGLAWI	Is descended from four great mares owned by a man of this name. Upon the man's death he gave his brother, Jedra, his favorite mare. Seglawi Jedran-horses of this family, of this ancestry, mostly bays in color, possessed the greatest speed of any Arab family.
SELFA	"Loan." An Arabian horse.
SELIMA	"In good health." Daughter of Godolphin. Imported from England. An Arabian horse.
SELLING FAST	Race horse.
SENSATION	A Percheron.
SERGEANT	Epsom Derby winner in 1784.
SEVEN KEYS	Race horse.
SEVEN CORNERS	Race horse.
SEVENTY-SIX	Race horse.
SHADOW WAVE	Race horse.
SHAMROCK SALLY	Pacer, champion in 1952.
SHANNON RIVER	Famous Steeple Chaser.
SHANNONDALE	Race horse.

SHAR-NA-LOU	Race horse.
SHARI KAY	Race horse.
SHARIF	"Noble one." An Arabian horse.
SHARIMA	"Generous." An Arabian mare. Champion 1939.
SHARP NOTE	Race horse. 3 year old trotter of year 1952 sired by Phonograph.
SHAYKHAH	"Chief." Arabian mare. Stallion name is SHEYKH
SHEER DELIGHT	Race horse.
SHEIK	"Chief." An Arabian horse.
SHEILAS REWARD	A Sprinter.
SHEPPERALK	A Stallion in Lord Dunsay's "The Book of Wonder."
SHERIFA	An Arabian mare meaning, "noble." SHARIF is name for the Stallion.
SHERMAN MORGAN	Son of Justin Morgan.
SHILOH	In 1848, one of the founders of the Quarter Horse.
SHIMMY DANCER	Race horse.
SHORT JACKET	Captured the 13th running of the $81,030 Del Mar Futurity by some two lengths. Credited with the speediest performance at the distance 6 furlongs in 1:09 flat, in America this year (Sept. 1960) by a 2 year old.
SHUETTE	Race horse.
SHINING HEELS	Race horse.
SHIRKER, THE	In "Caravan," by John Galsworthy.
SHOPPING BASKET	Race horse.
SHOT PUT	Made world record 1940 in Homewood, Illinois.
SHUE FLY	Race horse.
SHURABAT AL-RIH	"Drinker of the wind," Arabian horse in "Drinker of the Wind."

SHUT OUT	Kentucky Derby Winner, 1942.
SI KING	Race horse.
SIED ABDALLAH	"Servant of God." Arabian Stallion.
SIGNAL	Had an illustrious career.
SIGNORINETTA	Winner English Derby in 1908.
SILVER AGENT	Race horse.
SILENT MAGIC	Race horse.
SILENT WATERS	A Pacer, leading money winner.
SILVER	Horse on T.V., a star.
SILVER AGENT	Race horse.
SILVER FAITH	Trotter, leading money maker.
SILVER'S TAFFY	Race horse.
SILVER RIDDLE	Trotter, leading money maker. American Trotting Champion.
SILVER SPOON	Victor in Vanity Handicap at Hollywood Park, 1960, won $38,450.
SILVER TAIL	A Mustang Stallion. SILVERTAIL is descendent of Charles Kent Mare.
SILVERTONE	A Palomino, colored Quarter Horse.
SIMRI	"Certain shade of dark grey color." Means, "friend, inmate."
SINGING SWORD	A 2 year old Trotter, Arthur S. Tompkins Memorial winner, 1952.
SIR ARCHY	1805, by Diomed, out of Castianira.
SIR BARTON	Triple Crown winner - Kentucky Derby, Preakness, Belmont Stakes in 1919.
SIR SOX	Race horse.
SIR EVERARD	A Clydesdale.
SIR GALLAHAD III	Son of Man O' War.
SKIBBEREEN	Famous Steeple Chaser.

SKIP SKIP	Race horse.
SKOBELEF	In "Skobelef was a Horse," by Johan Bojer.
SLEEPY DICK	A Quarter Horse racer.
SLEEPY GEORGE	An American Pacer Trotter.
SLEEPYHEAD	Racing horse.
SMALL SECRET	Race horse.
SMALL TOWN GIRL	Race horse.
SMALL EFFORT	Race horse.
SMASHAWAY	Sire was Volomite.
SNARK	Sired by Boojuin.
SMILE TODAY	Race horse.
SNIPETTE	Mother of Snipper.
SNOWBALL	An Albino Mare.
SNOW STORM	An Appaloosa. A pattern, solid color with splashes of white over loins and hips. Sometimes called SNOWFLAKE.
SNUG BERTH	Race horse.
SOLAR FAIRE	Race horse.
SOLAR ORBIT	Race horse.
SOLID PINK	Race horse.
SOLID SHADOW	Race horse.
SOLOMITE	Sired by Volomite.
SOLVANG SUE	Race horse.
SONGBIRD	Race horse.
SONG GIRL	Won The Acorn, a Trotter mare.
SONGMAN	Race horse.
SONIC BLAST	Race horse.
SONOFAGUN	Race horse.
SONOMA GIRL	Fastest green trotting mare on 1909 circuit. Leading money maker.
SONOMA PASS	Race horse.

SOON WE'LL KNOW	Race horse.
SOOTHSAYER	An Arabian race horse.
SOTEMIA	Race horse.
SOUND OF RUM	Race horse.
SOUPED UP	Race horse.
SOUR CROUT	Imported in 1786.
SOUTH PACIFIC	Won Abbedale Stake, a pacing filly.
SPARKLE WAY	Race horse.
SPARKY PLUG	Dam.
SPEARMINT	Won English derby in 1906. Sire was Carbine.
SPECIAL BLUES	Race horse.
SPECIAL DELIGHT	Champion Cleveland Bay Stallion.
SPECIAL DEMAND	Race horse.
SPECIAL DIAMOND	Race horse.
SPICY	Race horse.
SPOKANE	Kentucky derby winner, 1889.
SPORTING BLOOD	Race horse.
SPOTLIGHT	Race horse.
SPREAD EAGLE	Won Epsom Derby 1795.
SPRINKLES	Race horse.
SQUIRE	An exceptional jumper, also white.
STAGEHAND	A Stretch runner.
STAND PAT	Race horse.
STAR	Queen Anne's horse, that won the first actual money-race in history.
STAR GAZE	Race horse.
STAR MILKMAN	Race horse.
STAR POINTER	One of leading sires of Pacers to 1918. Harness horse in 1897.
STAR RADIANCE	Race horse.

STAR'S PRIDE	Trotter, sire was Worthy Boy. Trotter of the year, 1952.
STAUNTON HERO	Shire.
STEAMBOAT	Top bucking horse of all time, owned by Buffalo Bill.
STEEL DUST	Is a magic name in Quarter Horse legend. The Steel family traces to the earlier Janus through the Celer and Whip strains.
STEEL MINX	Race horse.
STELLA	Hackney mare.
STEP A BIT	A thoroughbred filly in the book of the same name by Sam Savitt.
STEP NORTH	Dam of Step-a-Bit.
STIMULUS	Horse.
STENCIL	Horse.
"STEEPE HORSE"	Inhabited high places of Mongolia. Never found outside the cold, mountainous regions.
STEVERINO	Race horse.
STONE STREET	Kentucky Derby winner 1908.
STRICTLY CLASS	Race horse.
STRONG WIND	Race horse.
STUMP SUCKER	Horse in "Cowboy Reader."
STUMP-THE-DEALER	American Saddle Horse foundation stock thoroughbred.
STYLISH MAID	Race horse.
SUGAR FLUFF	Race horse.
SUMMER STORY	Race horse.
SUN ARCHER	American turf star.
SUN BEAU	True stayer; consistent; durable.
SUN DISC	Race horse.
SUNSTAR	Won English Derby 1911.
SUPERCHARGE	Race horse.

SUPER CHIEF	Quarter horse.
SURE CASH	Race horse.
SURVIVOR	Winner Preakness Stakes, 1873.
SUTTER'S CREEK	Race horse.
SUZY'S HONEY	Race horse.
SWALLOWSWIFT	Race horse.
SWAPS	Kentucky Derby winner 1955, thoroughbred Stallion, won $848,000.
SWEEP	A black pony.
SWEEP VESTAL	Won first race at Charles Town, W. Va. in 1934, but no win ticket had been sold on her. Sweep Vestal was ignored as winner in payoffs and those who bet on second horse, Tiny Miss-to-Win, were paid off.
SWEET AMEN	Race horse.
SWIFT BEAU	Race horse.
SWIRLING ABBY	Race horse.
SWORD DANCER	Race horse.
SYSONBY	Imported 1901, by Melton, out of Optime. A great one of earlier days. Defeated only once in his career; evidence since brought to light throws doubt on validity of that defeat.
T. FLYING DUTCHMAN	Winner Epsom Derby in 1849.
TACO	Means, "a rolled up tortilla," was mouse-gray, and so called because he looked like a Taco when he was asleep. In "Taco, the snoring burro," by Helen Holland Graham.
TAGALIC	Winner English Derby 1912.
TALK TALK	Race horse.
TAHALA	"sweeter" for either Stallion or

	Mare.
TAHIR	"Pure." Arabian Stallion name.
TALLYCOED	Race horse.
TAMRI	"Date colored one."
TAMWORTH	A Shire, imported to Canada in 1836, supposed to have been a Shire.
TANKARD	Race horse.
TAR HEEL	Pacer in 1952. Sire was Billy Direct. Won American National.
TARELLA	Race horse.
TATTON DRAY KING	In 1909 Champion Shire Society Show sold for $18,500 at dispersal sale.
TEA MAKER	A Sprinter.
TELEVISION	Won in 1948 Debutante Stake, 2 year old pacing filly.
TENNIS SLIPPER	Race horse.
TENSE INDIAN	Race horse.
TEMPESTUOUS	Race horse.
TETRARCH, the	Considered fastest horse to race in England in recent times.
THAT'S CANDY	Race horse.
THEME SONG	Sire was Algiers.
THINKING CAP	Race horse.
THISTLE BELLE	Won 286 races, a record for a mare.
THORNDALE	Sired by Mambrino Patchen. American Trotter and Pacer.
THUNDERCLAP	American National Stakes, winner. Sired by Chief Counsel. Leading money maker. Pacer.
TIGER	Quarter horse in 1816.
TIME SUPPLY	Race horse.
TINY TOWER	Race horse.

TIP ALONG	Race horse.
TIDES IN	Sired by Goose Bay.
TOLL GATE	A Pacer and leading money maker.
TOM FOOL	Race horse.
TONYWATHA	A Mustang.
TOP BRASS	An American Saddle Horse, gelding.
TOP CALIBER	Race horse.
TOP DECK	Outstanding sire of the $125,000 horse Go Man Go.
TOP DOUBLE	Race horse.
TOP GALLANT	Called Old Top. One of earliest and fastest trotters. A grandson of Messenger through Coriander. He had been a galloper of some repute, his trotting discovery came when as a hack horse in a Philadelphia livery stable. Startled, he ran away, trotting. Credited for winning the first trotting race on a regulation track in America and the victor in the Union Course trot in 1823. Age of 15.
TOP ROW	Race horse.
TOPSY	Mustang mare.
TORPID	Race horse.
TORRID SCOTT	Race horse.
TOSCA	Race horse.
TRAMP	Race horse in 1810.
TRANQUILIZER	Race horse.
TRAVEL BOOK	Race horse.
TRAVELER	General Lee's horse. Also a Quarter Horse in 1889.
TREMONT	Foaled 1884. One of greatest American thoroughbreds. In 1886 made racing appearance.
TRINKET	Notable Shetland pony sire.

TROJAN	In 1914 earned $16,010.
TROUBLEMAKER	The Gallant.
TROUGH HILL	Famous Steeple Chaser.
TRUE CHIEF	A Pacer and leading money maker.
TRUE KITTY	A Pacer and leading money maker.
TRUMPET	A Pacer and leading money maker.
TRUSTING SOULD	Race horse.
TRYCOOK	Highest payoff to players, U. S. 1934.
TUSTIN	Race horse.
TWENTY GRAND	Kentucky Derby winner 1931.
TWENTYONE GUNS	Race horse.
TWIGG	Quarter horse 1782.
TWILIGHT TEAR	Horse of the year 1944.
TWINKLE	A colt in "Twinkle, a baby colt" by Lawrence Barrett.
TYPHOON II	Kentucky Derby Winner 1897.
TYRANT	Epsom Derby Winner 1802.
UGLY	Named for dispositon. Breeding unknown. Would try to jump anything, anywhere.
UHLAN	A black gelding.
UNCUT DIAMOND	Race horse.
UNERRING	Race horse.
UPSET	Race horse.
URFAH	"The mane." Arabian name.
VAGRANT	Kentucky Derby Winner, 1876.
VAN METER'S WAXY	Thoroughbred; American Saddle Horse foundation stock.
VENDETTA	Race horse, thoroughbred.

VENETIAN WAY	Preakness favorite, on basis of early victory in Kentucky Derby. At Washington Park made $47,150. Won Churchill Downs Classic 1960, and Kentucky Derby, 1960. Won Wright memorial.
VESTA'S WORTHY	Trotter, won The Acorn.
VICTORY SPARK	Race horse.
VIDOCQ	A Percheron.
VOLO SONG	A Trotter, leading money maker. Won Arthur S. Tompkins Memorial, 2 year old.
VOLODYOVSKI	Sire was Florizel. Won English Derby 1901.
VOLGA	Daughter of Peter the Great; unbeaten during career.
VOLOMITE	Trotting sire.
VOLTAIRE	A Percheron.
VOLUNTEER	A famous don of Hambeltonian.
VOTING TRUST	Sire was Volomite.
VULCAN	A Shire, famous as a sire, has sired 41 prize winner.
WAGON MASTER	Race horse.
WAIST BANDIT	Race horse.
WAIT A BIT	Sire of Step-a-Bit.
WAIT AWHILE	Race horse.
WALTER DEAR	Trotter and leading money maker.
WAMPUM	A Mustang.
WAPAKONETA	Largest payoff on $5.00 win ticket, which was $1,078.20, in 1882.
WAR ADMIRAL	Horse of the year in 1937, Triple Crown winner. Sired by Man O' War. Only 3 horses had won the Triple heretofore.
WAR BATTLE	Steeple Chaser.

WAR GLORY	American turf star.
WAR PLUMAGE	Daughter of a dud in races for fillies; set new record for the race at Coaching Club Oaks. Is one of greatest race mares in turf history.
WAR RELIC	Race horse.
WAR TROUBLE	Race horse.
WARM UP	Race horse.
WAUSETA	Mustang mare.
WAVEAWAY	Race horse.
WAVERLY ANN	Winner Abbedale Stake, pacing filly.
WAY YONDER	Winner of Castleton Farm Stake.
WAYWARD JENNY	Race horse.
WAXY	Winner Epsom Derby 1793.
WEEKEND PASS	Race horse.
WEDDING GUEST	Race horse.
WELKIN, the	Famous Steeple Chaser.
WHALEBONE	Trotter in 1831. Another Whalebone won Epsom Derby in 1810. Sired by Waxy.
WHATS WANTED	A Famous Shire, sired 9 prize winners. Sire of Premier.
WHIP	A Quarter horse in 1809.
WINTER NIGHT	Race horse.
WHIRLAWAY	Horse of the Year in 1941; broke record in the Kentucky Derby.
WHIRLWIND	One of the greatest horses of Morgan blood foaled 1877, died 1908. An inbred Morgan. Sire was Whirlwind, by Indian Chief, by Blood's Blackhawk, by Vermont Morgan, by Sherman Morgan, by Justin Morgan.
WHISKER	By Waxy, 1812.

WHISKERY	Kentucky Derby Winner, 1927.
WHITE BELL	Race horse.
WHITE CLOUD	Pony in "Lightning," by Miriam Mason.
WHITE COCKADE	Race horse.
WHITE MOUNTAIN BOY	A Pacer.
WHITE STAR	Belonged to Little No Feather, a Navajo Indian boy in "the Little Horse," by Stan Steiner.
WHITE WINGS	An American Albino Stallion.
WHICHONE	Horse.
WHISK BROOM II	Saddle Horse.
WHITE KNIGHT	Race horse.
WHIZ BAM	Race horse.
WHY TRAVEL	Race horse.
WIDE OUTLOOK	Race horse.
WIFE, the	Race horse.
WILD DAYRELL	Won Epsom Derby 1855.
WILDFIRE	Important in history of development of the Hackney.
WILL BE READY	Race horse.
WINTER NIGHT	Race horse.
WIRE CUT	Race horse.
WISE JAX	Race horse.
WILLIAM THE CONQUEROR	A Shire that won some prizes in show ring; sired noted Stallions- Prince William Esquire and Staunton Hero.
WINTERGREEN	Kentucky Derby winner, 1909.
WIRE US	Race horse.
WISHING RING	Top payoff at Latonia.
WINNEPEG	Pacer 1928.
WOODBURY	Son of Justin Morgan.
WOODPECKER	By Herod, out of Misfortune, 1773.

WORKING GIRL	Race horse.
WOVEN WEB	Thoroughbred, sired by Bold Venture.
WRIGHT'S FARMER'S GLORY	Or the Attleboro horse; may have been a half-bred Suffolk. This strain existed from 1800-1880; used to improve Suffolk; couldn't overcome predominate Shire blood and character.
Y. ECLIPSE	Won the Epsom Derby 1781.
YANKEE MAID	Trotter, leading money maker; winner Arthur S. Tompkins Memorial, 2 year old trotter.
YELLOW STUD	Copperbottom Quarter horse.
ZAPE	An Arabian presented to the President of the Republic of Cuba by the King of Spain.
ZARIFE	"Beautiful." For an Arabian mare.
ZEV	Kentucky Derby winner, 1923.
ZERO NIGHT	Race horse.
ZAHI	Lit. "the flourishing one."
ZIPON	Race horse.
ZIYADAH	"Superb in speed."
ZOMBRO	1933 - Highest payoff to players- U. S. Charlestown, W. Va. Pacer, leading money maker.

INSECTS & SPIDERS

INSECTS & SPIDERS

Names

ANT

AUGUSTE

For Auguste Forel, who discovered that tiny ants, having passage ways to the nest of the big black ants would dash out of their galleries and devour the young of the big black ant.

BRAIN TRUSTER

The army ant has learned many things - to have slave ants, to cultivate agricultural crops, carry parasols on hot days.

DESTINY

The male ants fulfill their destiny when they die after the marriage flight; the princess fulfills hers when she becomes a queen.

GARDENER

The ant plants fungus on leaves, then tends this garden.

HAWKEYE

A Scout in "Last of the Mohicans," by James Fennimore Cooper. An ant scout wanders about to establish a trail for the other ants.

PHARAOH

The red house ant, so called because it might have been one of the seven plagues sent against Pharaoh, as told in the Bible.

PURSUED, the

Ants are pursued relentlessly by the ant lion.

SCISSORS

One kind of ant cuts leaves for their underground galleries.

SOLDIER

The worker major of the army ant.

SWEET TOOTH

Ants like sweet treats. They take the honey pollen from other

319

insects, feed it to their own workers.

ANT LION

GRISELDA	After Patient Griselda, character in Boccaccio and Chaucer, who was extremely patient. The ant lion patiently waits for its prey.
HUMPTY	They have hump backs.
IN REVERSE	They walk backwards.
LITTLE ENGINEER, the	They mark off a place where they dig a funnel trap, with great accuracy.
PATIENCE	For weeks they sit waiting inside the funnel with nothing to eat if no ant comes along.
SHOVELER	They have flat heads with which they mark off the pit margin, and shovel out the sand.
SNEAK, the	Their heads look sneaky, and they have fierce jaws, but appear to be innocent.

BACKSWIMMER

NIGHT FLIER	It flies and swims at night.
OUCH!	Swimmers know its painful bite.

BEE

ABUNDANT	Provides an abundance of honey.
BI	The American Indian name for 'bee.'
BOMB	Bumblebee's scientific name is Bombus Americanus.
DESTINY	He or she performs her destiny.
DIZZY	The way it dances to get off the pollen baskets.
FLIGHT MAPPER	Draws a map to tell the other bees where to find the honey.
KANXI	American Indian name for 'bee.'
PINCER	Part of leg of the honey bee worker.

BEE (continued)

SWEET TOOTH	Honey bee.
TUH MA GA	American Indian name for 'bee.'

BEETLE

ANDY	Name given to a beetle in the American Museum of Natural History.
BLACK KNIGHT	Ground beetle, for its color and armour.
CHEE MI	American Indian word of 'little.' Any small animal can be so named.
COUSIN SCARAB	The June beetle is related to the Sacred Scarab of Egypt.
CRASH DIVER	The whirligig beetle sees danger and he quickly dives deep under the surface of the pond until the danger is past.

BOOKLOUSE

CRUNCHER	It chews on paper.
THE INFORMER	Lives in books and papers.
RESEARCHER	Lives in books and papers.

BUTTERFLY

AURORA	Taken from Aurora Borealis which is the Northern Lights - all colors. Any bright colored butterfly, or winged insect.
CHERRY	The Tiger Swallowtail and the Blue Emperor like the wild cherry, prefers it to other plant foods.
CINDERELLA	The Tiger Swallowtail, is one of the ugliest of caterpillars, which becomes one of most beautiful butterflies.
CABBY	The Cabbage butterfly prefers the cabbage for food.
CLOVER	The preferred plant food of the

BUTTERFLY (continued)

	Clouded Sulphur.
DIRUNAL	Any day-active butterfly.
GLAMOUR GIRL	Any beautiful butterfly.
KI MA MA	American Indian name for 'butter-fly.'
NECTARINA	Any insect that likes to sip plant juices.
O WA NI YE TU	American Indian name for 'little wings.'
SPANGLES	The pretty clothes of any butterfly.
TAILS	The Swallow butterfly has tails on his rear wings.
TRIO	The cabbage butterfly has 3 pairs of round black dots on his wings. Sometimes only two pairs, so he might be called DUO.
VIOLET	Fritilleries like violets best of all plant foods.

CATERPILLAR

| ISABELLA | The scientific name for caterpillar is 'Isia Isabella.' |
| WOOLY | The caterpillar looks wooly because of his thick coat. |

COCKROACH

ARISTOCRAT	The cockroach has survived its present roach form for centuries.
HE WHO LEAPS	Name given to a cockroach in "Everyday Miracle."
MINNIE	Another in "Everyday Miracle."
PASSENGER	Cockroaches are found on all ships.
TRAILER	Several of the younger members of the family travel along with the adults.

CRICKET

| BROAD JUMPER | He makes wide leaps. |

CRICKET (continued)

BROADCASTER	The cricket chirps shrilly.
CHIN LING	A Chinese cricket in the book, "Chin Ling," by Alison Stilwell.
CHIRRUP	His shrill call sounds like this.
DANCING FIDDLER	He does both, dances and fiddles.
GOOD LUCK	A cricket on the hearth has been traditionally regarded as an omen of good luck. In the story "Cricket on the Hearth," by Charles Dickens, the cricket chirps when all is well, it is silent when there is sorrow.
GRYL	Taken from the scientific name, Gryllus campestris.
KIN CHUNG	"Golden bell." Name given to the Chinese cricket.
MANDOLIN	The cricket sings and chirps a little like a mandolin.
MUSIC MAN	He makes music by the friction of his leathery forewings.
OUT-OF-TUNE	Sometimes he is out of tune when the nights become frosty.
PATENT-LEATHER	His body has a smooth finish. (So has the beetle)
RASP	He makes noises like a rasp, or file.
THERMOMETER	"When a cricket chirps, take a watch, count the number of sounds in one quarter of a minute. Add forty to that count and the sum will be the approximate temperature. (Fahrenheit)."

DAMSEL FLY

AZURE	Its body is blue.
LACE	Its wings are dainty and lace-like.
SKY	The color of the fly is blue, a sky blue.

DRAGON FLY

BIG EYES	It has unusually large eyes.
BIPLANE	Looks like a biplane as it soars through the air. It is probably the strongest flyer of all insects.
DARK LACE	The wings are brown or black, some have solid spots making a pattern in the lacy wing.
DEVIL'S DARNING NEEDLE	Sometimes called this because it looks like a darning needle, but since it is not a stinger, is not a devil. Supersitition has accused it of having an intention to sew up the ears of bad boys and work mischief in the hair of naughty girls. In the South it is called a 'snake doctor' because it is said that it feeds and nurses ailing serpents.
GREEN DARNER	Another name for it, for it has a green body with black markings. "Green Darner," is the name of a book about it, by R.M. McClung.
GREEN JACKET	For its green body, which becomes blue when the insect becomes old, then it would be called BLUE JACKET.
LACE PETTICOATS	Her dainty, lacy wings.

FIREFLY

FAIRY LANTERN	The firefly has luminous segments in its abdomen which light up rhythmically. They are tiny and makes one think they could be fairy lights.
FLASHLIGHT	The body of the firefly is his flashlight as he skims through the night.
GLOWWORM	Another name for him.
LANTERN	His body lights up.
LIGHTNING BUG	Another name for firefly.

FIREFLY (continued)

LIGHT BULB	The firefly's ability to light up.
NEON	It's light turns off and on.
PETI	The American Indian name for 'firefly.'
TAIL LIGHT	For its ability to flash on lights.

FLEA

BLACK PLAGUE	A dog's flea, the color of which is dark. It is a black plague to the dog. Rat fleas may carry the dreaded disease Black Plague.

FLY

ACHILLE'S HEEL	Their weak point is that they can't see the color red.
FUZZY	The bee fly which has a body resembling a fuzzy bee.

GRASSHOPPER

CAREFREE	It seems to hop here, there, everywhere, without a thought in the world.
CATAPULT	It hurls itself into the air, landing anywhere.
CELLOPHANE	Their flying wings sound like the rustling of crushed cellophane.
CHIRPER	For its song.
EMILY	It keeps itself well groomed, for Emily Post.
FIDDLE AND BOW	Its hind leg and forewing are used to make music.
FIDDLER	It makes music.
FIDDLESTICK	Its hind leg is like a fiddlestick, with which to make music on its wing.
GAY HOPPER	Seems never to have a care.
HIGH JUMPER	Leaps high.
MUSIC MAKER	Could be used for any animal that

GRASSHOPPER (continued)

	sings.
POP CORN	It jumps suddenly, like the pop-corn in a pan.
RED LEGS	A kind of grasshopper.
ROVING FEET	Grasshopper is always on the go.
SOLO	He goes off by himself.
SPEEDY	He gets out of the way of his enemies fast.
TAKE-OFF	He takes off from the ground like a plane.
TITHONUS	Eos, Greek goddess of the dawn, turned her husband, Tithonus into a grasshopper, fed him nectar and ambrosia so that he would never die.
ZIGZAGGER	He zigzags through the grass to elude his enemy.

KATYDID

CACKLE-JACK	Name given to it in the South.
GREEN MANTLE	Wears a green suit of clothes.
MAKE BELIEVE	He looks like a leaf.
KATY DID	From its name.
MERRY, or MARY	A happy insect.
ZEEP	It sounds something like this when it talks.

LADYBUG

BEETLE OF OUR LADY	Lady bug was so called during the Middle Ages. Also, 'Our Lady.'
GREY LADY	The lady bug helps keep the insects down; the Grey Lady organization helps humans.
HALLOWEEN	It has the orange and black coloring of Halloween.
ON A TESKA	Or, just TESKA. This is the American Indian name for 'lady bug.'

MIDGE

    LARK · They look as though they were having a lark dancing above the surface of the lakes, the tops of the bordering trees.

MOTH

    GORGEOUS GEORGE · The Luna Moth. It is a sight never to be forgotten, for it is considered the most beautiful of all insects.

    MOONBEAM · Delicate, fragile, pale, like a moonbeam. This is the Luna moth.

    NOCTURNE · The Gypsy moth is active at night.

    REQUIEM · The Gypsy moth is harmful, so it is requiem for whatever it touches.

    SNOWHITE · The silkworm moth is white.

PLANT HOPPER

    JUMPING JACK · It is a great jumper

    PALE JACK · Its wings are a pale green.

PRAYING MANTIS

    CANNIBAL · It feeds on other insects. The female may eat its own male.

    FIGHTER · It is a good fighter.

    GREEDY · It buries its whole face in a meal worm.

    SPINY · Its forelegs are spiny.

    STEEL TRAP · The strong arms of the mantis is a steel trap to the bee or butterfly caught in them.

    TIGER · It has limbs of sharp cutting edges that can close like the blade of a pen knife.

    WHIPLASH · Its foreleg shoots out to grasp its prey, with a too-quick-for-the

PRAYING MANTIS (continued)

eye movement.

SPIDER

ACROBAT	Jumping spiders wander about in the open spaces.
ARACHNE	Arachne wove gorgeous tapestry picturing the gods love of adventure.
ATHENE	Was the goddess of weaving.
AUTUMN	The crab spider usually wears autumn colors.
AVIATOR	A spider plays out silk strands that float up and carry it to its future home.
BALLOON MAKER	He makes his balloon this way and rides in it.
BLACK SPINNER	From the color of the spider, and what he does.
BUILDER	He makes a balloon to take him over the earth.
CALLING CARD	The trap door spider leaves his hind legs and part of his abdomen in the trap door of his tube home so that he can open the door quickly when he returns.
CHARLOTTE	The spider in "Charlotte's Web," by E. B. White.
FLY PAPER	The bowl and doily spider builds two sheets of web for snares to catch its prey.
FLYER	The balloon spider.
GAY CABELLERO	The Jumping spider has gay colored hairs, plumed and spangled.
HARRY	From Harry-Long-Legs, another name for Daddy-Long-Legs.
HARVESTER	The Daddy-Long-Legs, or Crane Fly.
HINGE MAKER	Spider makes a trap door with a

SPIDER (continued)

	hinge on it.
JULES VERNE	The balloon spider floats through the air on its own web, like in a balloon. After Jules Verne who wrote "Around the World in Eighty Days," which was in a balloon.
JUMPER	The Jumping Spider has great jumping ability.
KING	The American tarantula is the largest in the spider world.
LITTLE CATCHER	The spider is small, catches its prey in webs.
MIRANDA	The scientific name for the spider, Miranda Agriope Aurantia.
MR. AND MRS. WEBB	The spiders in the Freddy stories by Walter Brooks.
MISS PARACHUT	The garden spider floats from its silk lines to find a home.
QUICKSILVER	The spider's eyes give off an intense silver-like glow at night, like the drop of quicksilver.
SILAS MARNER	Silas was a weaver in the book, "Silas Marner," by George Eliot.
SAFETY-FIRST or SAFETY BELT	The Jumping spiders secure a silk line at the jumping off place, so that if they fall by accident they can get back to their original position.
TORNADO	The Funnel web spider makes a funnel, a tube of web, like the funnel of a tornado.
TRAPPER	A spider traps his prey.
TURRET	The Wolf spider lives in the Arizona desert where he surrounds his hole with tiny pebbles where he sits waiting for his prey.
YELLOW SPINNER	The spider spins, he is yellow in color.

WALKING STICK

    I-DON'T-CARE

                  The walking stick is not particular about the way, or where, she lays her eggs.

    LITTLE TWIG

                  The walking stick looks like a twig.

    PATTER

                  When walking sticks group together, they may drop their hard shelled eggs into the leaves below, making a sound like the patter of rain.

WASP

    KNIGHT   It wears an armour.

    PILL BOX   A wooden pill box was used by Howes, the first biologist to use it as a method of housing solitary wasps nests. It suggests smallness too.

    YELLOW FACE   The face of the wasp is yellow.

WATER BOATMAN

    HICCOUGH   He jerks about when he swims.

WATER SCORPION

    SLENDERELLA   The water scorpion is slender.

WATER STRIDER

    SKATER   Looks as though he was skating on top of the water.

    SKI MAN   Glides and zigzags across the surface of the pond.

    SPEED DEMON   He is very fast.

    STITCHER   As he zigzags over the water he dips down as though he were stitching the water.

    THREADER   He looks as though he was threading the water.

SMALL & OTHER WILD ANIMAL PETS

SMALL & OTHER WILD ANIMAL PETS

Wild Animal Pets - Zoo Pets - Barnyard Pets - Pets of Science & the Naturalist

Names

ANTELOPE

    WHITE FLAG   In "Wild Animals of Five Rivers Country," by George Cory Franklin.

APE

    CHRISTINE   A Barbary ape in the St. Louis Zoo.

    PHILIP   A Barbary ape in the St. Louis Zoo.

    MONA   An ape in "Everyday Miracle," by Gustav Eckstein.

ARMADILLO

    ARMORED TANK   Armadillo is completely covered with armor.

    BASKET   He'll probably be one someday, for the natives make and sell the shell for baskets.

    BANDY   His armor has many bands.

    DIGGER   He is a good digger.

    DILL   The last part of his name, Armadillo.

    HINGES   The shell of the armadillo is hinged to allow movement.

    KNIGHT   A knight in the middle ages wore armor to battle.

    MOSAIC   The pattern on his coat looks like mosaic.

    WASHBOARD   His armored back feels like one.

BADGER

BOW LEGS	Badger is bow-legged and pigeon toed.
FLAT HEAD	He has a flat pointed head.
MISH TAN USK	American Indian name for 'badger.'
MUSSY	For his messy habits, in "Pets, Wild and Western," by Elmo N. Stevenson.
OLD GRAY COAT	His fur is gray and silver, grizzled with black.
OLD SILVER	His fur is silvery gray.
RAPIER	He can lash out with rapier-like claws.
TEJON	Name given to him in "Wild Animals of the Southwest."

BAT

DEXTER	Taken from "dexterity," which is a spectacular feature of bats when in flight.
ECHO	His high pitched squeaks are supersonic calls which echo back to warn him of obstacles and enable him to judge distance.
FLAPPER FANNY	A name given to him in "Illustrated Library of Natural Sciences."
MANG	The bat in the Jungle Books, by Rudyard Kipling.
PITCH	He is dark color, flies in the pitch black of night.
PUG NOSE	The nose of the bat is blunt.
MIGHTY JOE	Name given to him in "Illustrated Library of Natural Sciences."
RADAR	The bat's system of judging distances.
SILHOUETTE	He makes silhouettes against the moon and the night sky.

BAT (continued)

SQUEAKER	The way the bat calls, with high squeaks.
SULKY	A bat sulks in captivity.

BEAR

BALDY	The bear in "Wild Animals of the Southwest."
BALOO	In the Jungle Books, by Rudyard Kipling.
CHANG	A brown bear in the Brooklyn Zoo.
CHEK	A brown bear in the Brooklyn Zoo.
JO JO	An Alaskan brown bear in the Bronx Zoo.
MOM	A Polar bear in the Brooklyn Zoo.
NONOOK	A Polar bear in "One Day with Tuktu," by Armstrong Sperry.
NIKI	A cinnamon bear. American Indian name.
NIP & TUCK	Bear cubs in the book of the same name by George M. Dyott.
PADDY	A bear cub in "Paddy's Christmas," by Helen Monsell.
SONA	A black bear in the Jungle Books by Rudyard Kipling.
TUFFY	A bear in "Wild Animals of the Southwest."
WINNIE THE POOH	A bear in "Winnie the Pooh," by A. A. Milne.

BEAVER

AH MISK	American Indian name for 'beaver.'
BONNIE	A female bear in "Tuffy."
THE BROWN ONE	In "Here come the beavers," by Alice Goudey.
CROPPY	In "Tuffy."

BEAVER (continued)

ENGINEER	For he has extraordinary intelligence, industry and skill. Beavers trees, when felled, always face in the middle of the pond.
FLAT TAIL	In "Flat Tail," by Alice Gall.
KERSLAP	In "Here Comes the Beavers," by Alice Goudey.
LITTLE PADDLE-TAIL	He has a paddle for a tail. He is called this in "Here come the Beavers," by Alice Gall.
LITTLE TALKING BROTHER	The Indians called the beaver this in "Here Come the Beavers," by Alice Goudey.
MOSSA	American Indian name for 'beaver.'
NIGHT SHIFT	He works mostly at night or in the early morning.
SHARPTOOTH	Name given to a beaver in "Wild Animals of the Southwest."
SPLASHER	A beaver in "Flat Tail," by Alice Gall.
TUFFY	A beaver in "Tuffy," by George Cory Franklin.
WHISTLER	The beaver whistles to catch attention.

CAMEL

FRIEDA	The Dromedary Camel in the St. Louis Zoo.
HENRIETTA	The Bactrian Camel in the St. Louis Zoo.

CARIBOU

DANCER	The Woodland Caribou in the St. Louis Zoo.
RUDOLPH	The Woodland Caribou in the St. Louis Zoo.

CHIMPANZEE

ALPHA	"First." In 'Everyday Miracle,' by Eckstein.
AMI	"Love." In 'Everyday Miracle,' by Eckstein.
DIVINA	In "Everyday Miracle."
DUKE	In the St. Louis Zoo. A performing chimp.
FUNNY	A performing chimpanzee in the St. Louis Zoo.
HAPPY	A performing chimpanzee in the St. Louis Zoo.
JERRY	A performing chimpanzee in the St. Louis Zoo.
MESHIE	A Chimpanzee raised by the scientist, Harry Raven.
PAN	In "Everyday Miracle."
PANCHO	A performing chimpanzee in the St. Louis Zoo.
PATI	In "Everyday Miracle."
PETE	In the St. Louis Zoo.
TINY	A performing chimpanzee in the St. Louis Zoo.
WENDY	In "Everyday Miracle."
CONGO	A chimp in the Staten Island Zoo.
LOLA	A chimp in the Staten Island Zoo.

CHIPMUNK

AY ASHE	American Indian name for 'chipmunk.'
BRIGHT EYES	It has bright eyes.
CHIP	From the first part of 'chipmunk.'
CHIPPER	He is a chipper animal.
CHIPPIE, or CHIPPY	From the name. In "Pets, Wild and Western," by Elmo N. Stevenson.

CHIPMUNK (continued)

"CHIRRUP"	His call.
CHUCK	"Chuck, chuck," is his call.
COPPERHEAD	In "Pets, Wild and Western."
LITTLE CHIP	In "Little Chip," by Berta and Elmer Hader.
POUCHY	He stuffs his cheeks with food.
TIGHT ROPE	He can walk a tightrope.

COW

MRS. WOGUS	A cow character in the Freddy stories by Walter Brooks.
MRS. WURZBURGER	Also in the Freddy stories.
MOOLOO	A character in "Mister Penny," by Marie Hall Ets.

CUSCUS

MR. ODD SPOTS	He is as small as a kitten, and cuddly with odd spots over him.

DEER

BAMBI	The deer in "Bambi," by Felix Salten.
DASH	The deer in "Dash and Dart" by Mary and Conrad Buff.
JANGO	American Indian name for 'deer.'
JUDY	In "Wild Animals of the Southwest."
OLD HORNY	A buck in "Dash and Dart."
SPIKE	A whitetail deer in "Spike," by Robert M. McClung.
WAPI	An elk in "Wild Animals of the Southwest."
WHITETAIL	In "Here come the Deer."

DORMOUSE

SLEEPY HEAD	In "Twenty Little Pets from Everywhere," by Raymond L. Ditmars.

DORMOUSE (continued)

SLEEPY MOUSE   The meaning of dormouse.

EARTHWORM

NATURE'S PLOW   It plows through the ground.

RINGS   It is made of rings.

BRISTLES   It has hairs on its body.

ELEPHANT

ALICE   A performing elephant in the St. Louis Zoo.

ARTHUR   In "Barbar stories" by Jean de Brunhoff. He was a cousin of Babar.

BABAR   In "The Story of Babar," by Jean de Brunhoff.

BARNEY   In the Bronx Zoo.

CANDY   A baby elephant in the Bronz Zoo.

CLARA   A performing Asiatic elephant in the St. Louis Zoo.

CELESTE   Cousin of Babar in the Barbar stories.

CORNELIUS   In "The story of Babar."

FLORENCE   In the St. Louis Zoo.

HATHI   In the Jungle Books, by Rudyard Kipling.

HERMANN   A performing elephant in the St. Louis Zoo.

MARIE   A performing Asiatic elephant in the St. Louis Zoo.

MINNIE   In the Bronx Zoo.

MISS ZOO   In the Bronx Zoo.

OLIVER   In "Oliver," by Syd Hoff.

PEMBE   The bull elephant in "Tembo," by W. J. Wilwerding.

PINKY   In the Bronx Zoo. His real name is Doruma.

ELEPHANT (continued)

PUMIE
: A performing Asiatic elephant in the St. Louis Zoo.

TEMBO
: A baby elephant in "Tembo," who lived near the Kilimanjaro mountains.

THA
: In the Jungle Books by Rudyard Kipling.

TOOMAI
: In the Mowgli stories, by Rudyard Kipling.

TRUDY
: A performing elephant in the St. Louis Zoo.

WADDY
: In "Adventures of Molly, Waddy and Tony," by Paul Waitt.

FOX

JET
: A black fox in "Wild Animals of the Southwest."

MICKI
: In "Micki, the baby fox," by Astrid Bergman.

MOSBEY
: A gray fox.

NAKEE
: A red fox.

SILVER
: A grey fox.

GIRAFFE

CECILY G.
: In "Cecily G. and the 9 Monkeys," by H. A. Rey.

NYA
: In "Patches," by Joel Stolper.

PATCHES
: In "Patches."

YOUNG SPOTS
: In "Patches."

GOAT

ANNA-MARIE
: In "The Greedy Goat," by Emma Brock.

BIQUETTE
: In "Biquette, the white goat," by Françoise.

COCO
: In "Coco, the Goat," by Rhea Wells.

GOAT (continued)

ROCKY BILLY — In "Rocky Billy," by Holling Clancy Holling.

GORILLA

OKA — In the Bronx Zoo.

OM BOM — In the St. Louis Zoo.

RUDY — In the St. Louis Zoo.

SINBAD — In Chicago's Lincoln Park Zoo.

SUMAILI — Pronounced Soo-mah-ee-lee, and sometimes called Lilly. To the keeper the name was Sumalilly.

TRUDY — In the St. Louis Zoo.

GUINEA PIG

ALVIN — Goes to story hour at Mark Twain Branch Library, Long Beach, Calif. wrapped in a blanket, riding in a doll buggy.

CORNFLAKES — He likes cornflakes.

SQUEAKER — His voice is squeaky.

TIMID — He is shy.

UNTIDY — He isn't very tidy.

WHISTLER — He is a whistler.

HAMSTER

BROWNSWIGGLE — In "Hamlet and Brownswiggle," by Barbara L. Reynolds.

HAMLET — In "Hamlet and Brownswiggle."

NUBBIN — After his tail which is a nubbin.

BANK ACCOUNT — He stores his food for future use.

PERKY — He is a perky little fellow.

POUCHY — He has cheek pouches.

HARE

FURRY TOE — He has a furry toe.

HARE (continued)

HAYMAKER	The Pika hare carries grasses to a rock pile home, spreads them out to dry, then puts them in a crevice, like a silo.
HORACE	An Irish hare.
P SA WÁ	American Indian word for 'hare.'

HEDGEHOG

MRS. TIGGY WINKLE	In "Tale of Mrs. Tiggy-Winkle," by Beatrix Potter.

CHICKEN

CAESAR	Rooster in "How to Understand Animal Talk," by Vinson Brown.
CHARLES	The rooster in "To and Again," by Walter Brooks.
CHUKLUK	A fat hen in "Mister Penny," by Marie Hall Ets.
DODY	In "Mister Penny."
HENRIETTA	The hen in the Freddy stories by Walter Brooks. She is the wife of Charles.

HIPPOPOTAMUS

LITTLE PETE	A 259 baby hippo whose full name is Peter the Second, in the Bronx Zoo.
PHOEBE	In the Bronx Zoo.

IGUANA

TOLOK	Indian name for 'iguana.'

KOALA

FUNNY FACE	Silver wool hair, big furry ears, soft thick fur, eyes like a three cornered patch.
PATCH EYE	His eyes look like patches.
TEDDY BEAR	The Teddy part is in honor of Theodore Roosevelt. Looks like

KOALA (continued)

a little bear.

LAMB

HI HI | American Indian for 'soft, like down.'

BEANBLOSSOM | In "Danny's Pig."

DEBE | American Indian name for 'lamb.'

MIMKIN | In "Mister Penny."

LEOPARD

BRUTUS | In the Staten Island Zoo.

KIM | The snow leopard in the St. Louis Zoo.

EMPEROR | In the St. Louis Zoo.

REGINA | In the St. Louis Zoo.

SHADOW | The black leopard in the Brooklyn Zoo.

LION

BIG BOY | The performing lion in the St. Louis Zoo.

HERBERT | In "Herbert, the Lion," by Clare Newberry.

KING BOO | The performing lion in the St. Louis Zoo.

SUR DAH | In "Lions on the Hunt," by Theodore Waldeck.

TARNISH | In "Tarnish," By Osa Johnson.

MANATEE

MINNIE PEARL | In the St. Louis Zoo.

MAX PAUL | In the St. Louis Zoo.

MARMOT

WHISTLER | He whistles one single sharp whistle when he senses danger.

MIERKAT

NO CAT	The soft fur is marked like a tabby cat, but it isn't a cat. Miercat means 'no cat.'
SUN LOVER	It loves the sun and warmth.

MOLE

DIGGER	A mole digs tunnels.
EXCAVATOR	He is a tunneler.
LITTLE MINER	He burrows.
NO EYES	He has none, needs none.
OLD PLOWHEAD	He has a wedge shaped head for penetrating the loose soil.
PADDLES	His forefeet are big, shaped like paddles to help dig.
RADAR	The tail of mole guides him through his tunnel.
STAR	The star shape of his nostrils.

MONGOOSE

RIKKI TIKKI TAVI	In the Jungle Stories by Rudyard Kipling.
SPEEDY	He is quick.

MONKEY

BABY JENNY	In "Cecily G." by H. A. Rey.
CURIOUS GEORGE	In the "Curious George" stories by H. A. Rey.
DAVID	In "Cecily G."
DEVIL MONKEY	The Indians in Ecuador call them this.
EI-A	Little children in Ecuador call him this.
FEATHERTAIL	Because he has one.
JAMES	In "Cecily G."
KENNETH	The black monkey in the Bronx Zoo.

MONKEY (continued)

MOTHER PAMPLEMOOSE	In "Cecily G. and the 9 Monkeys."
OWL FACE	Name given to him in "Twenty Pets."
OZO	From the scientific name.
PUNCH & JUDY	The twins in "Cecily G..."
SAUERKRAUT	Monkeys love this food.
MISS BAKER	Squirrel monkey, first American traveller into outer space, won gold medal, now retired, living with her chum Spice, in Pensacola, Fla.

MOUSE

AMOS	In "Ben and Me," by Robert Lawson.
ANATOLE	The cheese taster in 'Anatole and the Cat,' by Eve Titus.
AUGUSTUS	In the Freddy stories, by Walter Brooks.
BONNIE	In "Mouse House," by Rumer Godden.
CHAMP	The jumping mouse. It is the champion broad jumper in its size class among mammals.
CHIRPY	It chirps like a bird. (the white footed)
DOUCETTE	Wife of Anatole in "Anatole and the Cat."
EEEE	The way a mouse talks, it squeaks.
EEK	The mouse in the Freddy stories, by Walter Brooks.
ELNY	A mouse in the Freddy stories.
FLANNELETTE	In "The Mousewife," by Rumer Godden.
FUR POCKETS	It has external fur lined cheek pockets.

MOUSE (continued)

GASTON — The mouse in "Anatole and the Cat."

HOP A LONG — He jumps.

JOHNNY TOWN MOUSE — In "Tale of Johnny Town Mouse," by Beatrix Potter.

LEAPER — The kangaroo mouse.

LITTLE WHITEFOOT — The field mouse in "Little White-foot," by Berta and Elmer Hader.

MRS. TITTLEMOUSE — "A most terribly tidy particular little mouse, always sweeping and dusting." In "Mrs. Tittlemouse," by Beatrix Potter.

NIGHT AND DAY — Two waltzing mice, which are black and white.

PATSY — In "Everyday Miracle," by Gustav Eckstein.

PEREZ — In "Perez, the mouse," by Coloma and Moreton.

QUIK — In the Freddy stories.

SINGER — The white footed mouse which is musical, chirps like a bird.

SNIPPY & SNAPPY — Two little field mice in Marjorie Flack's "Snippy and Snappy."

SPINNER — A waltzing mouse, which spins as it waltzes.

WALTER — In "Walter the Lazy Mouse," by Marjorie Flack.

WALTZ-ME-AROUND — Waltzing mice move in circles.

WHITE BOOTS — The white-footed mouse.

WHITE SHOES — The white-footed mouse.

YO YO — The waltzing mouse in "Because I Like Animals," by Dahlov Ipcar.

ZAP — Scientific name for the jumping mouse is Zapus hudsonius.

MUSKRAT

CHUCHUNDRA	The muskrat in "Jungle Books" by Rudyard Kipling.
MARSHA	The muskrat likes the marshes.

OKAPI

BILOTA	The name of the hut village in Belgian Congo from which this animal comes.

OPOSSUM

JOE	In "Edward, Hoppy and Joe," by Robert Lawson.
DIDEL	From the scientific name 'Didelphus.'
HITCHHIKER	The young ride on the mother's back.
MUYONI	Means 'heart.'

ORANGUTAN

JACK & JILL	Orangs in the Staten Island Zoo.
JANIE	Orang in the St. Louis Zoo.
LARRY	Orang in the St. Louis Zoo.

OTTER

FROLIC	Otter loves to play.
GRACE	It is graceful in action.
I HA HA	American Indian name for 'I bubble over and laugh like the river and stream.'
JOCHO	Given to otter in "Illustrated Library of Natural Science."
MOSES	In "Moses, my otter," by Frances Pitt.
NE KIK	American Indian name for 'otter.'
ROMPER	He loves to play.
SPORT	An otter will climb a steep snow bank, slide down with arms folded

OTTER (continued)

	back against his body.
TARA	Name given in "Illustrated Library of Natural Science." Means 'adamant, fortified.'
TETAWISH	Name given in "Illustrated Library of Natural Science."

PANTHER

BAGHEERA	The black panther in the Jungle Books by Rudyard Kipling.
LONG FANG	In "Wild Animals of the Sothwest."

PIG

ALBERT	In "Danny's Pig," by Janice May Udry. Sometimes called 'Old Albert.'
ALICE	A pig in "Danny's Pig."
ANNIE	The piglet in "Danny's Pig."
BETSY	A piglet in "Danny's Pig."
CARY	A piglet in "Danny's Pig."
GUB GUB	A pig in the Dr. Doolittle stories by Hugh Lofting.
PATRICK PUNK	"Pink" for short, in the "Story of Mrs. Tubbs," by Hugh Lofting.
PUGWUG	In "Mister Penny" by Marie Hall Ets.
WILBUR	In "Charlotte's Web," by E. B. White.

PLATYPUS

CECIL	In the New York Zoo.
FLAT FOOT	This is the meaning of Platypus.
GLUTTONOUS TEDDY	In "Illustrated Library of the Natural Sciences."
PENELOPE	Is in the New York Zoo.
PUZZLE	He has a beaver's shape, mole's fur, duck's webbed feet, flat bill, and

PLATYPUS (continued)

rooster's spurs.

PORCUPINE

IKKI	Appears in the Jungle Books, by Rudyard Kipling.
PORKY	In "Tuffy."
PORKY PORCUPINE	In "Wild Animals of the Southwest."
QUILL PEN	His quills remind one of quill pens.
QUILLA	For the quills.
RATTLETAIL	He flips his tail when he is frightened, rattled.
TREE DWELLER	He lives in trees in the winter time.
SAHI	Appears in the Jungle Books, by Rudyard Kipling.
WADDLES	He waddles when he walks.

PORPOISE

NOTTY	This porpoise belongs to the Naval Ordinance Test Station at China Lake. She gets her name from the initials of the Test Station.

PRAIRIE DOG

ARP ARP	Or, just ARP. This is their barking call.
BARKER	For the kind of sound they make.
BLACK FLAG	He has a black tail.
BUFF	The color of the animal.
BUMPY	Sister to Lumpy, and Stumpy, and Dumpy in "Prairie Dog," by Jene Barr.
METHUSELAH	Because he sleeps in winter.
PUDGY	This is his shape, round, dumpy.
SHORTY	It has a short tail.
SKIP, or SKIP SKIP	This is its warning call.

PRAIRIE DOG (continued)

WHISTLER	He can whistle.
WHITE FLAG	Some have white tails.
YAP YAP	For his sharp yaping bark.
YEK YEK	Some say his bark is like this, and high pitched.

RABBIT

BUNNYKIN	In "Mrs. Bunnykin's Busy Day," by Alan Wright.
CHUCK	A name given to it by a boy.
CROPPY	A snowshoe rabbit.
DESDEMONA	A name given to a black and white rabbit.
EDWARD	A name given to it in "Edward, Hoppy and Joe," by Robert Lawson.
HAJJA BA BA	A rabbit named by children who wanted a different name for him.
HARVEY	The famous white rabbit in the stage play of the same name.
MAUSTIN	In "Maustin, the Rabbit," an Old Indian Legend by Zitkala-Sa.
MRS. HOPPIT	In "Bounce and the Bunnies," by Ruth Carroll.
POWDER PUFF	A Cottontail, for his puff tail.
ROBBUT	In "Robbut, a tale of tails," by Robert Lawson.
SCAMPER	This is the way he runs.
TIPPETY	In "Tale of Two Bunnies," by Katharine Pyle.
WHITE JACKET	The snowshoe rabbit, for his coat.

RACCOON

AH SEE PON NA	American Indian name for 'raccoon.'
BLINKY	In "Blinky," by Agnes Atkinson.
BUSYBODY	A trait of his.

RACCOON (continued)

COLLEGE BOY	In the '20's college boys wore raccoon coats.
ES SEE	In "Wildfolk at the Pond," by Carroll Lane Fenton.
EWOONOTO	A Coati Mundi, related to the raccoon. Children of South America call him this.
HIGHWAYMAN	He is out at night, and looks as though he wore a mask.
HONEY BUNCH	The Kinkajou, a relative of raccoon. He is soft, yellow, brown, wooly with large shining eyes. "In Twenty Pets..." They are often called honey bears for they like anything sweet.
NIGHT CLOAK	He comes out under the cloak of night.
OLD BUSYBODY	He is a busybody.
NOSEY	The coati-mundi, related to the raccoon, has a long nose, comes from Mexico.
MISCHIEF	He is full of fun and mischief.
PEPPER	In "Pepper," by Barbara Leonard Reynolds.
PROCYON	In "Masked Prowler," by John Lothar George.
THA PA TI	American Indian name for the animal.
WITS	He relies on his brain to get him out of trouble.
ZEKE	In "Zeke, the raccoon," by Rhea Wells.

RAT

GRANDPA	An old White rat.
SUSIE	A tame white rat.
TA KA	The American Indian name for 'rat.'

RAT (continued)

WHISKERS	Rat wears long ones.

RHINOCERUS

HARRY	A rhino in the St. Louis Zoo.

SEA LION

FLIP	A baby sea lion in the Bronx Zoo.

SEAL

KOTICK	Appears in the Mowgli stories by Rudyard Kipling.
LITTLE FLIPPER	In "Here Come the Seals."
MABEL	An elephant seal in the St. Louis Zoo.
OLD SEACATCH	An elephant seal in the St. Louis Zoo.
SEA CATCH	In the Jungle Books by Rudyard Kipling.

SHREW

PIGMY	It is so small.
BEADY	Its eyes are tiny, like beads.
SHARPY	Its muzzle is very sharp.

SIAMANG

CHARLIE	Is in the St. Louis Zoo.

SKUNK

AH PEKI	American Indian name for 'skunk.'
KITTEN	Because they play like kittens.
CHARMION	It is pleasing, friendly.
MOH KUH	American Indian name for "skunk."
NIGHT CLOAK	It comes out under the cloak of night.
NO BEE OH	American Indian name for 'skunk.'
PERKEY	In "Biography of a Skunk," by Agnes Atkinson.

SKUNK (continued)

PLUMES	It has a tail like a plume.
SACHET	Often called 'sachet-kittens,' because of their offensive odor.

SLOTH

QUALANG	Pet name given to it by the natives.
UPSIDE DOWN	It hangs that way.

SNAIL

FLAT FOOT	The way it uses its foot to crawl.
HORTENSE	From the Scientific name, Helix Hortensis, the garden snail.
RAM	From Ramshorn, Scientific name.
SCAVENGER	It eats plants.
SLOW POKE	It moves slowly.
STICKY FOOT	Leaves a shiny, sticky trail.

STORK

HANSI	In "Hansi, the Stork," by Oscar Ludmann.

SQUIRREL

A RO	American Indian name for 'squirrel.'
ADJIDAUMO	"Tail-in-the-air," Hiawatha's name for the squirrel in Longfellow's poem, "Hiawatha." Pronounced, 'aw chit aw mo."
AVIATOR	The flying squirrel.
BLACK LEGS	The black-footed squirrel in "Pets Wild and Western."
BLONDIN	A pet squirrel the color of light tan.
BUSHY	For its tail.
BUSYTAIL	For its tail, in "Tuffy."
CHEEKY	It has pouch cheeks, acts cheeky.

SQUIRREL (continued)

CHICKY	After Chickaree, another name for it.
CHASER	The red squirrel chases the grey squirrel relentlessly.
CHIRR	The way it talks.
CLOWN	The flying squirrel is funny.
CUCK CUCK	The way it scolds.
EKORN	In "Ekorn," by Haakon Lie.
FLURRY	It is always in a flurry.
GLIDER	The flying squirrel glides through the air.
GOLDY	His color.
GORGEOUS	The tail of the grey squirrel.
HOARDER	Red squirrel especially is a hoarder.
HIGH JINKS	The flying squirrel flies high.
HURRY	In " Hurry, Scurry, Flurry," by M. M. Buff.
JERKY TAIL	He is always waving it about.
MIDNIGHT	The flying squirrel loves the night.
NIGHT FLIER	The flying squirrel.
NIGHT OWL	The flying squirrel.
NUTKIN	In "Tale of Squirrel Nutkin," by Beatrix Potter.
OLD MAN	The golden mantled ground squirrel looks like an old man.
ONE EAR	In "Pets Wild and Western."
PARACHUTE	The flying squirrel.
SASSY	The flying squirrel is sassiest of the squirrel family.
SAUCY	The flying squirrel.
SHADY TAIL	The large bushy tail of the squirrel.

SHARPY	He has sharp teeth, a sharp mind.
SI NA GO	The gray squirrel in American Indian language.
SKURRY	In "Hurry, Skurry, Flurry," by M. M. Buff.
SNUFFY	In "Pets Wild and Western."
TAKE OFF	The flying squirrel.
TRICKSTER	The flying squirrel.
TWINKLEBERRY	In "Tale of Squirrel Nutkin."
WHIPPER	The red squirrel whips about.
WHISK	In "Little Princess in the Wood," by Helen Dean Fish.

TARSIER

BIG EYES	In "Twenty Little Pets..."
MONKEY	It looks like a monkey.

TIGER

AAARH	The howl of the tiger in the Jungle Books by Rudyard Kipling.
DACCA	Tiger cub in the Bronx Zoo.
RAJPUR	Tiger cub in the Bronx Zoo.
SHERE KHAN	The big one in the Jungle Book by Rudyard Kipling.
HAM	A performing tiger in the St. Louis Zoo.
SLEIKA	A performing tiger in the St. Louis Zoo.

WALRUS

OLAF	In the New York Aquarium.
WALLIE	In "Wallie the Walrus," by Kurt Wiese.

WART HOG

CLARENCE	In the Bronx Zoo.

WHALE

GRAMPUS	In the Jungle Books by Rudyard Kipling.
MABEL	In "Mabel the Whale," by Patricia King, story of the whale that came to live at Marineland, California.

WOLF

AKELA	In the Jungle Book by Rudyard Kipling.
PHAO	In the Jungle Book.
SCARFACE	In "Wild Animals of the Southwest."

WOODCHUCK

FAT LADY	A lady woodchuck, for woodchucks are chunky.
FORAGER	They go on foraging expeditions far from home.
GREAT SLEEPER	It sleeps most of the cold winter in its burrow.
OT CHOECK	Indian name for woodchuck.
SOOTY	A black woodchuck.
WADDLES	The way the woodchuck walks.
WHISTLER	It whistles.
WOODY	From its name. Also CHUCK, from its name.
WE JACK	American Indian name for 'woodchuck.'

BIBLIOGRAPHY

AMERICAN KENNEL CLUB. Complete Dog Book. New
York: Halcyon House, 1938, 1961.
For breeds accepted by the American Kennel Club,
characteristics, habitat, coloring.

AMES, WINTHROP. What Shall I Name the Baby, edited by
Winthrop Ames. New York: Simon & Schuster, Inc. 1934.
For about 20 names and definitions.

ANDERSON, C. W. Black Bay and Chestnut. New York:
Macmillan, 1939.
For a few names and characteristics.

ANDERSON, C. W. Deep Through the Heart. New York:
Macmillan, 1940.
For a few names and characteristics.

ANDERSON, C. W. Thoroughbreds. New York: Macmillan,
1942.
For a few names and characteristics.

ANDREWS, ROY CHAPMAN. Nature's ways; how nature
takes care of its own. New York: Crown, 1951.
For characteristics.

ARTHUR, WILLIAM. An Etymological Dictionary of Family
and Christian Names. Sheldon, Blakeman & Co., No.
115 Nassau St., 1857.

AYMAR, BRANDT, ed. The Personality of the Cat. New
York: Crown, 1958
For characteristics.

BALLANTINE, JOSEPH W. Japanese as It Is Spoken.
Stanford University Press, n.d.

BALLARD, LOIS. True Book of Reptiles. Chicago: Children's Press, 1957.
For characteristics, color, habitat.

BARETTI, JOSEPH. Italian-English, English-Italian Dictionary. The first Leghorn edition carefully arranged
and corrected...with an abridged Italian Grammar. 2 v.
Livorno Dalla Tipografia di G. P. Pozzolini & G. 1829.

357

For Italian names, nouns suitable for names, definitions.

BARNHART, CLARENCE L. The American College Dictionary. New York: Random House, 1953.
For definitions in dictionary proper, comparison of names.

BARNHART, CLARENCE L. ed. The New Century Cyclopedia of Names...3 vol. New York: Appleton, Century, Crofts, Inc. 1954
For some Pre-names for comparison.

BAYNES, ERNEST HAROLD. Animal Heroes of The Great War. New York: Macmillan, 1929.
For a few names.

BETTERIDGE, HAROLD T. The New Cassell's German Dictionary. New York: Funk & Wagnalls, 1958.
For phrases, nouns suitable for names.

BEVANS, MICHAEL H. Book of Reptiles and Amphibians. New York: Garden City Books, 1936.
For characteristics, habitat, coloring.

BOIELLE, JAMES. A New French and English Dictionary compiled from the best authorities in both languages, revised and considerably enlarged by James Boielle, B.A., aided by de v. Payen Payne. New York: London: Funk & Wagnalls, Wm. T. Belding, 1903.
For names and nouns suitable for names.

BOULTON, RUDYERD. Travelling With the Birds, a book on migration. Chicago: New York: M. A. Donohue & Co. 1953.
For habits.

BRONSON, JULIEN L. Parrot Family. Wisconsin: All-Pets, 1950.
For characteristics, habits.

BROWN, CHARLETON, ed. New Book of Dogs. New York: Bobbs Merrill, 1954.
For characteristics, breeds.

BROWN, VINSON & HENRY G. WESTON, jr. Handbook of California Birds. California: Naturegraph Company, 1961.
For behavior, sounds, habitat, flight patterns.

BROWN, WILLIAM ROBINSON.   The Horse of the Desert.
New York: Macmillan, 1929.
For 5 horse names and meanings.

BRYANT, DORIS. Care and Handling of Cats.   Ives Wash-
burn, 1949.
For characteristics.

BULFINCH, THOMAS.   Bulfinch's Mythology; the Age of
Fable; the Age of Chivalry; Legends of Charlemagne.
New York: The Modern Library, 1934.
For gods and goddesses; their stories.

CARPENTER, FRANCES. Wonder Tales of Horses and
Heroes. New York: Doubleday, 1952.
For names.

CHRIST, HENRY IRVING, ed. Myths and Folklore...New
York: Oxford Book Co., 1954.
For comparison of mythical stories.

CLIFTON, E. A New Dictionary of the French and English
languages...by E. Clifton...remodeled and enlarged by
J. McLaughlin...Philadelphia: David McKay Company,
Washington Square. n.d. preface date, Paris janvier,
1904.
Names in text.

CROWELL, PERS. Calvacade of American Horses. New
York: McGraw Hill, 1951.
For comparison of names found in almanacs.

DAVIS, HENRY P., ed. The Modern Dog Encyclopedia.
New York: Stackpole & Heck, 1949.
For names in text; characteristics; habits.

DAVIS, MARS, AND PAUL NEWHALL. Pet Boxer. Wisconsin: All-Pets Books Inc. 1954.
For characteristics.

DENLINGER, WILLIAM. The Complete Beagle. Virginia:
Denlingers, 1956.
For characteristics.

DENLINGER, WILLIAM. The Complete Cocker. Virginia:
Denlingers, 1946.
For characteristics.

DENLINGER, WILLIAM.   The Complete Collie.   Virginia:
    Denlingers, 1946.
    For characteristics.

DENLINGER, WILLIAM.   The Complete Dalmatian.   Vir-
    ginia: Denlingers, 1947.
    For characteristics.

DICKEY, FLORENCE VAN VECHTEN.   Familiar Birds of
    the Pacific Southwest...Stanford: Stanford University Press
    and London: Geoffrey Cumberledge, Oxford Press, 1935.
    For characteristics, coloring, shape, size, etc.

DICTIONNAIRE GENERAL.   Francais-Anglais nouvellement
    redige de d'apres les dictionnaires Francais de l'academie,
    de anglais De Johson, Webster, Richardson, etc...par A.
    Spiers...ouvrage autorise par le conseil de l'instruction
    publique le 7 September 1849, dix-huitieme edition.   Paris:
    Baudry, Librairie Europeenne Dramard-Baudry et Cie,
    successeurs 12 Rue Bonaparte Pres le Palais des Beaux
    Arts, 1865.   Names and definitions.

DOBIE, J. FRANK   The Mustangs.   New York: Little, 1952.
    For characteristics, several names.

DUNN, C. J.   Teach Yourself Japanese by C. J. Dunn and
    S. Yanada.   London: The English Universities Press Ltd.,
    1958.
    For words suitable for names.

ECKSTEIN, GUSTAV.   Everyday Miracle.   New York &
    London: Harper & Bros., 1948.
    For names.

EDWARDS, THOMAS.   An English & Welsh Dictionary...
    London: H. Hughes, 1850.
    For names, words suitable for names.

ELIAS, EDWARD E.   Practical Dictionary of the Colloquial
    Arabic of the Middle East.   Elias' Modern Press, n.d.

ENCYCLOPEDIA AMERICANA.   Chicago, Washington: A-
    mericana Corporation.   Articles on Mythology: Stars:
    Birds: various Small Animals, for habitat, characteris-
    tics, authenticity.

EVANS, REV. D. SILVAN. Dictionary of the Welsh Language. Carmarthen: W. Spurrell & Son, MDCCCLXXXVII.

FANTIN, LORNA. Everybody's Book of Numbers. New
York: Brewer, Warren, & Putnam, 1931.
For comparison of names, no meanings.

FAYER, MISCHA H. Basic Russian. Pitnam Publishing
Company, c1959.
For names, words suitable for names.

FEDERAL WRITERS' PUBLICATIONS, INC. Birds of the
World. Chicago, Albert Whitman & Co., 1939.
For classifications; habits; color.

FENNENBERG, PAUL. Speak Danish; a practical guide to
Colloquial Danish. Copenhagen, G. E. C. Gad, Publish-
ers and London-New York: Oxford University Press, 1956.
First names of Danish kings. Words suitable for names.

FEYERABEND, CESSA. The Budgerigar, or shell parrakeet as a talker. American Budgergar Society, 1943.
For characteristics; colors.

FRAYHA, ANIS. The Essentials of Arabic. Khajjat's, 1958.
For words suitable for names.

FUNK & WAGNALL'S. Standard Dictionary of Folklore,
Mythology and Legend. New York: Funk & Wagnalls, 1949.

GAINES DOG RESEARCH CENTER. A Name to Fit Your
Dog, a pamphlet. New York: Gaines Dog Research Cen-
ter, 1951.
For names and definitions.

GARLAND, HAMLIN. The Book of the American Indian.
New York-London: Harper & Brothers, publishers, 1923.
For 8 Indian names.

GAYLEY, CHARLES MILLS. The Classic Myths in English
Literature and in Art. Boston-NewYork: Ginn & Co., 1911.

GORDON, DAN M. The Boxer. Chicago: Judy Publishing
Company, 1956.
For characteristics.

GRONICKA, A. V. and H. BATES YAKOBSON. Essentials
of Russian. New York: Prentice-Hall, 1958.
For words suitable for names.

GULICK, CHARLOTTE. A List of Indian Words from which
girls can derive their Camp Fire Names. New York:
The Campfire Outfitting Co., 1915.
For comparison and a few Indian names.

GULICK, CHARLOTTE V. The Name Book; a dictionary.
New York: Camp Fire Girls, Inc. n.d.
For comparison and a few names.

HAMILTON, EDITH. Mythology. New York: Mentor, 1942.
For comparison, stories of myths, gods and goddesses
names.

HARBOR CITIES KENNEL CLUB. Annual All Bred Dog Show
and Obedience Trial Programs for 1960 and 1961. Harbor
Cities Kennel Club.
For names of Kennel and Champion dogs.

HARRIS, ALBERT W. The Blood of the Arab; the world's
greatest war horse. Chicago: Albert Harris, 1941.
Characteristics, a few names.

HENRY, MARGUERITE. Birds At Home. Chicago: M. A.
Donohue & Co., 1942.
For habits.

HENRY, MARGUERITE. Justin Morgan Had a Horse. New
York: Wilcox & Follett, 1945.
For history of the Morgan Horse.

HOGNER, DOROTHY C. Farm Animals. New York: Oxford,
1945.
For breeds, characteristics, habits.

INGLEE, CHARLES T. Toy Dogs. G. Howard Watt, c1935.
For characteristics of toy dogs, breeds.

KELLINO, PAMELA and JAMES MASON. The Cats In Our
Lives. New York: A. A. Wyn, 1949.

For names, personalities, characteristics.

KOOLHOVEN, H. Teach Yourself Dutch. New York:
McKay, n.d.
For words useful as names.

KRAEUCHI, RUTH. The Cocker Spaniel. Chicago: Judy
Publishing Co., 1956.
For characteristics.

KROEBER, A. L. Handbook of the Indians of California.
Berkeley: California Book Co., c1923, 1953.
For Indian names, about 15.

LAROUSSE. Encyclopedia of Mythology...New York: Pro-
metheus Press, 1959.
For goddesses, gods and mythological names in various
myths in various countries.

LAUDER, PHYLLIS. Siamese Cats. London: Williams &
Norgate, Ltd. 1950.
For characteristics.

LUNT, HORACE G; Fundamentals of Russian...The Hague,
The Netherlands: Mouton & Co.'S-Gravenhage, 1958.
For words, definitions suitable for names.

LUTZ, FRANK E. Field Book of Insects. New York: G.
P. Putnam's Sons, 1935.
For habits, characteristics, colors.

LUTZ, FRANK E. Field Book of Insects of the U.S. and
Canada. New York: G.P. Putnam's Sons, 1948.
For habits, characteristics, colors.

MCCORMICK, JULIAN. The Child's Name. William H.
  Young & Co., 27 Barclay Street, 1899.
    For names and definitions.

MANDAHL-BARTH, G. Aquarium Fish in Color...New
  York: E. P. Dutton, 1959.
    For color, habits, characteristics.

MANDAHL-BARTH, G. Cage Birds in Color by Mandahl-
  Barth and Anthon. New York: Barrows, 1959.
    For color, habits, characteristics.

MARTIN, SAMUEL E. Essential Japanese. Rutland, Vt.
  Charles E. Tuttle Co., 1956.
    For words and definitions suitable for names.

MEARS, HELEN. First Book of Japan. New York: Watts,
  1953.
    For words suitable for names.

MEGARGEE, EDWIN. Dogs. New York: Harper and Brothers, 1942.
    For characteristics.

MENKE, FRANK. Encyclopedia of Sports. New York:
  A. S. Barnes, 1953.
    For Champions, Winners and the history of the horse
  in Shows. Characteristics of horses.

MENKE, FRANK G. Sport Tales and Anecdotes. New
  York: A. S. Barnes, 1953.
    For a few names.

MERRIAM, EVE. The Real Book About Amazing Birds.
  New York: Garden City Books, by arrangement with
  Franklin Watts, Inc. 1955.
    For characteristics, habits.

MILLELLA, DR. NICHOLAS J. Italian in a Nutshell. New
  Jersey: Institute For Language Study, 1958.
    Vocabularies for words suitable for names.

MITCHELL, LUCY S. Horses Now and Long Ago. New
  York: Harcourt, 1926.
    For breed characteristics.

MITCHELL, T. F. An Introduction to Egyptian Colloquial
   Arabic. London, Oxford: first ed. 1956.
   For words suitable for names.

MOORE, CLIFFORD B. The Book of Wild Pets. New
   York: G. P. Putnam, 1937.
   For life habits, identification, characteristics.

MORGAN, ALFRED. An Aquarium Book for Boys and Girls.
   New York: Scribner, 1936.
   For characteristics.

NELSON, VERA M. Siamese Cat Book. Wisconsin, All-
   Pets Books, 1956.
   For characteristics, habits.

NEWMAN, L. HUGH. The Fascinating World of Butterflies.
   New York: Random House, 1954.
   For characteristics, habits.

NICHOLAS, ANNA KATHERINE. The Pekingese. Chicago,
   Judy Publishing Co., 1952.
   For characteristics, habits.

OGRIZEK, DORE. Japan. New York: McGraw Hill, 1957.
   For an occasional word suitable for a name.

OZAKI, YEI THEODORA, comp. Japanese Fairy Tales.
   New York: Burt, n. d.
   For names.

PACA, LILLIAN GRACE. Introduction to Western Birds.
   Menlo Park: Lane Publishing Co., 1953.
   For names, characteristics, habits.

PEI, MARIO Getting Along in German. New York: Harper
   & Brothers, 1957.
   General vocabulary for words suitable for names.

PARKER, BERTHA MORRIS. The Basic Science Education
   Series: Six-legged Neighbors. Evanston, Row Peterson
   & Co., 1949.
   For habits, characteristics.

PERRY, VINCENT G. The Boston Terrier. Chicago, Judy
   Publishing Company, 1950.
   For characteristics of the breed, habits.

PIGNATARO, RUDOLPH I.   Ditelo in Inglese.   New York:
    Dover Publications, 1956.
    For vocabulary words suitable for names.

PLUMB, CHARLES.   Types and Breeds of Farm Animals.
    Boston: Ginn & Co., 1920.
    For characteristics, breeds, habits, history.

RAVENTOS, MARGARET H.   McKay's Modern Spanish-
    English, English-Spanish Dictionary.   New York, London:
    McKay Co., Inc., The English Universities Press, Ltd.,
    n.d.
    For names of Person, Animals & Mythological Names.
    Comparison with names found in other sources.

REGENSTEINER, HENRY.   German in a Nutshell.   New
    Jersey: Institute for Language Study, 1958.
    For occasional names, vocabulary for words suitable
    for names.

RENDEL, JOHN.   The Dog Book.   New York: Arco Pub-
    lishing Co., 1953.
    For characteristics.

RENIER, FERNAND G.   Learn Dutch.   Routledge & Kegan,
    1949.
    For words suitable for name.

RICE, FRANK A. & SA'ID, MAJED F.   Eastern Arabia, an
    introduction to the Spoken Arabic of Palestine, Syria and
    Lebanon.   Barut, Khayat's, D. C.: Georgetown Univer-
    sity, 1960, 1953.
    For words suitable for names.

RIDDLE, MAXWELL.   The Springer Spaniel.   Chicago:
    Judy Publishing Co., 1951.
    For characteristics.

ROSS, EDWARD S.   Insects Close Up...Berkeley, Los
    Angeles: University of California Press.
    For characteristics.

ROSS, MARVIN C., ed.   George Catlin: episodes from
    'Life Among the Indians' and 'Last Rambles.'   Okla.:
    University of Oklahoma Press.   1959.
    For a few Indian names.

ROWLAND, THOMAS. A Grammar of the Welsh Language.
London: Simpkin, Marshall & Co., D. Nutt, W. C.
Pennant-Melangell, 1876.
For names and words suitable for names.

SCOTT, ORAL E. The Stars in Myth and Fact. Idaho:
Caxton Printers, 1947.

SCOTT, RALPH W. Japanese. Vanni, 1944.
For words suitable for names.

SCOVIL, ELISABETH ROBINSON. Names for Children.
Philadelphia: Henry Altemus., 1897.
For names.

SEARS, PAUL MCCUTCHEON. "Fire-fly." ... New York:
Holiday House, 1956.
For characteristics.

STONG, PHIL. Horses and Americans. New York: Garden
City Publishing Co. 1939.
For characteristics.

SHERMAN, JANE. The Real Book about Bugs, Insects, and
Such. New York: Franklin Watts, Inc. and Garden City
Books, 1952.
For characteristics.

SHERMAN, JANE. The Real Book About Snakes. New York:
Franklin Watts, Inc. and Garden City Books, 1955.
For characteristics.

SHIPLEY, JOSEPH T. Dictionary of Word Origins. New
York: Philosophical Library, Inc., 1945.
22 words only.

SPEIGHT, KATHLEEN. Teach Yourself Italian. New York:
McKays, n.d.
For words suitable for names.

SPURRELL'S ENGLISH-WELSH DICTIONARY & WELSH-
ENGLISH. Carmarthen, W. Spurrel & Co., 1926.
For words suitable for names.

STEPANOFF, N. C. Say It with Russian. New York:
Dover Publications, 1958.
For words suitable for names.

SWAIN, SUZAN N. Insects In Their World. New York:
Garden City Books, 1955.
For characteristics, habits.

SWAN, HELENA. Girls Christian Names; their History,
meaning and association. New York: Dutton, Swan
Sonnenschein & Co., Ltd. 1900.
For names and meanings.

TABER, GLADYS. First Book of Dogs. New York:
Franklin Watts, 1949.
For habits, characteristics.

TATHAM, JULIE CAMPBELL. World Book of Dogs. New
York: World Publishing Company, n.d.
For characteristics, habits.

TELEVISION SPORTS-CASTERS, 1960-61.
For Champions and winners in various races.

TERHUNE, ALBERT PAYSON. A Book of Famous Dogs.
New York: Doubleday, 1937.
For characteristics, habits, a few names.

THATCHER, G. W. Arabic Grammar. New York: Fre-
derick Ungar Publishing Company, n.d.
For words suitable for names.

THOMAS, JOSEPH. Lippincott's Universal Pronouncing
Dictionary of Biography and Mythology. Philadelphia:
Lippincott, c1905.
For Christian names in separate index in back, with
meanings.

TINKLE, LON & ALLEN MAXWELL, eds. Cowboy Reader.
New York: Longmans, 1959.
For a few names.

TRITTON, A. S. Teach Yourself Arabic. New York:
McKay, n.d.
For words suitable for names.

U. S. DEPARTMENT OF AGRICULTURE. Insects. D. C.:
U. S. Dept. of Agr. 1952.
For characteristics, coloring, habits.

VELAZQUEZ DE LA CADENA, MARIANO. A New Pro-
   nouncing Dictionary of the Spanish and English Languages.
   New York, London: Appleton & Co., 1852, 1900.
   For English equivalent of Spanish names.

WEBB, ADDISON: Birds in Their Homes. New York:
   Garden City Books, 1947.
   For characteristics, habits.

WEBSTER'S BIOGRAPHICAL DICTIONARY. Mass: Merriam
   Webster, 1953.
   For some names.

WEBSTER'S INTERNATIONAL DICTIONARY OF THE ENG-
   LISH LANGUAGE, being the authentic edition of Webster's
   unabridged dictionary, comprising the issues 1864, 1879,
   and 1884 thoroughly revised and much enlarged under the
   supervision of Noah Porter ... Mass.: G. C. Merriam
   Company, 1905.
   For Christian names in separate list in the back. For
   biographical information in the separate list of biographies and for words in the text.

WEIDENHAN, REV. JOSEPH L. Baptismal Names. Mary-
   land: Kenmore Productions, n.d.
   About 20 names. Compared with other sources.

WEIR, ELIZABETH. Heath's New German Dictionary in two
   parts...Boston, New York, Chicago: D. C. Heath &
   Company, preface date, 1888.
   Names in Text.

WEYER, EDWARD M. ed. The Illustrated Library of the
   Natural Sciences. New York: Simon & Schuster, 1958.
   4 vol.
   For characteristics, habits, coloring, various animals.

WILLIAMSON, H. R. Teach Yourself Chinese. New York:
   McKay, n.d.
   For words suitable for names.

WILLIAMSON, MARGARET. The First Book of Bugs. New
   York: Franklin Watts, 1949.
   For characteristics, habits, colors.

WILSON, KIT and ADDISON WEBB. Cats. New York:
  Dover Publishing Company, 1952.
    For characteristics, habits.

WORLD ALMANAC. 1950, 51, 52, 53, 54, 55, 56, 57.
    For winners, champions, etc.

WOULFE, REV. PATRICK. Irish Names and Surnames...
  Dublin, M. H. Gill & Son, Ltd. 1923.
    For some names, comparison with other names found.

YONGE, CHARLOTTE. History of Christian Names, by the
  author of "The Heir of Redclyffe," London: Parker Son
  and Bourn, 1863. 2 v.
    For names and meanings, diminuitives, pet names, etc.

YONGE, CHARLOTTE. History of Christian Names. New
  ed. revised, New York, Macmillan, 1884. 1 v.
    For names and meanings.

ZIM, HERBERT S. Birds. New York: Simon & Schuster,
  1949.
    For habits, characteristics, colors.

ZIM, HERBERT S. Fishes. New York: Simon & Schuster,
  1956.
    For habits, characteristics, colors.

ZIM, HERBERT S. Frogs & Toads. New York: Morrow,
  1950.
    For habits, characteristics, colors.

ZIM, HERBERT S. Insects. New York: Simon and Schuster,
  1951.
    For habits, characteristics, colors.

MAGAZINES

DOG WORLD. All the issues in 1959.
    For breeds accepted by Kennel Club of America. For
    characteristics, some names.

POPULAR DOGS. December, 1959. "Know the Breed,"
  p. 56-63 inclusive.
    For breeds accepted by the American Kennel Club.

PARADE.   March 11, 1962.   "Top Dogs" by Jack Anderson.
   For the name of G-Boy, etc.

INDEX